Loyal Sisters

Loyal Sisters

Womanist Spirituality and the British Church

Doreen W. McCalla

WIPF & STOCK · Eugene, Oregon

LOYAL SISTERS
Womanist Spirituality and the British Church

Copyright © 2024 Doreen W. McCalla. All rights reserved. Except for brief quotations in critical publications or reviews, no part of this book may be reproduced in any manner without prior written permission from the publisher. Write: Permissions, Wipf and Stock Publishers, 199 W. 8th Ave., Suite 3, Eugene, OR 97401.

Wipf & Stock
An Imprint of Wipf and Stock Publishers
199 W. 8th Ave., Suite 3
Eugene, OR 97401

www.wipfandstock.com

PAPERBACK ISBN: 979-8-3852-0676-6
HARDCOVER ISBN: 979-8-3852-0677-3
EBOOK ISBN: 979-8-3852-0678-0

VERSION NUMBER 08/26/24

In loving memory to Dorothy, Cynthia, McCalla,
my biological mother and Loyal Sister.
RIP and rise in glory.

In dedication to Loyal Sisters of the Windrush Generation
who are part of the first cohort of formidable, diasporic,
British church women; who, without knowing it,
established womanist spirituality in the UK.

LOYAL SISTERS TELLS THE real-life story of diasporic, Black and Brown British church women in mainly two different denominations. They are Messa Pentecostal and High Parish. The book shows Loyal Sisters' spirituality, solidarity, immigration, and how they are overcoming adversity and in spite of patriarchy through spiritual transcendence and redemption. It shows that although church attendance is on the decline in Britain there is still a remnant of resilient and resistant Black and Brown Loyal Sisters in the church who are unmovable. There is therefore still hope for the continuation and refinement of womanist spirituality in the British church.

Contents

List of Tables | ix
Acknowledgments | xi
Abbreviations | xiii
Introduction | xv

1. Loyal Sisters: Black and Brown in the UK | 1
2. The British Church and the Spiritual Lifestyle of Loyal Sisters | 16
3. In the Spirit at Messa Pentecostal | 49
4. High Parish: The Spirit, an Intercultural Church, and a Multicultural Community | 70
5. Womanist Testimony Service | 92
6. BREAKING NEWS, 18th January 2023: CLAIMANT'S STATEMENT | 117
7. Sermon Reflection on Pentecost Sunday: What does this Mean? | 158
8. Loving Race and Accepting Self | 164
9. Spiritual Redemption and Transcendence | 184
10. Altar Service: Pneumatic Intercessions | 215

Bibliography | 225

List of Tables

Table 1: Generation by Age and Year Ranges | 2
Table 2: British Government Statistics on Immigration in the UK | 13
Table 3: My Discernment Process | 125

Acknowledgments

THIS BOOK HAS EMERGED from a wider project on womanism in Britain. Firstly, I thank God for her mercy and grace in granting me the social and economic means thus enabling it to come to pass. It was carried out under extreme difficulties as I attempted to find paid work, live on a meagre income and maintain my sanity by God's mercy and grace. I discuss some of this in chapter 5 in this book. Furthermore, at times, processing and analyzing the data from this study also took me on an enormously, painful but productive, emotional rollercoaster. The combination of the two happening meant that the speed of writing was somewhat slower than would normally be the case. God was constantly beside me when the burden was too hard to bare. I also thank God that through writing this book it has brought me some joy and fulfillment. Knowing that this book can prove invaluable to others warms my heart and grants me some peace.

Thanks to leaders, members, and visiting friends at Messa Pentecostal where years of service, leadership in, and visits allowed me to capture the spiritual environment of that church as a denomination and congregations in it for chapter 3 and other parts of this book. The Sisters there are truly amazing women of God.

Thanks to the vicar of High Parish who supported me in my ministry in the church he leads thus allowing me to collect data from which chapter 4 in this book developed, and where my ministerial outreach at High Parish also features in other parts of this book. Chapters 7 and 9 were originally delivered online for the church. I therefore also am grateful to High Parish congregants, parishioners and friends, many of whom are refugees and asylum seekers for the many conversations, some of which were agonizing to share but they did so as they saw me as a confidential confidant in their moments of immense difficulties. I hope my time with you was helpful and purposeful. My prayers for you is that this book will also enrich and encourage you.

Thanks to Mr. Ennis, a solicitor at Rees and Page Solicitors who represented me as my legal counsel in which chapter 6 emanated. He confirmed that I would be on safe, legal grounds if I chose to publish my findings on the claim, *Professor Doreen McCalla v Diocese of Lichfield*.

The inclusion of gospel songs in this book aids in my attempt to capture the womanist spirituality of the Black and Brown Sisters. I am therefore especially thankful to Christian, British Black composers and lyricists, Carol Wilson-Frith and Kevin Simpson and Velroy Bailey and Andrew Smith for granting me permission to print lyrics from their original songs, "Peace in My Soul," and "More Like You," respectively. May God's grace and mercy continually shine on you.

Special thanks to all academic colleagues who endorsed this book: to Margaret Aymer, Heidi Mirza, and Carlton Turner. May God continue to guide your work and devotion in higher education and beyond. Sincere thanks to Musa Dube who has been on this project-journey with me at various times since 2017; with all its twists and turns in trying to get it started, her invaluable contribution in recommending academic contacts such as Margaret Aymer, and her review of earlier work for an anthology which was later discarded. However, from that discarded anthology this monograph eventually developed.

Last but definitely not least, I am grateful to Wipf & Stock for publishing this book. I appreciate your guidance, clarity and support throughout the entire publication process. Thanks especially to Matthew Wimer and Robin Parry for your editorial advice, understanding, and patience when I asked for modifications to parts of the original plan in order to produce the book which has emanated. I trust that together we have produced a book which will be warmly welcomed by many people and therefore be read by a global audience.

Abbreviations

AIDS	Acquired Immunodeficiency Syndrome
AGM	Annual General Meeting
BAME	Black, Asian and Minority Ethnic
BAP	Bishop's Advisor Panel
BCP	Book of Common Prayers
BDO	Bishop's Director of Ordinands
BSA	British Social Attitudes
CoE	Church of England
CoGiC	Church of God in Christ
CoGoP	Church of God of Prophecy
DBS	Disclosure and Barring Service
DCC	District Church Council
DDO	Diocesan Director of Ordinands
DLT	Darton, Longman & Todd
DP	Discernment Process
EAT	Employment Appeal Tribunal
EDI	Equality/Equity, Diversity and Inclusion
ESOL	English for Speakers of Other Languages
FGM	Female Genital Mutilation
HIV	Human Immunodeficiency Virus

HMIC	His Majesty's Inspectorate of Constabulary
HMO	House of Multiple Occupation
IABRS	International Association of Black Religions and Spiritualties
ILTR	Indefinite Leave to Remain
LGBTQI+	Lesbian, gay, bisexual, transgender, queer (or those querying their gender identity or sexual orientation) and intersexual
LMP	London Metropolitan Police
LTR	Leave to Remain
NHS	National Health Service
NISRA	Northern Ireland Statistics and Research Agency
NIV	New International Version
NRPF	No Recourse to Public Funds
NT	New Testament
NTCG	New Testament Church of God
ONS	Office for National Statistics
OT	Old Testament
OWAAD	Organisation of Women of Asian and African Descent
PCC	Parish Church Council
PH	Preliminary Hearing
PPE	Personal Protective Equipment
RCG	Redeemed Church of God
UASC	Unaccompanied Asylum-Seeking Children
UK	United Kingdom
USA/US	United States of America/United States
VA	Vocation Advisor
WMB	Women's Missionary Band
WMP	West Midlands Police
YHWH	Yahweh

Introduction

Breathe, O breath Thy loving Spirit
Into every troubled breast!
Let us all in Thee inherit,
let us find the promised rest.[1]

THIS BOOK SHOWS US what it means to be diasporic, British, Christian, Black and Brown, Loyal Sisters in the British church and in two, contrasting, case study churches, Messa Pentecostal and High Parish. It goes beyond the conventional belief of ecclesiastical, Black women as only being salvific, hardworking servants and disciples of God and the church and therefore spiritual. They are depicted as Loyal Sisters to God and the British church and this is depicted in their spiritual lifestyles and womanist resistance. The womanist spirituality of Loyal Sisters is explored through some of their theological and ontological experiences. These are formulated in a context of community and solidarity; cultural religiosity, resilience and emotional encounters; ordination and ministerial licensing; leadership and discipleship; spiritual abuse; immigration, refugees and asylum-seeker living; racial acceptance and self-love for spiritual, collective, and personal well-being; and also for empowerment and resistance to oppression, discrimination, systemic patriarchy, and racism in the British church.

---

1. Wesley, "Love Divine, All Loves Excelling." Another song option can be the Grace Thrillers song, "Welcome . . . Blessed Holy Ghost We Welcome You" from their "Holy Ghost Power (Medley)."

Apart from their womanist lifestyle as practicing Christians and churchgoers, the significance of spiritual redemption and pneumatic transcendence enables Loyal Sisters to remain faithful to Jesus and the British church. It forms the basis of an understanding of their love and unreserved commitment to God and the church. It is this which enables Loyal Sisters to be devoted to a perfect God and an imperfect church. These Loyal Sisters serve a loving God who helps them to serve God and the church through the Spirit—womanist spirituality—to the best of their human abilities since they too are imperfect humans. Spiritual redemption and pneumatic transcendence allows them to stay with God and the church "come what may."

Although community womanism has emerged in the UK, in which womanist action functions outside and independent of the British church or in partnership with it,[2] there is still a remnant of Black and Brown, Loyal Sisters in the British church who are unmovable and operate in the British church (1 Cor 15:58). This means there is also hope for renewed womanist theology and religiosity through their spiritual agency inside the British church.

This introduction will proceed with a section on the methodology of the book. A section on the rational for writing the book will follow that section. Third, the structure of the book will be outlined.

Methodology

The book is part of a broader study into British womanist and Black feminist religiosity and theologies which started in 2017. The project draws on a variety of methodological approaches and tools. Ethnographical exploration and spiritual reflection are methodological approaches adopted.[3] The study is interdisciplinary and ecumenical. Without delving in-depth into the philosophy of the social sciences,[4] this study is therefore premised on data evidence—the language/concept and methodology generally used for field investigations as opposed to scientific research where

---

2. McCalla, *Community Womanism*, forthcoming.

3. Glesne and Peshkin, *Becoming Qualitative Researchers*, 199; Gold, "Roles in Sociological Field Observation," 217–23; Graham et al., *Theological Reflection: Methods*, 200; Lareau, *Home Advantage*, 288; Spradley, *Participant Observation*, 195; Swinton and Mowat, *Practical Theology and Qualitative Research*, 320.

4. Fay, "Philosophy of Social Science," paras. 1–21.

Introduction

the language, methods and tools of empiricism are used. It is explorative, experiential, descriptive and analytical rather than solely theoretical.

Black and Brown female praxis and experience in the British church combines to construct a religiosity, theology, methodology, ideology, and theory of the lived-experience of Loyal Sisters. As a practicing, ecumenical Christian, examples and illustrations are employed from my lifetime of immersion in numerous churches as mentioned above for data collection and analysis. My immersion in various congregations and among different congregants, at several church and community events, both in person and online, has equipped me to understand and thus interpret the meaning of the ecclesial communities and ethnical cultures of women's interactions in them through my participant observations and thus from which to construct a womanist spirituality of Loyal Sisters. Data is collected from a combination of literature review of Black and Brown women, textual analysis from documents and emails; many community, church, and academic conversations with mainly women but also men, in the churches mentioned above, and case study churches which I will detail in following chapters. I also noted reflections on current and historical autobiographical information—autobiographical ethnography or my womanist testimony. As far as possible, I selected appropriate Christian, songs: reminiscent of pneumatic outpouring and social justice from immersion in the churches, and therefore hope from oppression and discrimination. I have included my own creative poetries of emancipation, social justice, and empowerment. My own creative sermon and an intercession are also included in this book. I adopted an insider-researcher, participant observer role, that is, I am acquainted with the case study congregations. I was a congregant of them at some time throughout my lifetime. Data was gathered and notes recorded and analyzed using a combination of spiritual reflection and Staussian coding.[5] The chapters in this book are refinements of some previous substantive written drafts, some of which were presented and submitted as unpublished texts for former ministerial endeavors in the British church.

My testimonies throughout this book will show that I encountered some social and economic difficulties during the same time of carrying out lay ministry in the CoE and researching this book. Such personal tragedy and trauma may have impacted my theological reflection on the

---

5. Strauss, *Qualitative Research for Social Sciences*, 336; Strauss and Corbin, *Basics of Qualitative Research*, 272; Strauss and Corbin, "Grounded Theory Methodology," 273–85; Swinton and Mowat, *Practical Theology and Qualitative Research*, 320.

data in this book. Whilst as an experienced researcher, I have learnt to also examine and re-examine my analysis, to sound out my ideas and thoughts with church and community friends and kindly request rereads and comments on chapters from academic colleagues and confidants, which is a common practice in academic peer-reviewing anywhere. I think the balance between subjectivity and objectivity during the research process and amid my sometimes purling moments has been sufficiently maintained.

Case Study Churches

Unless otherwise stated, I draw most of my data collection and analysis from mainly two case study churches: High Parish and Messa Pentecostal. However, in addition to these two churches, spiritual reflection on what I call the British church also comprises the basis of data collection and analysis.

Rationale for This Book

This book emerged to account for a vast gap in world religiosity and theology on British, diasporic, Black and Brown females in the UK. It is an attempt to fill that gap. It surfaced from a wider investigation on Black and Brown females and religiosity in Britain. Secondly, a demand for such resources began when an active dialogue increased amongst female church and faith-community leaders, practitioners and followers, scholars and doctoral researchers, and teacher-academics and postgraduate candidates on this area. They expressed their interests in acquiring available resources in this area. For example, in February 2021 during COVID-19 lockdown, on an online Black Theology Forum, female postgraduate degree candidates at Queen's Foundation for Ecumenical Theological Education in Birmingham, UK, raised concerns that their master-degree course books on womanist theology only contextualized the American experience. It was apparent that these books were not accounting for the unique British context sufficiently for these students to identify their own experiences in them. The knowledge that university students had no books in an area which I specialized, such that they publicly complained, sometimes kept me awake at night even several days later. The fact that I was also experiencing financial and social hardship at that time and not in paid employment or receiving a liveable and regular income for my labour, a discussion I shall expand on in chapter 5 in the womanist testimony service, was unknown to them. Besides, their complaint was not levied at me personally but a general complaint that I certainly heard loudly and clearly. Notwithstanding, I still felt a burden to deliver publications for them in particular, and which would also help everyone in the world since I also knew there were limited available books in that area.

Apart from academic journal articles and other books mentioned in this book, some of which can be obtained only from theological colleges and university libraries, there are limited available sources which capture the British experience. This book confirms the students' observations. My forthcoming book, *Community Womanism*, also does the same since it demonstrates that British womanist religiosity and theological action is predominantly outside the church due to patriarchal sexism, racism, and other factors in it. It shows that womanist religiosity and theology is present in community organizations and parachurches.[6] This incident enabled me to recall another occasion when I attempted to also provide books for students—déjà vu. It was in my better economic times when, in 2007, I was academic dean and Distinguished Charles Boddie Professor at American Baptist College.[7] Some students at the college complained of not being able to afford to purchase books which were on their courses' reading lists. By negotiating with the business office's book shop staff for the removal of books from it which were unsold after several years, free of charge, and placing them in the college library, students were provided with ample books for their courses.

I trust that this book will add value to the supply of global, theological, and religious womanist resources. Secondly, I pray it also meets some of the demand for British womanist books for students who at Queen's Ecumenical College can afford to purchase books but are unable to do so since there are limited books on women of color in Britain from which such purchases can be made. The absence of books on women of color in religiosity and theology in the UK impacts on the advancement of knowledge and/or practice for everyone in Britain and globally too.

---

6. McCalla, *Community Womanism*, forthcoming.
7. This is the real name of the college.

The Readership

When engaging with scholars, students, practitioners, and anyone concerned with women's and/or racial equality, justice, inclusion, harmony, rights—and thus people involved in tackling inequalities, discrimination, injustices, exclusion, oppression, disunity and the wrongs of all Black and Brown females in attempting to decolonize communities—it was apparent that the exploration into this area and the dissemination of the findings from such work is certainly required. This book is therefore not just for Black and Brown women, females, and/or Black people. It is for anyone in and out of the British church. So, anyone involved in and concerned with women's and/or racial equality, justice, inclusion, harmony and rights will be audiences for the text. People concerned with tackling inequalities, discrimination, injustices, exclusion, oppression, disunity and the wrongs of mainly women and specifically women of color in attempts to decolonize communities will engage with this book. Practitioners and congregants in the church and other faith communities can read and apply the text to their learning, study groups, and practices. Scholars and doctoral researchers will also welcome it as a research base and higher education students in undergraduate and postgraduate teaching will find it a useful tool for their studies. This book is also for a global audience. Whilst some global experiences are similar, this book recognizes that there are nuances in the British context of church.

I am publishing this book with an American publisher with an international outlet. Whilst the context of the book is British, the American English spelling shall be used throughout the book in accordance with the publisher's house style. For example, mom rather than mum.

Book Structure

The structure of this book may resemble a service liturgy. This is normally presented in a service sheet or program in the Anglican tradition but rarely so in most Charismatic or Pentecostal Churches, apart from in special services where the convention, unwritten and known service-structure to regular congregants, deviates from the norm. I shall call this book structure a womanist liturgy to which, as the author of this book, I am the president or moderator of this liturgy. Apart from the discussion of the contents of each chapter below, chapters in this book are also laced with hymns and many gospel songs from around the world as well as my creative poetries. These add to the semblance of a service liturgy and my womanist liturgy.

The Introduction prepares the reader for worship as would be the case in a service. This is followed by chapter 1, Loyal Sisters: Black and Brown in the UK and chapter 2, The British church and the Spiritual Lifestyle of Loyal Sisters which could be likened to content and activities at the start of a service. Chapter 1 defines what is understood by a Loyal Sister in the book. It considers the racial, ethnic, and cultural identities of Loyal Sisters as Black and Brown and therefore the meaning of these indicators in the context of British demographics. Chapter 2 defines the British church and details what is considered as womanist spirituality in it.

The case studies in chapter 3, Messa Pentcostal, and chapter 4, High Parish, can be likened to the offertory in the liturgy since I see the data collection and analysis from these two churches as a donation or contribution to this book on womanist spirituality in the British church in the same way that a financial donation is a congregational collection in a church service. These two chapters present the spiritual lives of Loyal Sisters in both case study churches.

Chapter 5 is my creative womanist testimony. Testimony services are common to Pentecostal theology, spirituality, and service liturgy. I shall explore this tradition further in this chapter. Chapter 6 is another testimony of sorts. It tells the story of the malign side of spirituality, that is spiritual abuse, and how this testimony can be effective in changing policy and/or practise in the British church. The testimony service could sometimes occupy most of the remainder of the service in some Pentecostal services. At other times, there would be no testimony service.

The sermon would follow the testimony service in the Pentecostal liturgy or, if a soloist, choir, or musical ensemble is included in the service, after these renditions. If there is no testimony service, the sermon would occur after the offering and/or the musical rendition in the service.

Chapter 7 is a sermon reflection on scriptural references to Pentecost and for relevance and application to the spiritual lives of Loyal Sisters and anyone. Apart from the sermon reflection, chapter 8, *Loving Race and Accepting Self*, is also a reflection and is structured in the book accordingly, that is directly after the sermon. This chapter discusses the importance of loving and accepting oneself as Christian Black and Brown women and girls and as created in the image of God (*imago Dei*). It shows the failure to self-love and self-accept as Loyal Sisters, and that this can be spiritually redeemed. This brings me to chapter 9.

Together, chapter 9, *Spiritual Redemption and Transcendence*, and chapter 10, the *Altar Service*, are responses to the *Introduction* and chapters 1 to 8. A time for congregational respond is generally allowed in the liturgy of services. The response in chapter 9 is one of spiritual redemption and transcendence for Black and Brown women who suffer and are publicly oppressed and discriminated against in the church, but who can find peace, forgiveness, hope, be empowered, and gain eternal life. The womanist intercession or petitioning prayer as response for others and self, in chapter 10, is fashioned from the Anglican Church tradition which often appears before or directly after the sermon. However, in this book, it is structured at the end as would generally appear in a tradition, Pentecostal liturgy as the altar service or "altar call." However, an altar service may be automatically called by the prompting of the Holy Spirit throughout the service where congregants would readily flock to the altar to pray for themselves and/or others or if it is requested by the moderator of the service. Even if an "altar call" is planned in a Pentecostal service the moderator uses the oral traditional of prayers rather than a written intercession as is customary in Pentecostalism. In this book I have created a combined Pentecostal and Anglican intercession.

Service liturgies often end with a time of praise and thanksgiving to God and a brief encouragement to depart into the world with assurance of God's protection and guidance. This is mainly presented in song or words followed by, in Anglicanism, the procession of ministers and congregants from the service, and, in all traditions, the benediction or blessing and then the dismissal. In Anglicanism, congregants are given time to sit and further reflect on and respond to the service once the procession of ministers has taken place. In Pentecostalism, congregants can continue to "tarry[8] at the altar" or "tarry in my seat" with altar workers, or alone, after the dismissal.

In conventional written-form the conclusion summarizes all chapters. In academic writing it also presents findings and issues arising from the project and publication itself. Third, the conclusion of academic writing may also allow the author/s to make recommendations for developments, improvements, further research, projects and publications and, if possible, how other researchers and/or authors can act on any of the recommendations. In this book where it is symbolic of a church liturgy, I break from traditional writing. The book ends with the altar service since

---

8. Tarrying will be defined in chapter 3.

it is the usual completion of a Pentecostal service. The prayer not only includes all women of color and Loyal sisters in the book, but it is a prayer of petition and also demonstrates that there is hope for the progression of womanist spirituality in the British church. Furthermore, it is a prayer in which Loyal Sisters can action organic change in the British church through spiritual collectivism for each and all. Amen/So be it!

1

Loyal Sisters
Black and Brown in the UK

> All over the world
> The Spirit is moving.
> All over the world
> As the prophet said it would be.
> All over the world
> There's a might revelation
> Of the glory of [God]
> As the waters cover the sea.[1]

THIS CHAPTER RECOGNIZES THAT a unified Black identity or unified Brown and Black women of Asian, African, and Caribbean females does not exist in Britain and thus, the womanist spirituality conceptualization shall not treat Loyal Sisters as a universal/homogenous Brown and Black women's group. It presents the specifics of Black and Asian women's identity per se and therefore the formation of diversity and inclusion within and between Blacks and Asians of various ethnicities. The analysis of Black and Asian ethnic groups of women is appropriately captured and addressed in terms of their racial, national, ethnic, cultural, social, and

---

1. Author unknown. For this book, the word "the Lord" in the original song is replaced with the word God.

historical diversities in Britain and in terms of migration and what this means for each group.

I start with a definition of Loyal Sisters. This is followed by a section on racial indicators of identification and why I refer to Loyal Sisters as Black and Brown. The third section is about British Black and Brown diasporic women; followed by a fourth section on the use of the capital B in the words Black and Brown. A fifth section is on the racial, ethnic, and historical trajectory of Black and Brown women in Britain. The demographics of race and ethnicity are considered in section six. This chapter then concludes by drawing together everything on Loyal Sisters and Black and Brown in the UK.

Loyal Sisters Defined

Loyal Sisters (and Loyal Sistas[2]) are Christian Black and Brown[3] females who remain faithful to the British church, which is, mainstream churches and/or Black or multicultural/intercultural denominations, in the midst of all the church's deficiencies and in spite of systemic patriarchy. Loyal Sisters are the church Sisters who will attend as many church activities as possible and serve their church ceaselessly. They belong to church and Jesus "come what may." Whilst they are Sisters of all generations Loyalist Sisters are mainly Boomers and Generation X Black and Brown women, that is, older and middle-aged women between the ages of 50 to 80s or even 90s. However, some are younger Sisters too as demonstrated in Table 1.

Table 1 Generations by Age and Year Ranges[4]

Generations	Ages (in 2022)	Years
Alpha	Oldest 12 or (9)	2010 (2013)–2024 (or 2026)
Z	10–25	1997–2012
Y/Millennials	26–41	1981–1996
X	42–57	1965–1980

2. The word Sistas will be used for Sisters in Messa Pentecostal since, as chapter 3 will demonstrate, the majority of the congregation are of Jamaican-Caribbean origin and therefore the use of patois.

3. Black and Brown shall be defined below.

4. Table 1 is a construction based on figures from the generations defined by name, birth year, and ages in 2022, "Age Range by Generation," and "Understanding Generation Alpha."

Table 1 Generations by Age and Year Ranges[4]

Generations	Ages (in 2022)	Years
Boomers II	58–67	1955–1964
Boomers I	68–76	1946–1954
Post World War	77–94	1928–1945
WWII	95–100	1922–1927

Other Loyal Sisters are also carers of family and/or relatives such as children, elders, or the ill. Those who care for dependants would be regular church attendees if this activity did not consume all their time and energy. Church attendance is therefore a wrap-around pursuit to their caring responsibilities. They attend their regular congregation when they can and seldom visit other denominations due to their caring activities.

Loyal Sisters operate in the British church from the arrival of Blacks/the Windrush Generation from 1948 to 1973 and also the establishment of some of the nationalized Black churches at the same time. I will discuss this in chapter 2. Until relatively recently, the Black church did not consist of many Brown females of Asian origin. They belonged to other faith groups. So unless otherwise stated, much of what is said in this chapter about the Black church refers to Black females.

Loyal Sisters are also refugee and asylum-seeker, migrant women mainly from my case-study church, High Parish. A high proportion of women from High Parish are Loyal Sisters of various ethnicities since High Parish is an intercultural congregation of the Anglican Church which I shall explore further in chapter 6. Asian, African, and Caribbean women of color are Loyal Sisters at High Parish.

Why Black and Brown?

Reasons for the use of Black and Brown as racial indicators of identification in this book is firstly to avoid mixing the metaphors of Asian and Black with one being a color (Black) which denotes various meaning associated with culture and ethnicity also, and the other is a continent of Asia with its cultural and ethnic associations too. However, secondly, this Black and Asian binary assumes that peoples who are of Asian embodiment either come from the continent of Asia and/or so do their ancestors. This is not always the case. Asian people live in other parts of the world. For example, Asian native, indigenous, and migrant inhabitants are found in countries such as Trinidad and Jamaica in the Caribbean or Uganda, South Africa, and Kenya in Africa and are now diasporic UK residents. They may prefer to self-identify as Black although they are of Asian embodiment because of their Caribbean or African origin. Similarly, peoples of the darkest complexions may self-identify as Black but are not of Caribbean or Africa descendants and vice versa. For example, ancestries of Black peoples who would traditionally be associated with counties such as Africa and the Caribbean are found in Iran (Afro-Iranians) or Afghanistan (Hazara people) and some now populate the UK. The movement of people around the globe through colonization in the sixteenth, seventeenth and eighteenth centuries, and historically, more recently, through migration for economic purposes, such as work, in the 1940s, to the 1960s in the UK such as, through the Windrush Generation, or more recently due to refuge or asylum seeking, means that this Asian and Black binary may not be sufficient, adequate and/or helpful enough for women of color to self-identify in the UK.

The third reason for using the colors Black and Brown is primarily about enabling women of color to have a broader scope from which to self-identify and thus allow them greater appreciation to accept and own themselves and thus self-love—a point I shall discuss further in chapter 8. Over the past decade I have acknowledged that women of South Asian origin or biracial females are not always sure that being Asian qualifies them to self-identify as Black. So, in an act of defiance, for some females of South Asian and/or biracial descendants, they have self-identified as Black. In other cases, others have self-identified as Brown instead of Asian and/or because they are biracial.

Fourth reason for using Black and Brown is that, like my Sheroes book,[5] this book will show that there is not a homogeneous group of Black females. Common to the studies of Black and Brown women in the 1980s and beyond is the triple effects of racism, sexism, and classism and many other intersectionalities in terms of ethnicity, religiosity, class, and age.[6] In my book, *Unsung Sheroes in the Church,* I also acknowledged that there is not a homogenous group of Black and Brown females of Asian, Caribbean and/or African origin and biracial identities since ethnic, cultural and national diversity is apparent among and between Brown and Black females.[7] Similarly, this book will also demonstrate that ethnic,

---

5. McCalla, *Unsung Sheroes in the Church,* 201.
6. Brah, *Cartographies of Diaspora,* 292. Bush, "Gender and Empire," 77–111.
7. McCalla, *Unsung Sheroes in the Church,* 201.

cultural, and national diversity is apparent among Brown females too. Recent data-collection/sets such as in the 2021 census no longer conflates Asians as part of a racially Black ethnic group hence my separation in this book of females from Asian, Caribbean, and/or African origin whilst also conceptually acknowledging the ethnic diversity in and between Black and Brown girls and women too. This is demonstrated in the literature from around the world on Brown females also[8] and Black women too.[9] These studies also reveal many differences between these Black and Brown women during the same decades. Most of the studies on Black females were mainly about women from the Caribbean rather than Africa. There were also variations between East African Asian females and women from the Indian subcontinent.[10]

So, for the purpose of this book, I have decided to use the colors Brown and Black from which UK diasporic women of color who currently reside or were born in the UK can define themselves and therefore love themselves, that is, whether they are females from afro and/or indo peoples and wherever in the world they are descendants.

British Diasporic Black and Brown Women

This book is about Black and Brown women of the British diaspora. Why is it about the British diaspora and not the African, Asian, or Caribbean diaspora? I am centralizing my work in the historical and contemporary context of Britain since to focus solely on women of either the African, Caribbean or Asian diasporas is likely to exclude women and girls of the other continents who reside in the UK and are pertinent to the British church. It is about immigration to and settlement in Britain and its involvement with countries of peoples in relations to Britain. It is thus primarily about cross-culturalism, that is in relation to Britain although the broader concept of multiculturalism may also apply here too. It is about the usage of multi-ethnic inclusion or interculturalism of peoples with Black, Brown, and other origins of color.

British diaspora refers to immigrants and natives of the UK—the former British Empire and its links to British colonialism. It is important

---

8. Barton, *Liberation Spirituality as a Signal of Transcendence*, 26. Barton, *Scripture as Empowerment for Liberation and Justice*, 195. Pui-Lan, *Introducing Asian Feminist Theology*, 136.

9. Oduyoye, *Introducing African Women's Theology*, 132.

10. Brah, *Cartographies of Diaspora*, 292. Bush, "Gender and Empire," 77–111.

to note that most Black and Brown women of African, Asian, Caribbean, and biracial descent presently living in Britain are directly or indirectly of the British diaspora, that is, their ancestors were once colonized by Britain (or another European country) in the nations of their origin and many of these countries are part of the Commonwealth. It is about women of the Commonwealth and those who reside in Britain but also females who come from countries which are not Commonwealth nations but have settled in the UK. This book is also about current residents in the UK as asylum seekers and refugees with or without Leave to Remain (LTR) or Indefinite Leave to Remain (ILTR) as well as British women who were born abroad but are now citizens in the UK. LTR enables a non-UK citizen rights to stay in the UK for a certain time. There are different types of LTR such as, student, work and/or family visa and persons can reapply several times when their visas expire. ILTR entitles a person to obtain permanent "settlement" in the UK. With ILTR immigration controls are lifted and rights, to work, study, live and enter and leave the UK is granted. ILTR does not expire unless a person leaves the UK for more than two years. It is a prerequisite to British citizenship for people of different nationalities after a defined period of time.[11] This book is also about females who are automatic British citizens at their birth in the UK under the British Nationality Act 1981, section 11(1). I now turn to focus on the capital B in the racial identification of Black and Brown.

The Capital B

Historically, in the 1970s, the significance of the capital B, for the color Black, was a political mark of the anti-racist movement and solidarity amid gendered inequality and discrimination of African, Caribbean, and Asia British females.[12] Whilst not all writers of British Black females use the capital B, they are nonetheless either politically-driven and/or passionate about the emancipation of women of color.[13] Although this book is primarily about the womanist spirituality of Loyal Sisters, it will also show the activism of woman of color for their rights and justice in

---

11. Trinity College London, "Leave to Remain."

12. Swaby, "'Disparate in Voice, Sympathetic in Direction,'" 11–25.

13. Bryan et al., *Heart of Race*, 256. Feminist Review, *Many Voices, One Chant*, 1–117. Scafe, *Feminist Review*, 141.

the British church and women's rights of generations to follow hence the capital B shall be used for Brown and Black females.

Racial identification of Blackness may have differed overtime between British, Asian, Caribbean, and African females but this book will demonstrate that women of color are essentially still united in their struggle for women's Godly significance, emancipation, and rights in the church although with differing perspectives. For this reason, the capital B will be used for both Black and Brown Loyal Sisters. I now turn my attention to the racial, ethnic, and historical trajectory of Brown and Black females in the UK.

The Racial, Ethnic, and Historical Trajectory of Black and Brown Women in the UK

Whilst neither of my case study churches feature a long history of Asian people in Britain since most of the Asians in this study either are recent immigrants or still refugee and asylum seekers, I shall nevertheless provide a brief history and, in the next section, the demographics of Brown/Asian female present in the UK since some Christian Asian females also belong to the British church which I shall define in chapter 2.

In my Sheroes book,[14] I mentioned that Black in the UK does not mean the same as it does in the US and that by understanding the differences we can better relate to the ontology, that is, the experiences, existence, being, and realities of Black and Brown people in Britain and other countries. With regards to "black" in third wave womanist religious thought, Monica Coleman points out that our understanding of Black should not be constrained to the African American definition of Black as used in North America, but, in a global context.[15] Black has many meanings and within those meanings "ethnicity" and "color" must also not be assumed the same in geographical, religious, and cultural terms. For example, in South America, the Caribbean (and there are many countries that comprise of the Caribbean), and Australia, Black is understood differently in each of those countries and also differs to the definition in the US and Britain. In Britain, Black conventionally had its distinct definition to that used in other parts of the world. Traditionally, in the UK, Black included people of the Asian diaspora as well as from the African

---

14. McCalla, *Unsung Sheroes in the Church*, 201.
15. Coleman, "Introduction," 1–31.

diaspora that is, of the continent of Africa and Caribbean. In the 2011 Census Black people were of Asian, African, and Caribbean descent. So Asian people were united as Black in Britain until the 2021 census when Asian was identified separately.

It is now known that Blacks and Asians have been in Britain since AD 122 although not in any significant numbers.[16] African, Caribbean, and Asian women were invisible, outsiders to modern western civilization or marginalized in histories of empire, colonization, and slavery. There were significant differences in white stereotypes of Black and Brown women which emerged during colonialism and contrasted with the superiority stereotypes of white women. African women were seen as representatives of barbarism and Asian women represented the inferior traditional cultures of imperialism.[17] Dr. Suzanne Scafe reveals the lives of Black women living in Britain under slavery and beyond. Mary Prince from Bermuda was one such Black woman who eventually lived and worked at the home of the Scottish writer Thomas Pringle, the then secretary of the Anti-Slavery Society. Prince's personal account, which was published in 1831, was the first to depict the life of a Black woman in Britain: "The man that says slaves be quite happy in slavery—that they don't want to be free—that man is either ignorant or a lying person. I never heard a slave say so."[18] In 2014 an exhibition entitled, *Re-imagine: Black Women in Britain*, which was held at the then recently opened Black Cultural Archives in Windrush Square in Brixton, South London reveals Seaman William Brown as the first Black woman to serve in the Royal Navy. The 1815 Annual Register mentions, "her features are rather handsome for a black."[19] During the Crimean war, there is also a nurse, Mary Seacole.

It was during mass migration to Britain in the late 1940s from the Caribbean, Africa, and Asia that many found themselves in Britain, primarily England, and where the second, third, and in some cases, fourth generation of women of color are born. In a British Black feminist landmark text, *The Heart of Race: Black Women's Lives in Britain*,[20] Black, activist, feminists Beverley Bryan, Stella Dadzie, and Suzanne Scafe, and others who campaigned for females' rights in the late 1970s and 1980s,

---

16. Adewunmi, "Women in Britain."
17. Bush, "Gender and Empire," 77–111.
18. Scafe, *Feminist Review*, 141. Anim-Addo and Scafe, *I Am Black/White/Yellow*, 236.
19. Anim-Addo and Scafe, *I Am Black/White/Yellow*, 236.
20. Bryan et al., *Heart of Race*, 256.

draw on Caribbean women's promise of the "mother country" in the 1940s and 1950s in which their reality of Britain differed. The book talks about working women's experience of childcare and families, jobs, housing and communities, and how girls' educational, ambitious experiences are disregarded by racial, sexist, and classist intersectionality. An updated second edition[21] from the 1985 original book was published in 2018 with an introduction by Lola Okolosie and interviews with the authors were carried out by Heidi Mirza, a leading British Black feminist and academic sociologist. As emeritus professor of race, faith and culture, Mirza's work has shed many lights on the religiosity and praxis of Asian, Muslim females in white-majority institutions, such as schools and universities, and the perception of their race by the educational sector.[22] The pivotal leap from education settings of Mirza's work to the British church in this book is significant since they both explore the religiosity and lifestyles of women of color whilst the contexts are very different.

Suzanne Scafe also gives a detailed account of the Jamaica-born, Olive Morris (1952–1979) who contributed to community organizing and activism whilst living in Lambeth. She co-founded the Organisation of Women of African and Asian Descent (OWAAD), the Brixton Black women's group, which supported the setting up of the Brixton Law Centre. She was a member of the Black Panther Movement. Morris also helped to set up the Manchester Black Women's Co-operative whilst at the University in Manchester.[23] Seven years after her death of non-Hodgkin lymphoma, Lambeth council honored Morris by naming a building after her.[24]

In the 1980s, Pakistani and Bangladeshi women were "home workers," and as seamstresses, were poorer and periodically experienced racial harassment. They therefore had marginal options to work or not to do so.[25] Referring to the arrival of Caribbeans, almost every literature account makes mention of the West Indies and calypso music on Tilbury docks, Essex with the Empire Windrush, June 22, 1948 where the passengers numbered 490 men and two women with one stowaway. Whilst the naming of people after a ship is disliked by some people, the historic migration of the Windrush Generation to England from 1948 to

21. Bryan et al., *Heart of Race*, 304.

22. Mirza and Meetoo, *Respecting Difference*, 80. Mirza and Meetoo, "Empowering Muslim Girls?" 227–41.

23. Anim-Addo and Scafe, *I Am Black/White/Yellow*, 236.

24. Bryan et al., *Heart of Race*, 256.

25. Brah, *Cartographies of Diaspora*, 292.

1973; consisting also of children and men, is certainly significant. This is because, after 1973, immigration legislation changed in the UK which impacted other migrants to the UK as this book shall reveal, and also some of the Windrush Generation through the now notorious Windrush Scandal which started in April 2018. However, together Caribbean and Asian women organized through Black feminist organizations such as Southall Black Sisters, founded in 1979, to defend their rights, including the rights of better working conditions.[26]

By the 1990s and beyond, women of Hindu and Sikh backgrounds were beginning to occupy professional jobs outside the home and younger women were increasingly independent and liberated compared with their mothers. British Asian women such as Baroness Warsi (Muslim), Shazia Mirza, and Meera Syal have confounded popular perceptions by being prominent achievers in politics and the media and in various other areas in public life. Notable Caribbean women are politician, Diane Abbott, the justice campaigner, Baroness Doreen Lawrence, and publisher and Black Parents Movement activist, Jessica Hunley. It is within this historical British context that the British church was established and developed and where the womanist spirituality of Loyal Sisters was realized as following chapters will show.

Cultural and Ethnic Distinctions

Recent studies on culture and ethnicity in the public more generally, are demonstrating the differences between groups as apparent in a postmodernist age.[27] This and specific chapters in this book aim to appropriately demonstrate these ethnic distinctions. In the field of educational studies, when concentrating on some of the life histories and present experiences of two Black, professional women—one, a university, academic researcher (me—Doreen), and the other, a state nursery head teacher and research gate-keeper (Syble)—I showed in my paper that our stories sometimes varied substantially due to distinctive social, geographical, timeframe, career-choice factors, and personal and professional values. We united with a mutual purpose, that is, to embark on my research into the success of Black children, then and now adults, of a 1970s Black-led inner-city community nursery. Although sharing a research stage/agenda, the same

---

26. Gupta, *From Homebreakers to Jailbreakers*, 320.
27. Small, *Racialised Barrier*, 256. Hall, "Local and the Global, "173–87.

gender, racial, and social class grouping and thus seemingly having much in common, the paper concluded by emphasizing that among a homogeneous, gendered, and racialized group of apparent generalities, individuals exist—a frequent oversight, especially with regards to African-Caribbean people. This is with regards to issues of identity, culture, citizenship, and race and racism which featured strongly in the paper among some matters arising with regards to femininity and social class.[28] Audre Lorde and bell hooks also agree that while self-identifying with different national, cultural, and racial identities, which positions us with some people and not with others, is an indication of the varieties of humanities and identities that we share with some people and not with others, this variety is fine.[29] So whilst we may all differ and at times be the same it is still important to recognize these similarities and differences whilst loving ourselves, and by doing so, to also find ways to love and appreciate the worth and value of other Black and Brown Sisters in partnerships too.

I now address British racial and ethnic demography.

Racial and Ethnic Demography

The Office for National Statistics (ONS) which collates and analyzes the data from the 2021 Census, which was carried out at the time of writing this book, clearly shows a distinction between Black and Asian from which persons from the UK population can identify themselves. 19 ethnic groups are specified in the 2021 Census. According to the 2021 Census, Black now means people of African, Caribbean, and mixed racial or of other Black origins. Asian refers to people of descendants from the Asian Continent. The ethnic divisions of the Asian diaspora comprise of Indians, Pakistani, Bangladeshi, Chinese, and other Asian origin. Black people are Caribbean, African, Black British, and other Black backgrounds. This census also does not state the African and Caribbean diasporic ethnic population by countries. However other sources demonstrate a high concentration of West Africans such as Nigerians and Ghanaians and Caribbean persons. Caribbeans are disproportionately of Jamaicans, Barbadians (Bajans), and Trinidadians and Tabagonians who are often also referred to as African Caribbeans or Caribbean British.[30] For per-

---

28. McCalla-Chen, "Academic and Community Meet," 165–83.
29. Lorde, *Sister Outsider*, 187. bell hooks, *Sisters of the Yam*, 184.
30. See Small, *Racialised Barriers*, 256.

sons of mixed parentage, they can identify as white and Black Caribbean/Black African/Black Asian or any other background. Aside from these groups of Asians and Blacks, the 2021 British Census, collated by the ONS, also records an option in which people can identify themselves as Arabs or any other background.[31] These ethnic variations thus show that in Britain these Black and Asian ethnic groups are not homogeneous. The ethnic variations, in terms of culture, history, and geography between and within these Black and Asian nationalities, cannot be overlooked in this analysis. This is because these variants impact the life-course and Christian and faith experience of Black and Brown women.

The 2011 British Census demonstrates a population of Asian 5,235,154 and African and Caribbean 1,904,684 out of a total population of 63,182,178.[32] The Worldometres recorded a 2017 total population of 66,308,899 persons in the UK.[33] The World Population Review for 2021 gives a total UK population of 68,257,516.[34] At the time of writing the UK population from the 2021 Census for England is 56,489.800[35] and Wales 3,107,500.[36] The 2021 Census statistics for Scotland was 5,436,600 in 2022.[37] The 2019 figures show a Scottish population of 5,463,300.[38] The population of Northern Ireland is 1,903,175[39] and the Republic of Ireland, 5,123,536.[40] The 2021 Census for the population by ethnicity shows Asian ethnic groups comprising 5,515,455 peoples, Blacks consist of 2,409,283, mixed persons totaling 1,717,977, and the other ethnic groups calculation is 1,255,632 of the English and Welsh population.[41] The total ethnic groups is 10,898,347 in England and Wales. The ONS does not divide the population by ethnic genders only by gender so I am unable to say how many females comprise the England and Wales population by ethnicity.

---

31. ONS, *Harmonised Concepts and Questions*, 27. Gov.UK, *Population of England and Wales*.
32. ONS, *Ethnicity and National Identity in England and Wales*.
33. Worldometers, "UK Population."
34. World Population Review, *United Kingdom Population*.
35. ONS, *Population and Household Estimates, England and Wales*.
36. ONS, *Population and Household Estimates, England and Wales*.
37. Scotland's Census.
38. Wikipedia, "Demography of Scotland."
39. NISRA, *Northern Ireland Census 2021 Data*.
40. Central Statistics Office, "Census of the Population 2022."
41. Gov.UK, *Population of England and Wales*.

Table 2 British Government Statistics on Immigration in the UK[42]

Details	2022	2021	2019/pre-pandemic
Resettlement protection (5,792)	23,841 people (including dependants)		20,264 people (including dependants)
Humanitarian protection			
Refugee status			
Alternative forms of leave			
Asylum applications in the UK	74,751		37,376
Initial decisions on asylum applications	18,699	13,276	20,569
Decisions to extend a person's stay in the UK	571,815 people (including dependants)	331,652	80,054 people (including dependants)
Decisions on applications for settlement in the UK	133,451	101,422	78,736
People granted settlement in the UK	131,728		
Applications for British citizenship	190,741		173,574
People granted British citizenship	175,972		158,374 (including EU applicants)
Applications for citizenship by non-EU nationals	144,080		122,468
People entering immigration detentions	20,446		23,717
People leaving detentions	19,447		23,530
Detained for seven days or less	10,112		14,353

Notes:
- 2021 and 2019 figures in the table are approximate amounts of my calculations from percentages in the government statistics. The tabular blanks for 2021 and 2019 means that there are no percent figures given in the government statistics.
- In 2022, asylum applications in the UK were the highest number since 2003.
- In 2022, 14,211 initial decisions on asylum applications were granted that is, either refugee status, humanitarian protection, or alternative forms of leave.
- Of the top 10 nationalities applying for asylum in 2022, half were granted above 80 percent (Afghanistan 98 percent, Iran 80 percent, Syria 99 percent, Eritrea 98 percent, and Sudan 84 percent), partly because of the UK leaving the European Union (EU).
- In 2022, approximately 15,168 people leaving detention were bailed mainly due to an asylum (or other) applications.

---

42. Table 2 is constructed from government percentages and some of my calculations in the Gov.UK, *National Statistics*.

Table 2 shows the British Government statistics on immigration in the UK in 2022, 2021, and 2019. The Migration Observatory briefing on refugee and asylum resettlement in the UK shows an estimate of 5 percent of the UK's foreign-born population as asylum seekers and 0.6 percent of the total UK population. Between 2011 and 2021, 4,175 or 45 percent of women were granted initial asylum-related status or refugee family reunion. In 2021 Iranian nationals were the highest applicants seeking asylum (10,446) of which 78 percent were granted or other LTR in the UK, followed by Iraq nationals (7,721) where 50 percent of applicants were either granted asylum or other types of LTR in the UK. In 2021, 2,300 unaccompanied asylum-seeking children (UASC), that is children under age 18, were granted asylum or other LTR in the UK.[43] At my case study church, High Parish, congregants who are refugee and asylum seekers would be recorded in both of these statistics. By a lesser number but equally significant, so would some of the congregants of Messa Pentecostal. However, whilst women and children are amongst these, I do not know the numbers.

Conclusion

This chapter acknowledges that a unified Black and Brown identity or unified Black and Brown Sisterhood of Caribbean, Asian, and African Loyal Sisters does not exist in the British church because it does not exist in the British public at large. The analysis of Brown and Black ethnic groups of women shall be captured and addressed in terms of their race, ethnic, cultural, social and historical groups in Britain appropriately. It is about the specifics of personal and collective Black and Brown women's identity per se and thus an inclusive formation.

All of this racial and historical discussion about Black and Brown women in Britain, along with the mingling of their own traditional cultures from their once colonized land more generally, has influenced the way Loyal Sisters see themselves and interact with and function in Britain. It also shows how Loyal Sisters are treated in terms of their Christian faith and how it is practiced in the British church which I shall demonstrate in following chapters in the book.

---

43. Walsh, *Briefing*, 27.

For Discussion

1. Discuss the meaning, application and usefulness of Blackness and Brownness in the UK.
2. What is the relevance of modern history in terms of Black and Brown females today?
3. Are any church Sisters you know Loyal Sisters as defined in this chapter?

2

The British Church and the Spiritual Lifestyle of Loyal Sisters

Yet she on earth hath union
With God the Three in One,
and mystic sweet communion
with those whose rest is won.
O happy ones and holy!
[God], give us grace that we
like them, the meek and lowly,
on high may dwell with thee.[1]

THIS CHAPTER ADDRESSES THE relevance and importance of the British church, that is the mainstream, Black and multicultural/intercultural churches, for Black and Brown Loyal Sisters. It demonstrates Loyal Sister's spirituality or pneumatology, which is the study and praxis of the Holy Spirit, in terms of its historical context, the progress made in terms of womanism in the British church/Ecclesia overtime and what is happening now. It will take account of the nuances of diasporic Black and

---

1. Stone and Wesley, "Church is One Foundation," 545. For this book, I have changed the lyrics from "Lord" on line six to God. Another song-option can be Crouch's song, "Completely Yes."

Brown Loyal Sisters' experience in the British church but also draw on global similarities. It shall demonstrate the reasons for their spiritual resilience, resistance and staying power in the British church.

I start with defining the British church for clarity on what is understood as the British Ecclesia. This section will also produce research finding on the current context of religiosity and spirituality in the UK. The next section focuses on a literature review of existing studies on the British church and womanist spirituality, religiosity, and theology. The literature review of British texts is especially important since existing books are either unknown and/or whilst available and in circulation, are either in short supply or are no longer printed. Section three focuses on Loyal Sisters and their spiritual life-style of devotion to God, church, family, and community. The final section, prior to the conclusion, examines patriarchy in the British church and its impact on the lives of Loyal Sisters.

The British Church

The combined words, British church, naturally assumes a reference to some of the mainstream Anglican Churches of England, Wales, Scotland, Northern Ireland and Ireland in these devolved countries of the UK; and also the Catholic, Baptists and/or Methodists Churches. However, in this book, the British church to which British women of color belong, are also Black majority churches such as the traditional Black Pentecostal/Evangelical denominations which were established in the UK in the 1950s and 1960s namely, the New Testament Church of God (NTCG), The Church of God of Prophecy (CoGoP), The Church of God in Christ (CoGiC), and the Redeemed Church of God (RCG) to mention some. Brown and Black females are also from other apostolic churches like the Seventh Day Adventists. These congregations consist of mainly people of Caribbean and/or African origins.

In this book the British church also comprise of Black and Brown majority congregations of traditionally British, white denominations, for example, the Anglican, Catholic, Methodist, and Baptist Churches. Some of these Black and Brown women are minority-Black and Brown congregants of white-majority congregations and denominations. In chapters where the case-study churches are explored in this book, the British church will further be analyzed from a Black Pentecostal and a multicultural/intercultural Anglican perspective respectively.

Finally on this sub-section, by adding the word British before the word church in the title of this book and throughout, I am informing the reader that whilst Christian Black and Brown women in Britain are part of the diaspora simply because of either their African, Asian, Caribbean, and/or biracial origin, they are not guests of the British church but belong to the British church. I am saying that after over 75 years of mass migration and settlement in the UK, Christian Black and Brown women should now be accorded the same entitlements and treated with the same respect and dignity as any other citizen of the British church. I am saying that since the British church is now a racially and culturally diverse church, it should now be sensitive to the needs of different groups, but also allow for specific and separate racial, ethnic, and cultural groups to operate within it, like the monocultural Black churches, and the traditional Pentecostal Churches; as well as multicultural churches, such as the new Charismatic ones. The problem however, as this book shall demonstrate, is that Loyal Sisters have not been given the same rights and privileges as men, white females, and/or other groups. However, they remain faithful to it by practicing their spirituality regardless.

Research and the British Church

For the first time in British history the English and Welsh, 2021 Census found less than half of the population (46.2 percent/27.5 million) identifies as Christian. The second highest cohort of the population identifies as having no religion that is, 37.2 percent or 22.2 million.[2] In Scotland the total calculation of the population which identifies as Christian is 2,850,199 and 37 percent or 1,941,116 of the population identifies themselves as having no religion.[3] In Northern Ireland the census shows a calculation of 79.4 percent of the population being Christians. 17.4 percent of the population has no religion.[4] What is common in the population in all countries of Britain is that Christianity has markedly decreased compared with figures in the 2011 Census. Conversely, people are increasingly identifying as having no religion. This is a relevant factor in my study of Loyal Sisters since they comprise of the number of people in the

---

2. ONS, *Religion, England and Wales.*
3. Scotland's Census, "Religion, 2022."
4. NISRA, *Main Statistics for Northern Ireland Statistical Bulletin: Religion*, 11.

population of England who still identify as Christians and are *still* actively practicing their faith in their church, families, work, and communities.

Although there have been some in-depth qualitative studies on this phenomenon of no religion,[5] very little is known about them in terms of quantitative research. A recent national, demographical, representative sample of 5,153 adults surveyed by the think tank Theos provides a comprehensive account. It notes that more than half (53 percent) of adults in Britain identify themselves as having no religion. The study calls them "nones." A significantly high number of these "nones" are under 50 years young. In this study, of those under 50, millennials (37 percent) are disproportionately more likely to be "nones" than any other generational group. However, this empiricism, like all other studies, confirms that "nones" are generally young. More men (54 percent) than women (46 percent) are "nones." Some "nones" think the Bible is useful as a moral and social ethical compass for an instruction and direction to our lives but, for some of them, it is not the word of God/the *Logos*. To add, in my own encounters with atheists, some are also enriched by the lifestyles of genuine faith-believers, find comfort from pastoral advice offered by or requested of such people and, in some cases, contribute to their ministries in numerous ways whilst not believing in the God of their faith. The Theos study showed that no religion does not mean that all "nones" are antagonistic to religion. Notwithstanding, it also demonstrates that some "nones" have religious belief. The Report identifies three types of nones. One cohort of nones are the "spiritual nones."

The "spiritual nones" are most relevant to this book than other "nones" in the Theos Report since by name-definition they recognize the existence of spirituality, religion, and theology, although some are also agnostics and very few, atheists too. "Spiritual nones" are mainly females. Nevertheless, the Theos Report does not identify the participants by ethnicity and thus it provides no evidence of Black and Brown female "nones." However, two thirds of "nones" agree that religion has a place in the modern world and some "nones" believe that all faiths contain some truth.[6]

When referring to a demographic survey of both male and females, Linda Woodhead,[7] found that there is a significant decline in institutional

---

5. Lee, *Recognizing the Nonreligious*, 256.

6. Waite, *Nones*, 74.

7. Linda Woodhead has researched extensively on moral and social theology, religion, spirituality and church attendance.

churches as a whole and the rise in alternative spiritualities.[8] Woodhead's studies focus on all racial and gendered congregational demographics. My own research concurs that Christian Black and Brown females have sought alternative places and spaces of worship and/or means to express their faith in the general community and in public life.[9] What is apparent from my work also is that not only has attendance of Black and Brown women at mainstream British churches declined but this regression is apparent in Black churches too, with some exceptions, such as the continued church-attendance of Loyal Sisters.

In general, there has been a steady reduction in attendance in church services and Anglican congregations. According to Linda Woodhead and other colleagues, the British Anglican Church, in particular, along with other traditional, white churches, are in decline when compared statistically and qualitatively with the Pentecostal and Charismatic Movement in the UK. This is due to oppressive structures and various institutional abuses in the Church of England (hereafter CoE).[10] Akin to the reduction in CoE and church attendance generally, these studies also show church attendance consisting mainly of a middle-aged and aging population of congregants between ages 45–65.[11] A recent study by Stephen Bullivant has shown that the decline in Anglicanism is now beginning to stabilize with a modest rise from 16.3 percent in 2009 to 17.1 percent in 2015.[12] In 2018, the British Social Attitudes (BSA) research found seasonal increases in CoE attendance such as at Christmas and Easter. From 2010 my own experience as a congregant or attendee at several Anglican Churches over a twelve-year period shows large attendances every Sunday at those congregations, even on zoom or other online media during lockdown. However, that was only in one CoE diocese and even in that diocese some vicars murmured about low attendances in some parishes.

Whilst Woodhead's studies show a decrease in CoE attendance, some of her studies demonstrate a numerical increase in membership and regular attendance at traditional Black Pentecostal Churches.[13] Additionally, discipleship/volunteering and active, congregational participation in

---

8. Woodhead and Heelas, *Spiritual Revolution*, 226. Harvey and Woodhead, *Unknowing God*, 162. Cornelio et al., *Rouledge International Book of Religion in Global Society*.

9. McCalla, *Community Womanism*, forthcoming.

10. Brown and Woodhead, *That Was the Church that Was*, 272.

11. Wyatt, "British Social Attitutes Finds 'CoE' Respondents Halved in 15 Years."

12. Rudgard, "Anglican Church Congregation Numbers Have 'Stabilised.'"

13. Brown and Woodhead. *That Was the Church that Was*, 272.

the life of these churches were also apparent from Woodhead's studies. Woodhead would therefore be referencing churches such as the NTCG and CoGiC to mention two, along with more recently established Black Evangelical churches, which would therefore consist of Ruach Ministries and other newly established Charismatic churches in the UK such as Hillsong Church. Woodhead's research is not specific to Black and Brown females. However, from my knowledge of some of them, these Black churches: Pentecostal, Evangelical and Charismatic, consist not only of Black and Black mixed-raced women and girls of all ages, but a smaller number of Asian women too—Loyal Sisters. With this acknowledgment I now turn my attention to examine some studies on womanism, spirituality, and the British church.

Studies on the British Church and Womanism

In the US, Africa, and Asia, womanism and African and Asian feminism commenced in the 1980s with works by Delores Williams, Jacqueline Grant, and Katie Cannon, in the US;[14] Mercy Amba Oduyoye, Roxanne Jordaan, Rachel A. Kanyoro Musimbi and Musa Dube in Africa,[15] to mention some of them; and primarily, Kwok Pui-lan in Asia.[16] In contrast, Britain's commencement in the field of Black and Brown female ecclesiology and theology emerged a decade later, in the 1990s.[17] Whilst this book is about both Black and Brown Loyal Sisters, the presence of Christian Black females and its related ethnic diversities are greater in the British church compared with the presence of Brown female, diverse, ethnicities, where they are generally from other religious faiths. This is reflected in the lack of literature on Christian Brown/Asian female presence compared with the Christian Black female presence. As far as I am aware, there are limited existing books on Asian/Brown female spirituality, theology and/or the church in Britain with the exception of studies

14. Williams, *Sisters in the Wilderness*, 320. Grant, *White Women's Christ and Black Women's Jesus*, 282. Cannon, *Black Womanist Ethics*, 194.

15. Oduyoye, *Introducing African Women's Theology*, 132. Jordaan, "Emergence of Black Feminist Theology in South Africa," 42–46. Kanyoro, *Introducing Feminist Cultural Hermeneutics*, 99. Dube, *Postcolonial Feminist Interpretation of the Bible*, 232.

16. Pui-Lan, *Introducing Asian Feminist Theology*, 136. Pui-Lan, *Postcolonial Imagination and Feminist Theology*, 252.

17. A comprehensive account of Global Black and Asian feminisms and womanisms, and their relation to Britain, is recorded in McCalla, *Community Womanism*, forthcoming.

by Mukti Barton.[18] What we have in Britain is a limited number of books mainly on either the experiences of Christian African or Caribbean women or Christian Black and white women which are also authored by Christian, Black, Asian, white, or biracial women. What we also have are books, chapters in books, and academic journal articles which are written by people from a theological, methodological and/or ideological stance about women of color. Some works on British Black and Brown women in theology and the British church still exist although some are no longer in print.

These writings form the foundations of British womanist perspectives in the British church and theology. Given that some of these sources are no longer in circulation, this literature review is all the more important for epistemological reasons, that is, for informative knowledge to further the study into British womanism and theology and the church. In addition, these books are starting places for church leaders and congregants, and students' reading lists into womanist studies at universities and theological educational institutions and for other interested organizations and persons. The literature review will reveal that not only are there limited resources on womanism in Britain but very few spiritualize or religionize womanism. Some studies only focus on the theology of the church and its congregants. This book comes from the position of womanist spirituality and the church where religiosity and theology is also embedded in the analysis. It builds on existing and further develops British Asian/Brown female theology and religiosity in Britain for more, future research and content into this limited area. I shall therefore proceed with a review of womanist theologies and religiosity as I see them conceptualized in most of the existing but limited literature in the British context. I shall start with Black church studies.

British Black Church Studies on Christian Black Females

The first to show Christian Black women's disproportionate representation in the most senior ministerial and leadership positions in British Black churches was Elaine Foster.[19] This earlier demonstration of women's role in the church is found in one chapter of a book. Foster points out that Black women comprise the predominant membership of the Black

---

18. Barton, "Wrestling with Imperial Patriarchy," 7–25.
19. Foster, "Women and the Inverted Pyramid," 45–68.

church. They are the workers whilst men are the leaders. Foster's chapter demonstrates that Black churches are, in effect, guilty of racialized sexism and illustrate this observation through the analogy of the "inverted pyramid." The roles Caribbean and African Black women leaders play are often overlooked or devalued even when these women are prominent figures in local congregations compared with their male counterparts. Foster's work thus echoes many of the American womanist studies on Black women's experience in the American Black church and in Africa and Asia too as mentioned above.

Valentina Alexander discovered that when first arriving in Britain in the post-war period, the Black church was for many Caribbean, predominantly, Jamaican women, a place of liberation theology from oppression in the wider societal community, a space for spiritual development and a strategy of survival.[20] Alexander found that these women's spiritual, cultural, and social networks were often intra-church. They struggled to survive but nonetheless, learnt to hope in God, be faithful and God-fearing and ultimately initiated into a Christian Black female solidarity in the church. She argues that the Black church presently remains the space to openly express Black women's Caribbean spirituality and African-centric identity.[21] The Black church was important in terms of spiritual, religio-cultural, social, and psychological preservation-of-life for many Black women in a foreign land. However, in developing Alexander's earlier work, Selina Stone discovered that the Black Pentecostal Church also needs to be a place of "dual" spiritual living and engagement and, where embodied, liberation serves the social and economic well-being of Black women through religious, political action.[22] Diane Watt too echoes some of what Stone discusses in her work only that Watts's work focuses more heavily on Christian women in the community and their immense activism.[23]

Similarly, from an ethnographic, anthropological, and religious stance, Nicole Toulis, a white woman, explores the context of societal and cultural complexities and religious identities of British Caribbeans. Whilst focusing on their religiosity in the Black church, Toulis, explores women's oppression, power, advantage, and sexism and their relationship to their

20. Alexander, "Mouse in a Jungle," 85–106. Alexander, "Africancentric and Black Christian Consciousness," 11–18.

21. Alexander, "Mouse in a Jungle," 85–106.

22. Stone, *Spirit and the Body*, 233. Stone, "Toward a Holistic Pentecost, 21–39. Stone, "Holy Spirit, Holy Bodies?, 312.

23. Watt, "Praying, Playing and Praising," 84–104.

male counterparts, from a Black feminist position. She does not take a liberationist paradigm in her investigation unlike some of the American womanist theologians mentioned above and many British counterparts. She is concerned with gendered relations, discrimination and the difference between men and women's religiosity in the Black church. Black female gendered relationship in the church is diminished compared with their male counterparts.[24] Unlike Elaine Foster who demonstrated Black women's awareness of patriarchy in the Black church,[25] Toulis discovered that some Black women seemed to be either oblivious to or accepting of the patriarchal system which functions in the Black church. In other instances, she showed that women who were not accepting of misogynoir seem to be powerless to action change due to institutional sexism and unconscious bias. Instead, they adopted different identities, "identities mobilisation," at different strata within the Black church even if these identities meant being in constant subordination to and controlled by men. Overall, Toulis shows that whilst religious experience in the NTCG did not always resolve the issues of economic suffering in society it definitely provided a place of religious participation and racial identity for all congregants and especially women despite gendered discrimination.[26]

Although rare in the British context, Black theologian, Robert Beckford, has written about or focused on issues relating to Black women in the British Black Pentecostal Church and its relation to their spiritual emancipation.[27] Having published their monograph in which a chapter is devoted to womanist theology, to date Beckford and Reddie have yet to engage in publication of Black women's faith discourse, although they claim to include Black women alongside discussions of the Black Pentecostal Church and Black theology respectively in their books[28] and as editor of the *Black Theology* journal respectively. Notwithstanding, Beckford remains committed to highlighting the discrimination and emancipation of Black women in the church and society through a wider commitment to the African Diaspora and social justice. It therefore follows that for both Beckford and Reddie, womanism is a theological/religious tool in which to express womanist epistemology and advocacy for female

---

24. Toulis, *Believing Identity*, 304.
25. Foster, "Women and the Inverted Pyramid," 45–68.
26. Toulis, *Believing Identity*, 304.
27. Beckford, *Dread and Pentecostal*, 230. Reddie, "Bring on the Sistas," 83–112.
28. Beckford, *Decolonizing Contemporary Gospel Music*, 264. See Beckford, *My Theology*, 93. Jagessar and Reddie, *Black Theology in Britain*, 373. Reddie, *Black Theology*.

The British Church and the Spiritual Lifestyle of Loyal Sisters

inclusion and Black women's freedom although, in both cases, as men and by their own admissions, adhering to womanist praxis is personally an abiding struggle for them too. I believe this is partly because they also operate in systems of racist and sexist oppression and discrimination and partly because, as Black males in Britain, they too are succumb to the forces of racial oppression and discrimination which require the pneumatic intervention for all people of color.

Shirlyn Toppin's paper on soul food theology demonstrates how African Caribbean and African American meals are a focus of pastoral care and practice and indicative of African cultural identity and community in action. Toppin argues that these meals are important for cultural and socio-religious preservation as witnessed by herself and her Black female participants in a contextual and experiential study of a Black majority, inner-city church in East London.[29]

In addition to these more analytical and/or scholastic book chapters, journal articles and sections in books which address womanism in the British, Black church and society, there is also available a collection of devotional-type testimonials by Caribbean church women on reflections of their lives in Britain.[30] Although not in wide circulation and mainly unknown, that book is concerned with Black women's own personal stories about being Black women in Britain. It presents the lived-experience of mainly first generation, Christian Caribbean women who know what it means to be Christian, Black, women, church worshipers and poor; who, when arriving in an alien, white British country in the 1950s, 1960s, and 1970s, struggled to support their families, church, and community. As demonstrated by Valentina Alexander,[31] these women's spiritual, cultural, and social networks were often intra-church. They struggled to survive but nonetheless, learnt to hope in God, be faithful and God-fearing, and ultimately initiated a Christian Black lifestyle within the Black church in Britain. Similarly, there are works which document the autobiographical experiences of British Black women through their focus on "oral tradition," such as Rev Dr. Io Smith MBE,[32] Esme Lancaster collection of poems and Claris Nelson[33] which leads me to now discuss studies in mainstream British churches.

29. Toppin, "'Soul Food' Theology," 44–69.
30. Thompson et al., *Here to Stay*, 128.
31. Alexander, "Mouse in a Jungle," 85–106.
32. Smith and Green, *Ebony Cross*, 160.
33. Cited in Alexander, "Mouse in a Jungle," 85–106.

Black and Brown Female Studies in Mainstream British Churches

Being diasporic, British, Christian, Asian, female, a theologian, and a Anglican priest to first show the intersectionality of race, sex and class in theology as it relates to Asian females, Mukti Barton attaches her work to feminist theology and/or Black theology and feminist religiosity. It is hardly surprising therefore that she overtly confesses to siding with Black feminism in the British context[34] since Asian was defined as Black in the UK until recently as mentioned in chapter 1 of this book. Barton is therefore a selective exception who identifies as an Asian feminist theologian in the UK.

Barton's autobiographical intersectionality is demonstrated in her chapter, *Mukti's Story*,[35] and the combined racism, classism, and sexism associated with this. Similar themes and concepts are shown in her earlier paper, "Wrestling with Imperial Patriarchy"[36] and her other feminist studies.[37] Barton not only critiques western feminist theology for blindsighted imperial patriarchy towards Asian women but attempts to use her autobiographical and/or biblical studies to educate western society and the Church about feminist inclusion of Christian women of Asian origin, post-colonialism and decolonization.

In a writing by Eve Pitts she refers to Katie Cannon's famous book, *Black Womanist Ethics*.[38] Pitts demonstrates the similarities between the UK and US in term of ethics of survival and mutual support which Black women have created to cope with and combat the triple effects of racism, sexism, and classism in the CoE.[39] Similarly, Lorraine Dixon, provides an invaluable introduction to the theological and spiritual liberation of British Black women in the CoE through her then experience as a Black female deacon.[40]

By focusing on the predominantly African and Caribbean heritage women in her article about the spiritual and ministerial experiences of forty-two women ministers from over 300 churches in a large research

---

34. Barton, "From Victim to Victor."
35. Barton, "Mukti's Story," 96.
36. Barton, "Wrestling with imperial patriarchy," 7–25.
37. Barton, "Reflecting on the Story of Ruth," 236–38. Barton, "Race, Gender, Class and the Theology of Empowerment," 225–37.
38. Cannon, *Black Womanist Ethics*, 194
39. Pitts, "Black Womanist Ethics," 29–35.
40. Dixon, "Black Woman and Deacon," 50–64.

The British Church and the Spiritual Lifestyle of Loyal Sisters 27

project in the London Baptist Association, Michele Mahon draws on womanist theology and the tools of online questionnaires to discover that these female, ordained ministers faced many challenges of sexism, racism, isolation, lack of social capital and relevant information to help them progress in life and ministry. Nevertheless, they were thriving in their unique ministry-contexts through finding creative ways to fulfill their callings such as, through small-group, neighborhood, church meetings. Mahon also suggests ways to support these pioneering women in ministry through informal, women-only spaces for worship.[41]

More than an autobiographical narrative and social commentary, Chine McDonald's book, *God Is Not a White Man*,[42] is profoundly provocative but deeply honest about the racialized sexism of Black women's lives in the British church and society. As Baptist and CoE ministers, Kate Coleman and Lorraine Dixon respectively demonstrate some of the same racialized sexism in the British church and what it means to be human. They therefore attempt to belong to the church and adapt to ministry in it as Christian Black, females.[43] In her book, Chine McDonald reminds us that Black women are created in God's image (*imago Dei*) and thus are worthy of value and praise. In McDonald's book we meet a God who is not a Euro-British white male but a Nigerian-British female growing up in England as a practicing Christian and congregant of the CoE. She fully understands her own experience as a Christian Black woman with all its achievements and complexities.

From both Black and womanist theologies, Carol Troupe discovers liberationist church mission practices for descendants of enslaved Africans, like herself, through examining emergent themes from historical magazines of the Council for World Mission.[44]

Having examined Black womanist and Asian feminist works in mainstream churches, I shall now explore womanist texts in both British mainstream and Black churches.

---

41. Mahon, "Sisters with Voices," 273–96.

42. McDonald, *God Is Not a White Man*, 239.

43. Coleman, "Being Human," 63. Dixon, "Reflexion on Black Identity and Belonging," 22–27.

44. Troup, "Engagement with Mission Magazine Archives," 101–21.

British Black and Mainstream Church Studies about British Black Women

In 2008, *Unsung Sheroes in the Church* was published; the first book to address the issues of British Black females in both mainstream British churches and British Black churches. It is also a volume where most chapters are authored by me, and an interdisciplinary documentation where all other chapters are written by Black women.[45] We introduce the complex issues of racism and sexism and other intersectionalities experienced by Christian Black females in the mainstream British church and Black church.[46] Whilst there are copies of this book in circulation, *Unsung Sheroes in the Church* is no longer in print and thus the need for this book, Loyal Sisters, which expands some of the spiritual issues in that book and extensively goes beyond it.

Having explored the literature in the UK I now turn my attention to a section on the spiritual lifestyle of Christian Black and Brown Loyal Sisters. That section will demonstrate what is similar and nuanced from studies either no longer in print or are still in existence and what is also similar and dissimilar to womanism globally.

The Spiritual Lifestyle of Loyal Sisters

Godly Spiritual Living

A prominent tenet of womanist spirituality is how spirituality is defined by Black and Brown Loyal Sisters in the British church. Alice Walker says a womanists "loves the Spirit."[47] The Holy Spirit or pneumatology, that is, the third person and the femininity of God, is primarily the Spirit which Christian Loyal Sisters worship. However, beyond this, as shall be discussed in the chapter of spiritual redemption, some Loyal Sisters may also acknowledge the spirits of their African and/or Asian ancestors or deceased relatives in their daily spirituality as do some Jewish worshipers. They recognize Jehovah as "the God of Abraham, Isaac and Jacob," as did Moses in Exod 3:1–6. To acknowledge their deceased relatives

---

45. See Further Reading for a review of books which include either both Black and white women or books for all women not specifically for women of color or solely about womanism.

46. McCalla, *Unsung Sheroes in the Church*, 201.

47. Walker, *In Search of Our Mother's Gardens*, xi-xii.

and ancestors is not to worship them as Loyal Sisters' worship only God. However, by recognizing their ancestors and relatives, they are saying that they are aligning themselves with the same God of their relatives and lineages; are following similar religious and spiritual traditions of their deceased souls and saints; are of the same racial and/or cultural family as their ancestors; and/or are making some other relevant and spiritual connection with their deceased loved ones or descendants.

Christian Black and Brown Loyal Sisters possess a genuine love for God and the church. Their conviction and passion for God is based on a commitment and acceptance of the Christian faith through some form of conversion, baptism, and/or confirmation depending on the denomination. Conversion, baptism, or confirmation immediately follows an intimate relationship with *their* God and it is this relationship that drives them into spiritual actions within and beyond the church. They demonstrate an unceasing commitment to God and the church which is reflected in their prayers, conversations, and Christian living; all of which are superimposed on each other. Valentina Alexander's work on Christian Black women[48] emphatically verifies this. What was evident from the spirituality of the Loyal Sisters in the Black Pentecostal Churches in the 1960, 1970s, and 1980s is that it transcended the worship of church services alone, that is, their spirituality was manifested everywhere they went: in home, the wider community, and work. Impromptu church services led by Christian Loyal Sisters were normal where encouragements from Scripture and speaking in tongues (*glossolalia*) occurred in home gatherings of Christian and unchristian friends and family. These services would often occur during casual discussions about everyday life whether these were testimonies about good or bad occurrences.

In the 1970s and 1980s, many first-generation Caribbean women occupied domestic work and/or worked in the clothing, food, and other similar industries. They were often poorly paid. Others found it difficult to find work and even trained teachers took menial jobs and nurses served as ancillaries in the National Health Service (NHS). They frequently experienced racism from patients.[49] Whilst occupying these often low paid and manual labor jobs at that time, it was typical to witness brief prayer meetings led by Loyal Sisters at work in the canteen or corridors during break-times as someone expressed a personal need for a

48. Alexander, "Mouse in a Jungle," 85–106.
49. Webster, *Imagining Home*, 268. Mama and Williams, "'We Are a Natural Part of Many Different Struggles,'" 148–66.

family-member. It was standard to hear praise-singing and merriment in the community craft-sewing gatherings. Loyal Sisters created a womanist spiritual community anywhere and everywhere they assembled. Whilst in today's secularized world many of these spontaneous outward expressions of Christian faith and Pentecostal spirituality may not be appropriate and acceptable, nevertheless, Loyal Sisters today would demonstrate their spirituality by saying to someone who requested a need for pray or shared a concern with them, "I shall pray about this tonight" and either offered a quiet and brief word of encouragement on the spot or a brief prayer. These women were "filled" with the Holy Ghost. Loyal Sisters are therefore practicing Christians in the sacred and secular places and spaces. From different denominations of either Black-majority or white-majority churches, these Loyal Sisters of Asian, Caribbean, and African origin are found to be tremendously spiritual and inspirational.

In Britain it is not unusual to ascribe to Christianity and specific denominations through family-ties, child-dedications/baptisms, a previous conversion, or other affiliations such as voluntary and community involvement and the like, whilst not actually practicing Christianity. However, among British Black and Brown Loyal Sisters you are likely to find them fully immersed into practical Christianity and they are unlikely to make claims to Christianity unless conversion and/or baptism and practice are absolute. In such cases, their Christian faith is about a personal encounter with the Divine and thus experiential. It is based on specific faith standpoints and adherences. Many Loyal Sisters are therefore committed to their faith. They are paradigms of fidelity, faithfulness, and integrity, especially noted among Generation Xs, Boomers and Post World Wars women. They are zealous and innovative as witnessed by younger women. Loyal Sisters' devotion to spirituality is also pointed out by Io Smith in her experience as a minister in the New Testament Assembly,[50] Nicole Toulis in her study of a congregation of the NTCG,[51] Valentina Alexander in her study of Black Christian women in Britain[52] and Roswith Gerloff on Pentecostal, Black Churches.[53] For example, Io Smith was a community activist, church pastor, and ecumenical enabler in Britain and abroad. When she died in May 2008 at the age of 70, she

---

50. Smith and Green, *Ebony Cross*, 160.
51. Toulis, *Believing Identity*, 304.
52. Alexander, "Mouse in a Jungle," 85–106. Alexander, "Africancentric and Black Christian Consciousness," 11–18.
53. Gerloff, *Plea for British Black Theologies*, 1086.

had founded a school in Ghana, a Christian Institute for adults, day care centers, sheltered housing for the elderly, the New Testament Assembly church in England, and a children's fundraising project for disadvantaged children in Jamaica.[54] The tropes of Black church "passive radicalism" that is, the personal sphere of religious social polity without communal interaction and "active radicalism" where the wider world is collectively engaged in religious activism[55] are evident among these Loyal Sisterhoods. Notwithstanding, examples of the political, social activism witnessed in the American, Civil Right Movement in which campaigning expanded to street marches for social, racial and gender justices, is rarely, if at all seen in the history of British womanism. That said, however, in CoGoP during the 1970s to 2000s, in major cities in the UK, it was commonplace for the WMB to conduct street marches and door-to-door pamphlet-dropping for evangelistic, outreach purposes. Dressed in their all-white dresses and royal blue capes and caps with red lining, this was especially apparent during the annual, national convention where, accompanied by Sussex Police, who controlled the traffic, and led by the CoGoP brass band, hundreds of Sisters marched on Brighton streets, along the seafront, singing gospel songs as they waved their CoGoP church flags.

The Black church was the community for Black women in the 1960s and 1970s to express their separatist, African-Caribbean cultural spirituality and find solidarity and association from a hostile racist environment/public life when they first arrived in Britain. They created Christian, Black women's groups inside their churches for that purpose. These Loyal Sisters were not only faithful to their churches, such as the Black Pentecostal denominations, but faithful to their cultural and racial identity also as seen in Valentina's and Nicole Toulis' studies,[56] and demonstrated by soul food.[57] African American women scholars and practitioners also found liberation through cultural religiosity in the Black church for their elevation, survival, and existence.[58] Through African female theology, Mercy Ambo Odyoye also shows the importance of cultural religiosity in the daily lives of Christian African women from mainly Nigeria and Ghana but also the whole continent.[59] This is also demonstrated in the

54. Smith and Green, *Ebony Cross*, 160.
55. Alexander, *Breaking Every Fetter?*, 427.
56. Toulis, *Believing Identity*, 304. Alexander, "Mouse in a Jungle," 85–106.
57. Toppin, "'Soul Food' Theology," 44–69.
58. Williams, *Sisters in the Wilderness*, 320.
59. Oduyoye, *Introducing African Women's Theology*, 132.

British African churches which were established at the same time and later too. So race and culture are central to Loyal Sisters' Christian discipleship and spirituality.

For purposes of cultural expression, although patriarchy existed in the Black church, it was not necessarily only patriarchal oppression that brought these women together but it was also for reasons of female spirituality, sociality, economics, culture, personal religiosity, and family. Their limited economic and social resources at that time also meant that they shared their skills and resources and therefore created a social collectivist, theocratic and democratic womanist community in the church. In present days Loyal Sisters stay in some Black churches although some of them are not socially or economically deprived. They therefore have a genuine choice to stay or leave and/or seek alternative ways to worship from their conventional places of worship. However, these Loyal Sisters remain and continue to faithfully serve their denominations. This is because serving God is a lifestyle they have either adopted or, since their conversion to Christianity, is a natural progression of their faith. This clearly demonstrates that for these Loyal Sisters God and church is not a crutch—a metaphor which is often applied to people who use religion to lean on for their weak, broken or needful lives. Secondly, on arriving in England in the 1950 and beyond, senior Loyal Sisters have experienced racism and sexism in public life and the church and have trusted God and supported each other through those times. They have invested too much time, resources, and energy into the church because of their love for God and people. These Loyal Sisters will therefore not leave the church now. For younger Loyal Sisters, they want to build on the foundations of their spiritual mothers and seek God for a spiritual vision in their era to do so, so that they can also make a meaningful difference to the church and community like their spiritual mothers. From this ecclesiological place of belonging these Loyal Sisters, young and older, can make and have made positive womanist change from within the church. It is with this understanding of womanist epistemology that I now focus on church matriarchs.

Matriarchic Church Leadership

These Loyal Sisters are sometimes amongst the first to create a space for other Black and Brown women (and men) in the church to freely worship through the establishment of churches, congregations, leadership

The British Church and the Spiritual Lifestyle of Loyal Sisters 33

systems and/or church departments in them. Brown and Black women's faithfulness and spiritual discipleship in this area, is outstanding. Without them, others would not know God, find love and comfort, be prayed for and encouraged in times of need, be housed when homeless, supported when without a family, or, when hungry, be fed in Godly, friendly environments. An example of this is found in the CoGoP as the example below demonstrates:

> The Women's Missionary Band (WMB)[60] was one of these exceptional cases of voluntary action operating in the formal organizational structures.... In the WMB, the Darcus Club— a subsidiary women's sewing and social club, where non-Christian women also attended—social activities foregrounded proceedings of the religious event. Christian women used this opportunity to share the gospel message of Jesus Christ with non-Christian women with the hope that they would eventually accept the Christian faith. The religious goal was the underlying intention of this social activity....Women's Missionary Band (WMB) 1928—Introduced in 23rd CoGoP General Assembly • For women to be engaged in missions endeavour both at home and abroad...within a setting in which they could socialize with people of the same ethnic and religious culture.... Further research is nonetheless needed to discover the extent to which Darcus clubs... served a cultural, gender-specific and social welfare purposes for CoGoP congregants and non-members during this internal period.[61]

In other words by saying, "Further research is nonetheless needed to discover the extent to which Darcus clubs . . . served a cultural, gender-specific and social welfare purposes for CoGoP congregants and non-members during this internal period"[62] and the WMB ministry as a whole, I meant then that I could not ascertain if these established Pentecostal Church women's ministries were set-up to serve the interest and well-being of women alone or were intended to serve the spiritual and social requirements of the whole church, that is, men and women alike. I also meant that more research was required to demonstrate womanist social action in the church.

60. In CoGoP, the WMB is now called the Women's Ministries.
61. McCalla, "Black Churches and Voluntary Action," 137–75.
62. McCalla, "Black Churches and Voluntary Action," 137–75.

During the internal period of CoGoP, that is, a time from 1953 to the 1990s when the denomination was very exclusive, myopic, and insular of ecumenical church associations, the WMB and Darcus Club were led by women. I believe that these women's ministries sought to support women's pastoral and social flourishing whilst serving the requirements of the whole church and others outside the church too. They were therefore very collectivistic, theocratic, democratic, and practical. On reflection, I would thus now say that woman's ministries in the internal period of CoGoP were womanist ministries although patriarchy was prevalent in the church. However, these woman's ministries were also supported by church men—the "bodyguards." Loyal Sisters were therefore regarded as important. So, when it came to WMB programs, bodyguards served at Loyal Sisters' beckoning requests and for Sisters' devotion and not the other way round. Bodyguards ensured that Loyal Sisters were protected and came to no harm. This was often observed in support for fundraising and outreach in the WMB; attending the WMB, Sunday services and should Loyal Sisters ask for and require escorting for WMB ministries, church men supported them. Bodyguards were there for the Loyal Sisters and not to serve their own agendas or as unwanted chaperones. Whilst there were instances where Loyal Sisters would be escorted alone with a bodyguard, in many cases they would work in groups of other Sisters and assisted by bodyguards. Similarly, unless occasionally asked by Loyal Sisters to participate in WMB services and activities, or suggestions by men were agreed by Sisters, WMB was led and functioned by Sisters for Sisters. Loyal Sisters who had "unsaved" husbands also recalled receiving genuine support from their husbands for WMB, other women's services and church in general, although their "unsaved" husbands never attended church or were congregants.

From observation of the CoGoP today, it is evident that some womanist spirituality still exists in CoGoP at the national-UK level since the women's ministry team is implementing programs both in person and online. They are also female-led. However, in some cases, I can only assume that all these programs are for church and community women as some appear to be for the whole church and are very generic. Whilst the topics are often very well delivered they do not always directly serve the interests of women. These programs are often delivered in CoGoP's annual women's conferences and in health and well-being services and so forth. However, beyond the national church, women's ministry seems to have regressed in CoGoP in the UK. Some congregations still operate

The British Church and the Spiritual Lifestyle of Loyal Sisters 35

excellent women's spiritual services on Sundays and midweek, and community programs, such as mother and toddler groups, health and wellbeing sessions and, interestingly, the old partner[63] schemes for its female congregants, of which some younger Loyal Sisters are also participants. However, some congregations do not even have local women's ministries anymore and neither do they specifically serve the spiritual and social interests of females in other church ministries.

Loyal Sisters believe that "the family who prays together, stays together." They are the prayer warriors and intercessors. So, Loyal Sisters pray together about their callings, projects, and visions, whilst supporting each other and others too, in/for pastoral action. They are passionate, wise, and productive. They are often ordinary Christian Black and Brown women in the British church and society. Brown and Black women recognize the invaluable contribution they give to the world. Similarly, Loyal Sisters appreciate and value others' work and contributions to the world; especially those who suffer the most in it of whom Brown and Black women definitely comprise of those who suffer the most.

Keri Day points out that whilst Azusa Street was rooted in US Pentecostalism, it embraced an "erotic" community orientation and environment. Day clearly demonstrates that this community was void of and resistant to radical capitalism; free, market forces; systemic, individualistic, religiosity and the practices of US white Evangelicals. Azusa Pentecostals favored communal and democratic service empowerment. Whilst Selina Stone argues that the dualism of spirit and body is absent from British Black Pentecostalism, that is, they only practice the manifestation of the spirit in daily worship but not political activism,[64] Day shows that it is possible to be both Pentecostal and communitarian[65] and therefore as Stone states, possible in British Pentecostalism.[66] I demonstrate this realization in this book and others have done so elsewhere and in the review section above. That said, womanist political and social action is

---

63. Partner schemes are money saving programmes which operate among Jamaicans. They were introduced in England by the Windrush Generation who, on arriving in England in the 1950s and sixties, were refused bank accounts. These schemes enabled Jamaicans to obtain savings, housing and other assets which they were unable to obtain otherwise due to racism.

64. Stone, *The Spirit and the Body*, 233.

65. Day, *Azusa Reimagined*, 218.

66. Stone, *The Spirit and the Body*, 233.

now lacking in British Black Pentecostalism because it has regressed as I shall develop further below and elsewhere.[67]

If It Wasn't for the Women[68] describes the important role African American women play in society and the American Black church. CoGoP originated from the Holiness Movement and started in 1903 in the US. It was then called the Church of God. Its name changed to CoGoP in the 1920s with a legal dispute. CoGoP is also Pentecostal. Although its white male founder, Ambrose Jessop Tomlinson, was formerly a Republican and Populist Party political persuader,[69] when it came to spirituality, the General, Church of God in the US seemingly adopted a Quaker evangelical theology but simultaneously practiced "plainfolk" liberal compassionate conservatism (or liberalism) and religiosity for the working class.[70] Whilst not being poor himself, Tomlinson followed in a spiritual tradition of Pentecostalism which was observed globally during the Rival Movement. That was a gospel to the poor.[71] In studying CoGoP in Britain, I learnt that it was theologically closely connected to the Pentecostal Movement in the late nineteenth and early twentieth centuries. However, I would argue that a direct link between CoGoP in Britain and the origins of Azusa Street, which started by the working class male African American preacher William J. Seymour in 1906, is unclear. Nevertheless, the grass-root, social communitarianism of Azusa which Day demonstrates[72] and is similarly seen in Wales in 1904 and elsewhere in the world, was apparent in the infancy of British Black Pentecostal Churches during the 1950s to 1980s.[73] In the 1970s, the context of Caribbean theology was similar.[74] Azusa Street commenced and later became the Church of God in Christ (CoGiC),[75] at the same time as the beginnings of the Church of God in the US. I therefore think that the communitarianism, philanthropic, collaborative, and/or grass-root models of CoGoP in Britain may have historically come from cultural communitarian practices in

---

67. McCalla, *Community Womanism*.
68. Townsend Gilkes, *If It Wasn't for the Women*, 266.
69. Wikipedia, "Ambrose Jessup Tomlinson."
70. Robins, *A.J. Tomlinson*, 336.
71. Anderson and Hollenweger, *Pentecostals*, 181. Hollenweger, *Pentecost between Black and White*, 128. Hollenweger, *Pentecostals*, 588. Hollenweger, *Pentecostalism*, 512.
72. Day, *Azusa Reimagined*, 218.
73. McCalla, "Black Churches and Voluntary Action," 137–75.
74. See Turner, *Caribbean Contextual Theology*, 224.
75. Day, *Azusa Reimagined*, 218. Stone, *Spirit and the Body*, 233.

the Caribbean as well as the spiritual praxis of its founder thus meshing Jamaican culture with Pentecostal Christianity. My study of CoGoP also reveals that social and economic collectivism, that is, to each and all Loyal Sisters (and others in the church and neighborhood too), also empowered CoGoP's Sisters despite patriarchal practices in the same time period. Nonetheless, my own observations show that some of the Pentecostal Churches have now shifted to Evangelical neoliberalism. This religiosity is critiqued by Day.[76] It can be argued that whilst British Pentecostal Churches were never spiritually and practically perfect, they have moved from their traditional Pentecostal spirituality of social and/or liberal collectivism. Their stance on women was always restrictive in terms of certain roles and ministries. However, womanism has generally regressed. Whilst woman are now able to minister in more roles in the church than their spiritual mothers before them, to some extent, less is seemingly done by them especially at the local church level in CoGoP and this has not always been the case in all British Pentecostal Black churches. My observations also reveal that systemic patriarchy, as I demonstrate in this book, is also responsible for this womanist regression which I further explore in *Community Womanism* and one of the reasons for the rise in community womanism.[77] It is this shift and regression which is now detrimental to each and all Black female congregants, effective partnerships and communities alike. However, there is spiritual redemption for Loyal Sisters of British Black churches as I discuss later in this book. It is for that reason they are avid givers to the church and others and to that discussion I shall now focus my attention.

Personified Generosity

In the lives of many Loyal Sisters we see spiritual virtues come alive. They are personified generosity. They provide for their families and people in their communities; for their neighbors and strangers alike. To generalize, Black and Brown women are found amongst the poorest in society, although this is changing for some in church-life as shall be discussed in the chapter on Messa Pentecostal. Their willingness to contribution to others freely in the British church and community in terms of time, skills, talents, calling, and sometimes money (tithes and offerings) especially

---

76. Day, *Azusa Reimagined*, 218.
77. McCalla, *Community Womanism*.

noted in the 1950s to late 1980s, is often astounding. More importantly, they are faith-givers or they give willingly by faith. Like the widows in 1 Kgs 17:8–16 and 2 Kgs 4:1–7, they give from what little economic and material resources they have and, in some cases, they impart from nothing and they request nothing in return for their kind and generous giving.

> Incomes that were primarily generated for voluntary action through more formal networks were raised in the WMB for "home and world missions"[78] at national, regional and local levels: The missionary in those days, they knew everybody in need, they would get money, or some groceries and take to whoever was in need. (Interview, senior member) And: Her [Vera Rodney[79]—former national WMB leader] passion was for raising funds and people did it willingly. There was no qualms about where the money was going or who it was going to, but people raised—all the churches—raised hundreds and hundreds of pounds. (Interview, adult member)[80]

Loyal Sisters believe that if they "give as unto God," God shall reward them in this world and in the eschatology (see Mark 10:30). For these women their reward in this life may not be physical but spiritual. In other instances, it is received through the next generation—their offspring (children and grandchildren) as seen in my book, *Community Womanism* on Black female success—who in turn, give back to their mothers and grandmothers. Some Black and Brown Loyal Sisters are fulfilling their mission of giving in secret (see Matt 6:3–4). They are real, living examples of godly charity.

Apart from my observations of CoGoP, studies by Toulis,[81] Foster,[82] and Alexander[83] reveal that the British Black churches would not exist without British Black women. These women have done and are doing extraordinary spiritual, social, and economic things; even those who face adverse spiritual, social, and economic circumstances of which the women in the church attempted to address at that time and some are still

---

78. Bible Training Institute (BTI), *Bible Training*, 323. BTI was CoGoP's training ministry.

79. Vera Rodney is the real name of the WMB leader. I am quoting directly from McCalla, "Black Churches and Voluntary Action," 137–75.

80. McCalla, "Black Churches and Voluntary Action," 137–75.

81. Toulis, *Believing Identity*, 304.

82. Foster, "Women and the Inverted Pyramid," 45–68.

83. Alexander, "Mouse in a Jungle," 85–106.

doing the same today. However, the shift to neoliberalism as mentioned above, means that social and economic action is limited when individuals and groups experience such hardship and devastation. Instead, a culture of denunciation and victimization may persist whilst I acknowledge that, in some cases, some individuals and groups may be at fault. Nevertheless, collectivism is strong on intervention, compassion, and pastoral care and in the faith-action of support for others and less about blame and shame and sink or swim *laissez-faire*. A return to womanism in praxis is required where action and care for the necessities of others is balanced with one's own responsibility and agency for one's own well-being. However, all is not lost for a return to greater womanism in British Black churches through womanist, spiritual redemption which I demonstrate later in this book, and for expansion of it where womanism still exists in the church. Maternal and child-caring is often realized when womanism exists and the next section will demonstrate this.

Maternal and Childcare Responsibilities

Black and Brown women carry an extra responsibility in the world. Whilst not exclusively, Black and Brown women champion the struggles and needs of women and children specifically whether they are practitioners, academics, activists, or church-leaders/goers. Many Christian mothers assume main responsibility for child-rearing since women are the child-bearers. If a male partner is present, child-rearing is still often performed by the female mother irrespective of both spouses being economically active in the public domain of paid employment. Childcare responsibilities are seldom equally shared between Black and Brown Christian heterosexual parents. Fathers may adopt a leadership role in the family but it is Black and Brown women who carry the greater share of child-rearing. In a patriarchal church, spouses still believe that child-rearing is a woman's God-given role. This is despite living in an advanced liberal democracy, such as capitalistic Britain, where, in the twenty-first century, gender specific roles are not necessarily upheld or adhered to but men and women both occupy public (work/out-of-home) and private (domestic/home) spaces.

Tracey Reynolds points out that the success of Caribbean mothers (I would add, Christian ones too) is in their child-rearing skills and practices in developing four strategies that enable their children to advance through life in a predominantly white-majority Britain. These strategies are first, mother's guidance in psychologically and emotionally preparing their children to challenge racism; second, monitoring their children's education to ensure they have the best chance of succeeding; third, the celebration of Black diasporic culture to instill in their children a positive sense of self; and fourth, the regulating of their children's activities in the public sphere in order to safeguard them from danger.[84] I would argue that in addition to these strategies, Christian Black and Brown mothers are also found to be children's readers of Bible (and secular) stories, instructors on Black cultural awareness in relation to Christianity and moral living. These mothers understand and practice their ethnic culture which is intermingled with their Christian culture. Lorraine Dixon shows Caribbean mothers' creativity in creating a Christian Caribbean environment at home through "open pot."[85] "Open pot" refers to the seemingly endless servings of Jamaican cooked food which would be offered to visitors who attend the homes of Jamaican Loyal Sisters; foods such as rice and peas, and curried goat; and/or ackee and "salt fish"; and soul/hard food, like yams and plantains. Thus the home is an integral, Black and/or Brown female-facilitative space and is thus children's space too. It is where most of the child-rearing occurs, therefore Christian, Black and Brown mothers attempt to generate alignment in the home for their children and themselves, and if a male spouse is present, they provide a comfortable place for him also. Even when parents are engaged in different public activities beyond the domestic realm, and where alternative and adequate childcare cannot be arranged unless at least one parent is present, children are more likely to be in the care of their mothers and not their fathers.

The historical and spiritual context of Dixon's mothering spirituality is provided in the section entitled "Spirituality? What Spirituality?"[86] This section provides the theological grounding to the chapter and gives the historical and geographical progression of African-centric spirituality and its link to Christianity and the African diaspora. Direct connection is made between the historical section and the practical spiritual experiences of the women in their contemporary church, home, and community

---

84. Tracey Reynolds, "Success of Our Mothers," 85–100. Reynolds, *Caribbean Mothers*, 206.

85. Dixon, "At My Mother's Feet," 69–83.

86. Dixon, "At My Mother's Feet," 69–83. Although this book is in circulation it is no longer being printed. This paragraph is a summation of the chapter in the book.

lives. The interplay of African-centrism and the impact of the church on Black women's spirituality are portrayed by very good use of Jamaican phrases, language, and culture which are demonstrated through concepts such as "Messa Jesus" and "open pot" which are skillfully interpreted and explained by the author to aid comprehension and thus meaning to the text. This evidence allows readers to get a sense of the life of participants and invites them to be part of their religious and cultural spaces. Through comparing and contrasting the spirituality of the author's mother's generation of immigrant Caribbean woman (first generation) with the author's generation of Caribbean descendants (second generation), the chapter demonstrates why the discussion of spirituality is liberating for Black women, how this relates to the British church, and what makes Black women Loyal Sisters. It is evident that Black women's spiritual praxis is manifested through their cultural ontology in conjunction with their passion for Jesus. Their religious salvation and social and cultural empowerment, agency, and enfranchisement are interwoven and inseparable. Their liberation is found at the merging of the two positions.

Despite making their influence felt in the church, home, and community through their spiritual lifestyle as discussed in the sections above, the investigation into the lives of Loyal Sisters also revealed that they serve God, church, family, and community in the midst of a patriarchal British church. I shall now focus on this in the next section.

Patriarchy and the Church

In the section above, I demonstrated that Christian Black and Brown women take action when required and exhibit spiritual living in words and deeds. However, a contradiction exists. Whilst the Christian faith has for a large majority of Black and Brown women provided a vehicle for their spirituality and they have come to love the church, patriarchy, misogynoir, sexism, and racism, as basic intersectionalities, are features which simultaneously act as oppressive and discriminatory forces against Loyal Sisters. By their actions and deeds mainstream British churches thus have still to really love Black and Brown women. The Black British churches are no exception on this point. They are not always racist but are still misogynistic and sexist. A recent example from the CoGoP illustrates this point.

CoGoP still does not ordain/license female bishops simply because they are women and for no other reason. This contrasts with some mainstream, British churches, such as Anglicans and Baptists where females are bishops and presidents respectively. However, the most senior position of archbishop, in the Anglican Church, is still only held by men. This and other similar examples are clearly instances of sexual discrimination although the British church would argue that it is spiritual. So does God favor men over women when it comes to the office of bishops and the most senior offices in the ecclesiology? Are we still not "all one in Christ?" (Gal 3:26–29).

In CoGoP, there is no secret that Pastor Daisy Bailey was the overseer of Region 6. In CoGoP UK, overseers are the most senior, administrative, ministerial leaders in a local region. Region 6 is the Great Manchester region in CoGoP UK. Pastor Bailey was appointed into this position in 2016 by the former National Overseer, Bishop Wilton Powell, who attempted to go as far as possible to installing her to a bishop's role although without the title and office so as not to overrule CoGoP doctrinal guidelines. She was the only female in CoGoP UK who held such a title in relations to her female gender. However, whilst she did the same ministerial administration as male regional overseers who are appointed purely on their spiritual credentials, and is equally spiritual as the male appointees, Daisy Baily did not hold the bishopric office. On November 20, 2023, just before making her ministerial appointments at the CoGoP, National Convocation, Daisy Bailey informed the convocation that she plans to resign the regional overseer position because she hoped she would have become a bishop when she accepted the title as overseer and having waited for over five years, it did not materialize. Pastor Bailey clearly acknowledged that God also calls women to the office. Speaking directly to the General Presbyter, Tim Coalter, who was present at the convocation and to whom she called directly by name as she spoke, she expressed her love for God and the church and asked him if the denomination would reconsider its stance on the ordination of women. Pastor Bailey also thanked Bishop Wilton for appointing her to the regional overseer position. She has resigned her title as regional overseer since May 2024. In 2024 on another occasion, Daisy Bailey also announced her official, ministerial retirement. She finished strong. Pastor Bailey leaves an awesome example of godly, female ministerial legacy for younger, female ministers to follow.

> Hand in hand we walk each day,
> Hand in hand along the way,
> Walking thus I cannot stray,
> Hand in hand with Jesus.[87]

Like other ministers and congregants of CoGoP, I totally agree that Pastor Bailey should have been a bishop. Something is very wrong and it is not Daisy Bailey. Bishop Coalter did not reply to Pastor Bailey's question as he sat on the first row in the pews; flanked by other international bishops and their families of CoGoP. However, two days later at the commencement of his sermon at the same convocation, Bishop Coalter announced that Pastor Doreen Makaya is appointed to the international church, doctrinal committee in the US. Whilst this does not mean that the office of female bishops will be considered by this appointment, it does say that a Black female from the UK shall be holding a senior position at the international head office of CoGoP. Being a godly minister, if Pastor Makaya is allowed to influence doctrinal change for women of color globally in the CoGoP, no less, in relations to female bishops, I think this will be a womanist spirituality appointment for good. The adverse to this is that if this appointment does not result in womanist change it could just produce a Black female figurehead who assumes the role of womanism but, in fact, only continues to represent the patriarchal status quo. The global CoGoP would then have succeeded in getting a Black female from the UK to keep women in their place.

Apart from the example of hierarchical misogynoir above, when Black churches are racist, this is often in the areas of ethnicities, nationalities, and colorism and the like, which I address in another chapter on self-love. Another primary reason for continued sexual discrimination and inequity in the British church has much to do with churchgoers' appreciation and misinterpretation of Scripture and/or failure to contextualize the Bible in terms of history, timeframe, culture, and country. This is where biblical hermeneutics and contextual biblical theology is important. A fourth reason Black churches demonstrate the intersection of racism and sexism is in an unwillingness to action change for the amelioration of all Black and Brown women and the whole church too. It is for these reasons that some Black and Brown women find it hard to really love, accept, belong to, own and even stay in the British church whilst loving God, community, and family with a dedication and passion

---

87. Oakman, "Hand in Hand with Jesus." Oakman composed over 3000 hymns during his lifetime from 1856–1922.

which is insurmountable. Notwithstanding, this chapter shows that many still stay in the British church whilst some of these Loyalists also fully understand the reasons for the boycott of and departure from it by others as I demonstrate in my *Community Womanism* book.[88] This is due to Loyal Sisters' Christian spirituality which enables them to transcend and resist the manifestations of institutional racism and sexism in the British church for the sake of the British church itself since the presence of Black and Brown women help the British church. That is not to say that those who leave the church are necessarily less spiritual or committed to God as *Community Womanism*[89] will show. It often means that their callings and convictions for God, the church and religiosity, in this current, sacred-secular time, is different.

Findings from this project demonstrated the invisibilities and difficulties Brown and Black Loyal Sisters encounter and how they overcome them through their avid devotion to their Christian spirituality. Although many devoted Loyal Sisters of the British church and community are hard-working, sadly, but unsurprisingly, many have never been recognized and praised for their outstanding contribution to church life, faith communities, and society. They give their time, finances, and spiritual gifts and talents to the church and the wider community unreservedly despite sexist and racist patriarchy that exist in these churches and communities. Close examination of their lives, challenges the misconception of Brown and Black women in the church as uninspired. Lorraine Dixon's words say it perfectly:

> Christian books on spirituality often use the wise words of "celebrity" gurus or mainly white, male, Western historical figures. Thus the perspectives of Black [women] are left out of the equation. Our church is the poorer for this.[90]

Similarly, for Loyal Sisters in the mainstream British church in the 1970s to 1990s, church was where they practiced their faith and loyalty to Jesus and the church although the church was not necessarily a place to escape from patriarchal racism or indeed sexism, as both existed in the church too. They sometimes experienced open verbal racist and sexist comments about, at best, their clothes, hairstyles, skin color, and romantic

---

88. McCalla, *Community Womanism*.

89. McCalla, *Community Womanism*.

90. Dixon, "At My Mother's Feet," 69–83. Although this book is in circulation it is no longer in print.

relationships, which were often degrading comments. At worse, Loyal Sisters were politely but patronizingly asked to leave the church as they were not welcomed. From my experience of some mainstream British churches, whilst carrying out this research study, the same kinds of racism and sexism still exist in some of them today. However, the resilience, grace, humility, and faith in God by Black and Brown Loyal Sisters is strong, consistent, although constantly tested by racism and sexism. Loyal Sisters are sometimes blamed for the sexualized racism which they experience. I observed this being demonstrated by comments made by a white woman to a Black woman in a British Anglican congregation when I attended the service. She said, "Our warden was so disappointed last week when you refused to sit in the other aisle," when, in fact, I later discovered that the warden had approached the only Black person in the congregation and asked her to give up her seat because an aisle seat was required for easy access to the pulpit for a congregant who was reading one of the Scriptures for the service. However, the warden could have spoken to other congregants who were also sitting in aisle seats. I recall a similar thing happening to me at a CoE church too. A white women wanted two seats; one for her and another for her husband to sit beside her. Like Rosa Parks who refused to give up her bus-seat to a white man in Montgomery, US on December 1, 1955 and the Black woman in the CoE congregation, I also did not vacate my seat when I attended that church. Seeing only a few vacant aisle seats for one person and where my row of seats was also full, I told her that I didn't know where she was going to sit. This prompted the reaction of a white, male assistant priest to swiftly vacate his front-row seat for another congregational seat. She occupied that front-row seat and her husband therefore had to sit elsewhere. Problem sorted! I discovered that in some of these mainstream British churches the white congregants believe that their entitlement in the church is greater than the people of color and especially when it comes to females of color simply because they are white. Notwithstanding, I discovered that these Black and Brown Loyal Sisters stay at the mainstream British churches regardless:

> I/[We] have decided to follow Jesus.
> I/[We] have decided to follow Jesus.
> I/[We] have decided to follow Jesus.
> No turning back.
> No turning back.[91]

91. God TV News, "I Have Decided To Follow Jesus." See also Job, *Why God Why?*, 199. The hymn was composed from the dying words of an Indian, Nokseng, who

Conclusion

This chapter features British diasporic Black and Brown Loyal Sisters in the British church and their spirituality in it. It shows the womanist spirituality of Loyal Sisters in terms of their godly lifestyle of prayer and worship in the church, home, work, and community which is mingled with racial and cultural expressions of faith. Their womanist spirituality is also demonstrated through matriarchic church leadership, generosity to the church and society through giving of their time and finances to God and the church, and finally by maternal and childcare responsibilities. Whilst active womanism has regressed from some British Black churches and many younger Black and Brown women are leaving the mainstream British churches, it is important to observe that Loyal Sisters have given their entire lives to God and therefore, in many cases, this is demonstrated through their lifetime investment to the British church whether that is mainstream, intercultural or Black churches. Despite oppressive and discriminatory patriarchy, racism, sexism and misogynoir in the church, they remain resilient and are committed to God and therefore the church. They have decided to stay in/with the church, "come what may." It is with this knowledge that I shall concentrate on the womanist spirituality of Loyal Sisters in the case study congregations, Messa Pentecostal and High Parish, in the next two chapters.

Questions

1. What can we learn from known and existing sources in the British context about the relationship of Black and Brown women: their spirituality, theology, religiosity, and the church in Britain?

2. Nicole Toulis's book, *Believing Identity*,[92] depicts the experiences that Black women play in the Black Pentecostal Church and their invaluable role. What important roles do Black and Brown Loyal

---

converted to Christianity during the Welsh Revival when missionaries traveled to India in the later nineteenth and early twentieth centuries. Nokseng was requested by the Chief of his Garo tribe in Assam to denounce his Christian faith. Refusing to do so, Nokseng and his family were executed. The lyrics were then composed into a hymn by an Indian missionary named Sadhu Sundar Singh.

92. Toulis, *Believing Identity*, 304.

Sisters play in your church-families and communities? What would your churches be like without them?

3. You are the women's ministry leader in your local church. How would you create a womanist theological program for your congregation and community?

Further Reading

Publications on British Christian Black, Brown and White Women

Whilst not focusing exclusively on Black or Brown women, but women generally, in *7 Deadly Sins of Women in Leadership*[93] Ghana-born British citizen, Kate Owusua Coleman, explores several unique encounters which women leaders experience and demonstrate in their ministry and work as leaders. As my first PhD student in 2004–2006, the first Black woman to become an ordained Baptist minister and six years later in 2006–2007, the first Black female president of The Baptist Union of Great Britain, Kate states that her book is "the book I could have done with reading before I started on the road to leadership, and came face to face with some of my own deadly sins."[94] It is a book Kate commonly uses in her training of female leaders. Many women have advanced in their ministerial and career leadership through learning from it.

A more general, highly significant anthology about Christian women, both Black and white,[95] edited by a Black male Christian, exists. It demonstrates the inclusion of men in women's discourse. The topics for inclusion were at the discretion of the individual authors of chapters, many of whom were publishing for the first time. This book thus provided for them an ideal opportunity to address a wide array of topics on hegemonic structures in the church and society and their role as women in it. They thus looked at issues such as patriarchy, leadership, resistance, ministry, the Bible, professionalism, cultural restoration, singleness, womanhood, and the worth and assets of Black and Brown women. This book does not focus solely on Black or Asian women. It is not solely a Black feminist or womanist publication but Lorraine Dixon's chapter on

---

93. Coleman, *7 Deadly Sins of Women in Leadership*, 320.
94. The Baptist Union of Great Britain, "Kate Coleman."
95. Aldred, *Sisters with Power*, 165.

womanism,[96] nonetheless, provides an invaluable introduction to British Black women and the British church. However, having published his anthology which featured white, Black, and Brown women in 2000, Joe Aldred has not published anything again that solely includes women.

The *Black Theology*[97] journal has provided a space for academic papers on Black and Brown faith, theology, religiosity, and spirituality to take place by many British academics and practitioners as well as international contributors. It is where articles by British females are published too.

---

96. Dixon, "Black Woman and Deacon," 50–64.
97. Reddie, *Black Theology*. Lartey, *Black Theology*.

3

In the Spirit at Messa Pentecostal

[God], you are worthy
[God], you are worthy
[God], you are worthy
We give you the praise.¹

HAVING CONSIDERED WOMANIST SPIRITUALITY of Loyal Sisters and the British church more generally in chapter 2, this chapter considers the first of two case-study churches in this book, Messa Pentecostal. This chapter adds to the spirituality of Loyal Sisters in the British church by presenting the spiritualities of them which are unique to Messa Pentecostal. Spiritual, emotional experiences and cultural religiosity are characteristic of Black and Brown ecclesiological lifestyle which is also captured in this chapter.

The chapter starts with an examination of Messa Pentecostal itself as both a denomination and an individual congregation in that denomination. The second section explores the spirituality of Loyal Sistas² in Messa Pentecostal. The third section analyzes patriarchy in Messa Pentecostal

---

1. Composer unknown. The word God replaces Lord in the original song for the purposes of this book. This song has three verses. The first verse is as written. In the second verse, the lyric "worthy" is replaced by "Holy." In verse three, the lyrics "you are worthy" are replaced with the lyrics, "We adore you."

2. Sistas will be used for Sisters in Messa Pentecostal since the majority of the congregation are of Jamaican-Caribbean origin thus the use of patois.

before the conclusion where the spirituality of Messa Pentecostal Loyal Sistas is summarized.

Messa Pentecostal

Messa Pentecostal is a typical congregation of the Pentecostal denomination investigated and would therefore represent some churches in that denomination or the denomination itself. It is a congregation of a nationalized, Black-led, and Black-majority church in England. Messa Pentecostal is its pseudonym. The denomination is a predominately Jamaican church consisting of Windrush Generation congregations who immigrated to England in the 1950s and 1960s. It also consists of the descendants of the Windrush Generation. However, some congregations are populated with smaller numbers of Africans and Asians. They are either economic migrants who arrived in the UK since the 1990s and gained ILTR statuses and/or later British citizenship through professional or semi-skilled employment in England or are converts to Christianity from other religions. Messa Pentecostal is part of a multiracial and multicultural, international, Evangelical, Pentecostal Church of the Holiness Movement with its headquarters located in the US.

In addition to the dominant Jamaican presence, as a denomination in the UK, some congregations also comprise of congregants from other Caribbean islands who are also part of the Windrush Generation and their offspring are congregants too. The monoculture of the UK denomination is certainly apparent. An even smaller number of white and Black European congregants and white Brits also comprise the racial demographics of the denomination.

The current numerical demographics of the denomination in the UK is about 4000 regular congregants. However, over the history of its existence in the UK, which dates back to the early 1950s, it rapidly grew to a population of nearly 6,000 regular congregants. This 4,000 and 6,000 respectively does not include persons who attended the denomination but were not members. With the nondenominational attendees added to the membership-total, the denomination is considered much larger than 6000 people. There are approximate 80 formal congregations located in mainly inner-city urban and suburban areas, in six administrative regions in England and Wales. The findings for Messa Pentecostal would clearly reflect the majority of traditional congregations in this denomination in

England and Wales which consist of approximately 50 to 250 congregants since they tend to be religiously similar. Other congregations were either smaller than 50 members, such as 10 to 20 or even larger than 250 regular attenders such as 300 or more people.

The denominational structure is both patriarchal and hierarchical where the doctrinal policy allows only male bishops in which national and regional overseers are male also. Local congregations are led by a mix of full-time and part-time, paid and unpaid, ordained ministers which mainly consist of Black male senior pastors. I know this denomination well because of my ethnic origin and through my immersion in numerous congregations and among various congregants at several church and community events, both in person and online. Unlike the CoE, this church is not as diverse in terms of religious tradition. Every congregation is recognizably Pentecostal and/or Pentecostal-Evangelical although there are identifiable variations of these Pentecostal traditions amongst it. Congregations ranged from conservative to progressive/liberal Pentecostals. The Pentecostal traditional is manifested in the womanist spirituality of Loyal Sistas at Messa Pentecostal as I shall now explore in the next section.

Loyal Sistas and Messa Pentecostal

Whilst the indwelling, filling, and practical manifestations of the Holy Spirit are important to all Trinitarian Christians, they are especially significant in the Pentecostal theology[3] of Messa Pentecostal. Messa Pentecostal Sistas are represented among the older and middle-age range that is, mainly Generation X and Boomers, but the congregation also consists of younger and older generation females as demonstrated in Table 1. Many of them are females who either immigrated to England as part of the Windrush Generation in the 1950s and 60s and are now British citizens or are the daughters of first generation, British-born, Jamaican parents and are therefore automatic citizens under the British Nationality Act 1981 since they were born in the UK before 1983.[4] Those born in Jamaica intended to return to the Caribbean after five years. However, like the biblical Judeans who were exiled in Babylon as recorded in books such as Jeremiah and Ezekiel, and who eventually settled there, the Windrush

---

3. Cox, *Fire from Heaven*, 372. Gerloff, *A Plea for British Black Theologies*, 1086. Land, *Pentecostal Spirituality*, 239. Toulis, *Believing Identity*, 304.

4. British Nationality Act 1981, 2.2.1, Section 11 states which peoples are automatically British citizens if they are born before January 1, 1983.

Generation too found that their plans to return to their homeland after five years extended into a lifetime. Many of the Windrush Generation Loyal Sistas and their descendants also settled in the UK. They will not act on the racist orders by others in the wider society to "go back to your country." Britain is now their residential home. Remaining in the UK for a lifetime also resulted in a lifetime of service to Messa Pentecostal for these Christian Loyal Sistas. To leave Britain would be through their own choice. However, for them, their commitment to God and the church is for a lifetime regardless of their choice to stay in the UK or return to their country of origin.

The 1950s to Mid-1990s

There was an era in Messa Pentecostal, from the 1950s to mid-1990s, where the Black Loyal Sistas (and the limited Christian, Brown Loyal Sistas present at that time) were very active in mainly traditional women's ministries and roles in the British church such as leading or supporting children's and childcare ministries, sewing/dressmaking, woman's groups, and hospitality such as culinary work and stewardship. These were often voluntary unpaid roles which demonstrated women's commitment, discipleship and service to Jesus and the church. These Loyal Sistas attended church as regular as possible and also engaged themselves in community ministry such as volunteering in soup kitchens for the homeless or visiting shut-ins for the disabled or elderly. Apart from caring for others in community activism and services, there was a strong sorority among them. They supported each other and had each other's backs whether they were partnered in marital relations or unmarried. The sorority was evident in childcare, shopping, cooking, housecleaning, financial help, doctor and hospital appointments, praying, and encouragements to mention some things. These Loyal Sistas knew their hearts' desire. Some even found their vocation through the discipleship and Sistahood. They therefore did what they were born to do. Loyal Sistas worshiped together at church and would support each other through home groups too.

The spirituality of Loyal Sistas at Messa Pentecostal confirms the experiences of Christian Black women by Alexander and Toulis[5] as a place to share their faith and general well-being when the Windrush

---

5. Toulis, *Believing Identity*, 304. Alexander, "Mouse in a Jungle," 85–106. Alexander, *Breaking Every Fetter'?*, 427.

Generation first arrived here in the 1950s to 1970s. Many Loyal Sistas also remained in the same congregations in the denomination in question. They are possibly more representative of the Classical Pentecostals mentioned in Stone.[6] However, their economic and social activism was demonstrated in the sorority, the church, their families, and community-relationship such as work and residential neighborhoods. Much of what is said about Loyal Sistas in the Black church in chapter 2 can therefore be said of Loyal Sistas in Messa Pentecostal. I thus turn to address the womanist pneumatics of prayers and testimonies.

Prayers in the Holy Ghost

Whilst Loyal Sistas are often the prayer warriors and would lead prayer meetings at church and in homes for the whole church, in the early days mentioned above, Messa Pentecostal Sistas were especially seen as intercessors and not just for their Sistas and the church family but for secular friends and families too. Common to Pentecostal spirituality, Loyal Sistas would "tarry" at the altar, in and between the pews/benches, during worship, or in home groups. Unscripted prayers are also characteristic in Pentecostal spirituality and the oral tradition. Whilst tarrying may feature in other denominations, it is especially evident in Pentecostalism. Tarrying is commonly associated to Black Christian spirituality of waiting on the manifestation of God's presence and the pneumatic outpourings.[7] Tarrying occurs through either audible individual prayers or when all the congregation prays together. In the Garden of Gethsemane as Jesus prayed in preparation for his death, burial, and resurrection, which would follow as recorded in Matt 26:40–43, he asked his disciples if they would tarry with him. Although their spirit was willing to tarry in prayer with Jesus, being human, their embodied weariness prevented them from doing so. Jesus therefore tarried alone.

Messa Pentecostal Sistas sing as the music plays, clap, and display ecstatic body movements in the Holy Ghost. Loyal Sistas would dance and praise God, speak in tongues (*glossolalia*), and rejoice through noise-making. Loyal Sistas would pray and sometimes lay prostrate on the ground until they sensed the "breakthrough" of the Holy Spirit in their lives, homes, or church/spiritual circumstances and then there would be

6. Stone, *The Spirit and the Body*, 233.
7. Stone, *Tarry Awhile*, 191.

more singing, clapping, dancing, tears of joy, and jumping in the Holy Ghost. But then there were times of silence—a pause in anticipation of what the Holy Ghost would do or say next. Loyal Sistas' prayers were common to Pentecostal spirituality[8] and in this they were the leaders. Loyal Sistas are currently blazing the Holy-Ghost fire in prayer in Messa Pentecostal.

Womanist Testimonies

According to Toulis, unlike prayer, testimonies are communication with the congregation rather than with God. They are autobiographical accounts of events and experiences, a time to give thanks and praise for God's blessings and often a time in the service for call and response between the testifier and the congregation.

> Epithets such as "Hallelujah," "Glory," "Praise the Lord," and "Thank You Jesus!" are all expressions of praise. Testimonies and epithets convey the mood and emotions which belief engenders in the saint.[9]

Testimony services are traditional to the liturgy of ecclesiastical worship in Pentecostalism[10] and some Black churches. However, testimony services are seldom practiced in many other Christian traditions. At Messa Pentecostal, and in numerous British Pentecostal Churches, testimony services occur mainly in Sunday evening worship. They either occupy the entire evening service or are part of it. If testimony services are part of a worship liturgy, they often occur after the devotion, which commences the service, and prior to the sermon. It is a liturgical practice that may also take place in midweek services and group meetings and occasionally a few testimonies would happen in morning worship too. Occasionally special testimonies are asked of congregants who are planning a permanent or temporary departure from Messa Pentecostal for residency elsewhere or holidays abroad such as Jamaica. At Messa Pentecostal, Sistas are often asked to lead testimony services by the moderating minister.

---

8. See also Cox, *Fire from Heaven*, 372. Gerloff, *Plea for British Black Theologies*, 1086. Land, *Pentecostal Spirituality*, 239. Toulis, *Believing Identity*, 304.

9. Toulis, "Believing Identity," 304.

10. Calley, *God's People*, 182. Lawless, "Rescripting their Lives and Narratives," 53–71.

Testimony services are an open opportunity in the service where congregants (and anyone) can also interact and participate in the service. It is a democratic engagement which, apart from being randomly asked to pray by the moderator in the congregation or prompted by the spirit to do so, and/or to engage in collective, congregational singing, it is an opportunity for congregants to partake in the service. Without testimony services (and congregational singing) only leaders of the church and/or others who are often only asked by leaders to participate in the worship, would participate in it. Although at some churches testifiers speak from their pews (or "bench") as they are prompted by the Holy Spirit or during the testimony service,[11] at Messa Pentecostal testifiers are required to create a line at the front of the church and face the congregation. They take it in turns to testify and after doing so, return to their bench. The testimony leader instructs the congregation on how many testimony lines they require for the testimony service and sometimes how many people are to occupy each line. For examples, a testimony line of 10 congregants. In between each line of testimonies the testimony leader either leads (or "raises") a congregational song or asks the congregational, song-worship leaders to "raise a chorus" for congregational singing. At Messa Pentecostal testimonies usually start with similar words such as,

> Testifier: To the whole house of faith, visiting friends, greetings *or*
> To the pastor, ministers, saints in Christ and visiting friends, greetings *or*
> Greetings to the whole house of faith and visiting friends *or*
> Greetings in the might name of Jesus
> Congregational response: Greetings!

At the end the testimony service the testifier says similar words as, "Pray for me as I prayer for you in Jesus's name" and the congregational response is "Amen!" or "Praise the Lord!"

Similar to prayer, when Messa Pentecostal Loyal Sistas testify, their stories are revealing of the joys and sorrows of their ontology, that is, their lived-experiences, realities, and being—the hopes and dreams as well as the pains and traumas. Testimonies are either spoken-narrative and/or sung recital of Scriptures, usually from the Kings James version of the Bible, or poetries, musical renditions and/or a combination of these verbal and visceral forms.

---

11. Toulis, "Believing Identity," 144.

Testimonies are worship opportunities for Loyal Sistas to update the congregation about their spiritual standing and relationship with God; remind the congregation when they were "saved" or converted to Christianity, "sanctified" or received a deeper cleansing from sin, and made their private or public confession to "set apart" their lives for holiness, and/or were "filled with the Holy Ghost." In some cases, some Loyal Sistas mentioned the exact dates of their Christian salvation, sanctification and/or Holy-Ghost filling. They will testify their faith journey throughout the week, share personal or professional news such as obtaining a new job or the birth of a baby, and/or their brokenness from the death of a loved one. They sometimes comment on a former or present worship service. Testimony services are also times to request for congregational prayers and support in times of trials and/or economic and social hardships and for the restoration of broken relationships with church members or family and friends. There are times of confession for sins committed and appeals for forgiveness from God and the congregation. There are other times of apologies for wrongs done to congregants and restitution and restoration of severed relationships. Like prayers, the testimonies of Loyal Sistas invokes the presence of the Holy Spirit. There shouts of glossolalia, impromptu songs, cries, screams, laughter, dancing, hugs, and so forth. Healings from physical, emotional, mental, and spiritual brokenness all occur during testimony services. They are experienced by testifier and congregations alike. Womanist testimonies are encouraging, expressive, informative, honest, emotional, and spiritual regardless.

Cultural Religiosity in Song

Cultural religiosity in song is just as salvific and spiritual to Loyal Sistas in women's worship and home meetings as congregational Sunday services. Messa Pentecostal is a predominately Jamaican denomination so Jamaican hymns and songs would often be sang in women's and Sunday services where the song leaders are often females in Sunday worship and, as is normal, in women's meetings. Singing is accompanied by clapping, musical instruments, and notably the tambourine-playing by Loyal Sistas:

> Let the Spirit move.
> Let the Spirit move.
> [Come on all Sistas,][12]

12. I have changed the words of this line from "My brother and sisters" for the purpose of this book on womanism.

Let the Spirit move.
When things go wrong,
And the way seems [bleak],[13]
Get on your knees (and pray)
And let the Spirit move.[14]

Worship in Food

Another expression of cultural religious worship at Messa Pentecostal is through food. Jamaican women cook and bake traditional Jamaican food in women's meetings such as: rice and peas; "curry goat" and plain rice; ackee, "salt-fish" and hard food; curry patties; okra, peas, and Saturday soups;[15] gizzada; toto; grater cake;[16] coconut and peanut drops; carrot cake; sweet potato or cornmeal puddings; carrot juice; and Irish moss to mention some items. Prior to the 1990s the only doctrinal forbidden beverage to Messa Pentecostal congregants was alcohol. However, since there was an accepted belief that cooking and baking destroyed the alcohol in food and drinks whilst the flavor remained in them (and was later scientifically proven when some Loyal Sistas took culinary classes at colleges), some Loyal Sistas used alcohol in cooking and baking. From the mid-1990s, like adornment discussed below, Messa Pentecostal members are no longer required to abstain from alcohol for the same reasons given in the case of apparel. However, some Loyal Sistas clearly continue to abstain from the consumption of alcohol. Although I am an ecumenist, I am and have always been teetotal. However, for me, this is a personal preference rather than a religious or spiritual adherence to any doctrine. I am therefore unopposed to the consumption of alcohol for practicing Christians.

Food items are either donated to church and Sistahood fellowships for democratic and collective bring-and-share and/or for social entrepreneurial sales at woman's gatherings and, after services on Sunday or midweek, to fundraise for global, national, regional, and/or local, church missions. Loyal Sistas often welcomed other Sistas and brothers to their

---

13. I have changed the word "dark" in the original song to bleak for the purpose of this book.

14. Author unknown.

15. The Saturday soup is named as such because Jamaicans often make and eat it on Saturdays. However, it is a popular dish for any day. It is essentially a vegetable soup. Meat, usual beef or chicken, may be added.

16. All cakes are made with coconut.

homes for worship and meals too. "Open House" was very commonplace in the 1950s to 1990s. Common to these meetings were occasions for singing which also invoked the Spirit into mealtimes. Praises, thanksgiving, glossolalia, dancing, and raising of hands to God all followed. Their womanist rights, political freedom, and empowerment allowed Loyal Sistas' cultural expression through their worship and service to Jesus which still exists in Messa Pentecostal and other congregations of this denomination now.

Adornment, Apparel, and Tobacco

Apparel has traditionally been a symbol of pietism and purism in many religions and denominations.[17] Another marked symbolism of spirituality for Messa Pentecostal females from the 1950s to mid1990s was in the area of adornment and apparel. Smoking tobacco was another forbidden sin in Messa Pentecostal for all members. As pointed out by Calley, Gerloff, and Toulis, there was definitely a clear division between what was considered Christian and spiritual such as regular church attendance and church-life, in that historical period and trajectory of congregants in many Pentecostal Black churches, and what was considered secular or "worldly," such as the party-life which practicing Black Christians did not do[18] including Loyal Sistas.

A sign of spirituality in Messa Pentecostal for females was in the wearing of "high enough necklines and low enough hemlines" and not the other way round; long-sleeved dresses and tops; skirts and no trousers or shorts, and no makeup and jewelry, including the wedding band. No cleavage, thighs, knees, arms, navels, and armpits should ever be on public display. Forbidding the wedding band for legally married women sometimes called into question their marital status in the wider public domain and beyond the church. Some women expressed their disapproval of being "scorned" by paediatric medical professionals especially during their pregnancy, nursing, and baby-care. Others talked about feeling ashamed when people falsely accused them of cohabitation or being singletons and having children out of wedlock for not wearing a wedding band whilst child-rearing. This was especially apparent for some women

---

17. See Arthur, *Religion, Dress and the Body*, 203.

18. Calley, *God's People*, 182. Gerloff, *Plea for British Black Theologies*, 1086. Toulis, *Believing Identity*, 304.

when they attended their children's school for parents' evenings and other visits with their husbands or alone. Their spouses were often referred to as their "boyfriends" and "partners" whilst other married women's spouses were called "husbands." Some even admitted to carrying a ring in their handbags and putting it on for occasions like these to hide their shame. However, others were proud to represent their faith through their adornment and sometimes used this as a missional opportunity to share womanist spirituality in their church and/or as evangelistic expressions of their faith and belief to nonbelievers or people of other denominations and religions. Interestingly, whilst the wedding band was forbidden, some Loyal Sistas were frequently seen wearing fancy broaches on their garments, hairclips, and hatpins. Extravagant watches were also a commonly-worn accessory by all Messa Pentecostal members. Similarly, whilst makeup was generally outlawed, skin-colored foundation was worn by some Sistas.

From the mid-1990s, adornment in Messa Pentecostal changed. Apart from the wedding band, it is unclear if all other areas of doctrine on adornment was officially changed. However, women and girls then wore all the forbidden garments, makeup, and jewelry, since there was then a general belief that a person's spirituality was not necessarily demonstrated by their dress-code but by the conditions of their heart and how this was manifested in their good Christian living and their godly values towards others. Scriptures such as Matt 15:11–20 and Mark 7:20–23 were significant. Ironically, whilst standardized adornment was an indication of womanist spirituality in Messa Pentecostal pre-1990s, post-1990s demonstrated that this doctrine was more about religious legalism than spirituality. In *Faith and Fashion*, some of the same issues which were raised in Messa Pentecostal about adornment, pride and modesty are also questioned along with issues of vanity and the cost of clothing which often leave practicing Christians with experiences of guilt, and the effects of certain clothing on the environment. Cole and Cole concludes that there is synergy between God, beauty, and clothing when they give glory to God[19] Similarly, pre-1990s, female adornment was often also linked to female embodiment and therefore the need to not only protect women from male lust and their unwanted attention but also about the control of female sexualization which can also be expressed through their adornment.[20] At Messa Pentecostal this belief was extended to the forbidding

---

19. Cole and Cole, *Faith and Fashion*, 162.
20. See also Arthur, *Religion, Dress and The Body*, 203.

of shared male and female bathing/swimming facilities since almost all of females' physical embodiment is exposed in a bathing suit in this leisure activity. There appeared to be a failure of the often all-white, male, General church, doctrinal decision makers in the USA to appreciate the social, gendered and racial impact their adornment policies would have on women globally. Of course times have changed and so too have cultural norms internationally and in the UK. From mid-1990s, at Messa Pentecostal it was therefore clear that giving women choice in their dress-code, where practical and shrew advice and guidelines were administered, was more spiritual than religious dogma. Diane Watt's research on Christian Black female attendance at a Manchester leisure center demonstrates that type of female choice in terms of their embodiment to a women's only space.[21] Furthermore, I would add that changes to the beliefs on adornment in Messa Pentecostal also directly or indirectly removed some of the blame of victims/the females for the unwanted actions of men in terms of female dress-code, and instead, the blame was rightly placed on perpetrators. So rendering your heart rather than your garment was subsequently an attempted practice at Messa Pentecostal. See Joel 2:13.

Some Loyal Sistas are frequent, jewelry and make-up wearers and have adjusted their dress-code also from mid-1990s. Boomers and Generation X Sistas are still dressed very smartly, in their Sunday best, for church on Sunday and midweek services too. Some say that this is how their mothers taught them to dress in public and not just on Sundays. However, younger Generation Y, Z, and Alpha, Loyal Sistas are often seen in casual or causal smart clothing such as jeans, T-shirts/pullovers, and trainers for Sunday services and during the week. Notwithstanding, they remain committed to Messa Pentecostal. Conversely, smoking tobacco is still forbidden. This is arguably for health reasons and therefore a symbol of spiritual abstinence.

Despite the changes in the church doctrine, some Loyal Sistas remain faithful to the pre-1990s adornment practices because they genuinely believe that that doctrine was spiritually right, and in some cases, think that the doctrine on adornment should never have changed. In other cases, some Loyal Sistas (and men too) have persuaded but failed to enforce their continued beliefs on other Sistas who have changed. It is with this divergence of opinion that I shall now consider the patriarchy in Messa Pentecostal.

---

21. Watt, "Praying, Playing and Praising," 84–104.

Patriarchy[22]

The women's fellowships and worship mentioned above provided opportunities for womanist solidarity in which Loyal Sistas could develop and flourish in their faith spiritually, culturally, and socially. They were void of men and therefore were both liberating and empowering for Loyal Sistas in a way that no other church setting could give them in Messa Pentecostal. All or most of the social-community activities, such as sewing club, comprised of only females where men were not in attendance. However, on many occasions men supported the Sistas in the background such as with buying and transporting supplies and equipment to and from venues for meetings and services. They assisted with childcare responsibilities if children were not with their mothers which was often the case, and for transporting Sistas to women's activities if they did not drive as not all Sistas drove in the 1950s to 1970s. Like all systems, there were rare cases when church men took advantage of their role and function and Sistas were not always protected or supported which is beyond the scope of this book. However, generally, church men served the Sistas and were sincere allies with them in women's programs. That said, not all women's ministries were women-exclusive. Some services, especially those held on Sundays, consisted of both female and males but women led women's ministries and moderated the services.

From the 1950s to early 1990s, formal church policy and decision making was governed by men as it was denominational doctrine that church trustees were only men. Whilst Sistas attended church business meetings and annual general meetings (AGMs) they could not speak in these meetings and had no legislative or decision-making powers, not even the women's ministry director who was female. Her voice was only heard when the women's ministry report was read which she was allowed to present in church business meetings. Men sat on one side of the room, often closest to the chair of the meeting which was nearly always the pastor of the church, and women sat on the other side or men sat at the front of the church and women sat at the back so the men could interact with the chair, each other, and vote in these decision-making arenas. Unless women spoke with men who would speak for them during or before the business meeting, they were completely inactive in decision-making and church governance. I noticed similar practices of

---

22. Messa is a Jamaican patois word for Mr. or Master. The acronym, Messa Pentecostal, is intended to epitomize the patriarchy of this case study church.

excluding women from committees at regional and national gatherings. Messa Pentecostal then misinterpreted Scriptures such as 1 Cor 14:33–35 and 1 Tim 2:12 to mean that Sistas could not speak in business meetings since these were the only contexts in which church members assembled as opposed to church services and community events where anyone from the public could attend. For this reason, patriarchy still existed in the women's ministries, although indirectly, since decisions about funds raised for mission through the women's ministries were made by only male church governors at local, regional, national, international, structural, and systemic levels. So Elaine Foster was right in demonstrating the disproportionate representation of Christian Black women in the most senior ministerial and leadership positions in the British Black church in her study although, as Foster also pointed out, Black women comprise the predominant membership of the Black church. They are the workers whilst men are the leaders. Foster shows that Black churches are, in effect, guilty of racialized sexism. She illustrated this observation through the analogy of the "inverted pyramid."[23] Whilst today woman are allowed to be church trustees, participate in business meetings and lead their own church services, systemic patriarchal hegemony and other factors prevent these woman from completely operating womanist theology in some Messa Pentecostal congregations at the UK level. However, even so, Loyal Sistas continue to faithfully serve their God and the church.

Although women knew they had no governance-rights in Messa Pentecostal apart from in their women-only contexts they remained loyal to the church. Loyalty was expected of them to be "good Christian women/girls" so they continued to serve the church, often in various lay ministries, through discipleship and in some cases, ordained ministry too. They remained in hospitality ministries and other ministries commonly occupied by women as mentioned above. For example, they were caterers although in some congregations, the head caterers were men since men were often ordained or lay deacons in the church, whilst women assisted them. Church cleaning was another hospitality role commonly held by women in Messa Pentecostal. This contrasts greatly to the practice at the Black Pentecostal congregation where I was converted to Christianity as a child, flourished as a congregant, and first served as lay leader. There, church cleaning was done by the entire congregation through a weekly cell-group rota. This ensured that everyone, including men, participated

23. Foster, "Women and the Inverted Pyramid," 45–68.

in the hygienic upkeep of the church even if in their domestic sphere of the home, this was not happening.

The roles Christian Black women leaders played were often devalued or overlooked even when these women are prominent figures in local congregations compared with their male counterparts. Until the mid-1990s, female ordained ministers were disallowed to perform the ordinances[24] of Lord Supper, baby dedications/christenings, weddings, funerals, and immersion baptisms without a male ordained pastor being present who would officiate the service and ordinances. Ordained females could only preach and teach in congregational services which were open to the public. Unlike some denominations which forbid women from preaching in the pulpit or "from the rostrum," Messa Pentcostal females were not disallowed from such sacred engagement. Females were then ordained to serve mainly as local pastors of congregations. However, there was an occasion in which a male pastor could not be ordained as a bishop because Messa Pentecostal said that the wife was not "filled" with the Holy Ghost, that is, never spoke in tongues (*glossolalia*). In Messa Pentecostal there was then a common theological doctrine that speaking in tongues was the only evidence of the indwelling of the Holy Ghost. For reasons either related to this or others, this pastor would publicly humiliate and "put-down" his wife in the congregation with misogynistic jokes, such as saying that his wife was not like the other pastors' wives because she was unable to sing, preach, and/or teach. However, he said she was "very beautiful." The congregation would roar with laughter at his comments and in the presence of his wife who humbly said nothing. Instead, she often bowed her head in embarrassment and/or produced a nervous chuckle. These misogynistic comments towards his wife went on throughout this pastor's entire ministry and life. In terms of being a role model of equity and womanist justice and rights to others in the church, he was far from that. His comments were not banter. However, he remained admired and praised for his faithfulness to Messa Pentecostal.

Another pastor's wife recalls being told by her bishop to comply with the sudden and unplanned appointment of her husband to a new church which was out of town and furthermore, to be supportive of his ministry. She was then also rearing two children under the age of five years. Her views in the matter were not sought. Another pastor's wife described herself as a "living widow" because her husband, like many ordained husbands

---

24. Ordinances is the official language used in Pentecostal traditions for sacraments in Anglicanism and some other churches.

of the post World War generation, believed his ministry was a calling to serve God and the church completely and the family should take a secondary role. She never worked but became a stay-at-home mom for their large family of eight children. The first two incidents mentioned above, occurred in the 1970s and 1980s and the last one started from the 1950s (when Messa Pentecostal started) to the death of the couple in the 1990s.

Misogynoir is still prevalent and accepted as normal in Messa Pentecostal although it is questioned far more now by younger Loyal Sistas than prior to the 1990s. In today's church and in world contexts, the examples mentioned above would arguably be encounters of spiritual abuse. Notwithstanding the impact that the ministries of some of these men had on both the church and the world, in some cases, was formidable. Questions of devotion to God where their wives and families are sacrificed are therefore raised. In addition, in some cases these men chose to sacrifice their lives for God and the church too, that is, some gave up lucrative jobs and opportunities to serve God and Messa Pentecostal and in other cases forfeited wealth, material possessions, and their physical well-being to serve Messa Pentecostal locally, nationally, and internationally. For example, they worked for little economic remunerations and social bounty. In England new-field Sunday Schools were established for local children, food social enterprises and luncheons for local communities, mass-scale social housing for senior citizens, and new congregations for local residences. They were provided through these male ministers' endeavors. These male ministers led fundraising projects for water wells in remote villages in Africa and new buildings and school products for school children. They collected clothing and other items from congregants and friends of the church in the UK, and for postage of barrels to destitute congregants in Jamaica. This is to mention only some of their social activism,[25] let alone their sacramental and worship ministries. Debatably, if they and their families were not ultimate sacrifices, intentionally or unintentionally, the church and world would not have been so impactful and changed by their suffering and/or selflessness. Furthermore, in some cases, for the male ministers, at least, it is for this

---

25. Messa Pentecostal, like some other congregations in the UK denomination, operates many community and charitable projects. Like many of the denominational social projects, Messa Pentecostal's community center functions for the local community whilst some congregants also participate in the community center. It is a distinctive social business entity from the church charitable status but is owned by the church unlike the community womanist organizations in McCalla, *Community Womanism*, forthcoming.

reason that their sacrifices have ironically also brought them peace with God. Secondly, they also admit their love for their wives and children and look forward to the rare and limited family times away from ministerial passion and duty. Third, on rare occasions, the price some ministers pay for the church has sadly also cost them their ministerial licenses and sometimes their marriage when any infidelity is disclosed due to months away from their wives for church ministries, thus resulting in them falling prey to improper relationships.

Whilst it is important for ministers to marry spouses who are also compatible and sensitive to the godly callings of their partners, the positions and opinions of families are more likely to also be considered in ministerial appointments today for safeguarding regulations if for nothing else. This may even reduce the number of their children, now adults, who left the church and cite the infrequency of seeing their fathers as children due to their fathers' ministerial service, as a contributory factor to their departure from Messa Pentecostal. Conversely, back in the day, as was expected of them, Loyal Sistas remained devoted to their pastor-husbands, their husband's ministry, and their children all of their lives. In some cases, due to misogynoir in the church, their sacrifices were often overlooked and unrewarded but, nonetheless, I believe it is for this reason that their sacrificial lives are spiritually redemptive in ways which I shall discuss in chapter 9 where they are rewarded and highly favored by Jesus.

Prior to the 1990s Loyal Sistas would stay with the church because to leave Messa Pentecostal implied that they had "backslid" from their commitment to their Christian faith although, in reality, the church was lacking in allowing female agency to their Loyal Sistas whilst it voiced its total commitment and support to them. Like some Pentecostal Black Churches in Britain in which "exclusivity" existed, in researching Messa Pentecostal, I found that in the years of exclusivity, to be a good Christian female meant staying in the church despite patriarchy. Exclusivity was the period in the church's history where it remained insular and separated itself from all other denominations and ecumenist engagement; and all "worldly"/secular activities except for paid work and schools. To leave the church would render Loyal Sistas "backslidden" and un-saved/unchristian even if members departed for allegiance to another denomination. Besides, going to another denomination was rare since the church was insular and a doctrine of exclusivity operated between the 1950s to mid-1990s. Furthermore, most if not all close associates, friends, and families of Loyal Sistas were in Messa Pentecostal. To leave

Messa Pentecostal in that period of the church's history would mean that a Sista would be isolated especially if her marital status was single. She would have to build new friends with people who were not members of Messa Pentecostal whilst she may keep distant ties with some friends and families in Messa Pentecostal. However, from the mid-1990s many Sistas knew that to leave Messa Pentecostal for alternative churches would not render them "backslidden" or traitors since the values and beliefs of the denomination regarding Christianity changed. Some Generation X and Boomer Loyal Sistas admit that they would leave if they were younger due to the church's imperfections, some of which are sexist. However, given their longevity in Messa Pentecostal and their age, they stay as unfamiliarity elsewhere is likely to lead to unhappiness and an eventual return to Messa Pentecostal. Messa Pentecostal is familiar to them and hence they stay although they acknowledge it is imperfect. In fact, some Sistas left Messa Pentecostal for pastures green only to return soon after leaving when realizing that the Loyal Sistas' reticence were that "the grass is greener on the other side" until you get to the other side. Other Loyalists stayed and resisted patriarchy from within the church. There is no point requesting them to "move on." They only dig their heels in as they continue to pursue for patriarchal change either through Bible studies, women's programs, leadership, and change to policy and practice of the church. Messa Pentecostal is their church. They are going nowhere else. Their commitment to God and Messa Pentecostal is therefore similar to the conversation Jesus had with his disciples in John 6:67–69 (NIV) when other followers of Jesus had left Jesus:

> "You do not want to leave too, do you?" Jesus said to the Twelve. Simon Peter answered him, "God, to whom shall we go? You have the words of eternal life. We have come to believe and know you are the Holy One of God."

This spiritual says it too:

> Give me that old-time religion.
> Give me that old-time religion.
> Give me that old-time religion.
> It's good enough for me.[26]

---

26. Hays Daily News, "Give Me That Old Time Religion," 1889 and Wikipedia, "Old Time Religion." The lyrics of one of the verses is "It was good for our mothers" and therefore a fitting hymn for this book. Jamaican gospel artists, Grace Thrillers, also produced a rendition of the song on their album, *I Will Worship You Forever*.

Some Loyal Sistas rarely complained about their unfulfilled female agency since rocking the boat was not the thing to do. Second, other Loyal Sistas failed to challenge patriarchal injustices in the church as they did not regard themselves as activists for women's rights and change and were therefore less concerned about discrimination of Black and Brown women in the church. Third, other Loyal Sistas were not called or wanted to lead. They preferred to serve as active Christian disciples than lead. For these Sistas, church is a place of worship only. For example, they were happy to gather on Sunday morning, volunteer in the women's ministry, and go about their daily lives at other times. Fourth, in other instances, I discovered that some men and women in Messa Pentecostal failed to challenge the discrimination as they believed that such inequality was biblically correct although they never examined the biblical accuracy and therefore did not challenge sexist patriarchy. Fifth, other Loyal Sistas who were lay leaders or ordained ministers in circles of male leaders and pastors, were supported and encouraged by them to faithfully serve in the church. They were informed that women should "wait" until it was their turn to be recognized and appointed to church office and leadership instead of contesting for their rights against the status quo. They certainly did not acknowledge that social action for female change could simultaneously occur whilst waiting, hoping, and preparing oneself spiritually, psychologically, and socially for female ministerial agency and vocation. In her exploration of religious identities of British Caribbean women in the Black church, Toulis discovered that Black women seemed to be either oblivious to or accepting of the patriarchal system they function in.[27] This seemed to be the case in a specific time in Messa Pentecostal and still the situation for some Loyal Sistas today.

Other Loyal Sistas did voice dissent about the lack of female agency quietly, that is, in safe spaces such as, with other church female dissenters. However, there were others who openly aired their disapproval of female discrimination and oppression. Those who dared to publicly challenge patriarchal misogynoir were verbally scolded to submission, humiliated, and sometimes publicly. For peace's sake, most Loyal Sistas therefore conformed to church doctrine on women and so systematic patriarchy continued. Female leaders found that they could not change the structures once they were in positions of authority and any influence they had

---

27. Toulis, *Believing Identity*, 304. I also observed the same when considering power and decision making in schools, which Steven Lukes called "false consciousness." See McCalla, "Theoretical Framework of Benign Power," 39–57.

was marginal amid systematic and structural sexism. Toulis also discovered the same in her study of the Pentecostal Black Church mentioned above. In her study she found that women who were not accepting of misogynoir are seen to be powerless to action change due to institutional sexism. They adopted different identities, "identities mobilisation," at different levels within the Black church even if these levels meant being in constant subordination to and controlled by men.[28]

So until the Black church (and mainstream British church) acknowledges sexism and racism against Black and Brown women in its midst and public at large, its willingness to change, act on its acknowledgment, and not retreat after starting its endeavors when the going becomes difficult to accomplish, Brown and Black women will remain loving and faithful to their Jesus, family, community, and in many cases, even the Black church (and mainstream British church). Loyal Sistas will remain faithful whilst resisting the church's oppressive systems of racism and sexism, and, in some cases, also seek for welcoming, alternative places and spaces such as community womanism which operate as independent organizations or churches outside mainstream denominations and Black churches. However, this study found that whilst remaining faithful to their church, a small number of Loyal Sistas occasionally engaged in the community womanist movement although their devotion to it is minimal. This is because community womanism also serves their spiritual and social well-being especially for training and allows them womanist activism as volunteers in causes they are passionate about, such as Black women in leadership.[29] Notwithstanding, Loyal Sistas stay faithful to Messa Pentecostal because serving God and the church is a lifestyle-choice and not just a casual pursuit. They have dedicated their lives to Jesus since their conversions and to their church too. They "have decided to follow Jesus" and church so, as the songwriter says, "no turning back, no turning back."[30]

---

28. Toulis, *Believing Identity*, 304.

29. McCalla, *Community Womanism*, forthcoming.

30. God TV News, "I Have Decided To Follow Jesus." See also Job, *Why God Why?*, 199.

Conclusion

This chapter explores church-as-usual in terms of the worship, service, and commitment of Loyal Sistas in Messa Pentecostal. It shows the consistency in the spiritual lifestyle of Loyal Sistas to God, the church, their families, and community and their community solidarity as witnessed in their support for each other. The chapter demonstrated their staying power with the church in spite of discrimination, oppression, and patriarchy in the church. For example, women were prohibited to moderate over trustees and business meetings in the years prior to the 1990s. They are sometimes publicly humiliated when they voice their dissent to gendered inequity. However, the chapter recognizes that for some Loyal Sistas change is not required or welcomed both in terms of doctrinal practices and womanism, such as in clothing. Notwithstanding, the 1990s marked a change in some doctrinal practices thus enabling female agency to perform the ordinances as ordained ministers. Despite these changes, the chapter shows that Messa Pentecostal has some way to go before women are regarded as equal with men.

Besides, adopting a spiritual lifestyle which enables them to remain with Messa Pentecostal, Loyal Sista stay with Messa Pentecostal for spiritual redemption and to enact womanist change for the betterment of women which will ultimately benefit everyone as will be discussed further in chapter 9.

For Discussion

1. What do we learn about Christian Black and Brown females from the spirituality of Loyal Sistas at Messa Pentecostal?
2. The doctrinal changes in Messa Pentecostal since the 1990s are sufficiently womanist. Discuss.
3. Patriarchy exists in every church. Loyal Sistas are right to stay at Messa Pentecostal. Discuss.

4

High Parish

The Spirit, an Intercultural Church and a Multicultural Community

> Breath on me, Breath of God,
> fill me with life anew,
> that I may love the way you love,
> and do what you would do.[1]

IN 1989 I SPENT several weeks in German with a white German congregation from the Pentecostal denomination I was raised in. Although I now define the British Pentecostal Church I was raised in by the national, Black-majority, demographics of its congregants, and thus to align it with the international body of literature on the Black Church as it relates to race and racism, this was not always the case. I was raised with the understanding that my Pentecostal denomination was an "all nations" church due to its international, multicultural composition and its then, global exclusivity from associations with other denominations both nationally and internationally. My biological sister was then doing her year abroad in Germany as a modern language student. After graduating from university she became a French and German schoolteacher—the profession she still practices. Although all the congregation were fluent bio- or multi-linguists, like my

---

1. Hatch, "Breath on Me, Breath of God."

sister, the services were all in German. My sister is a practicing Christian and was nearly always my interpreter for the services.

Other early recollections of intercultural worship occurred in Portugal and Spain. Interculturalism is the term sometimes used in the sacred arena instead of multicultural and refers to various cultures in relations to diaspora or a national culture, in this case Britain. I was then an undergraduate Erasmus student undertaking a four-month course in Portugal for my undergraduate applied social studies degree. I attended both church, national conventions respectively and traveled to Spain from Portugal for that national convention. Thankfully most of the three-day weekend conventions proceeded in Spanish, Portuguese, and English, as I spoke no Spanish and only basic Portuguese which is unchanged to this day.

Beyond these occasional events, in my twenties and early thirties when I was a member of the Pentecostal Church, during the summer I also spent one or two weeks in Paris immersed in missionary endeavors with an intercultural congregation of mainly Black Haitian immigrants who spoke French and Creole. However, there were some French-speaking Africans too. These mission trips were organized by my then husband[2] and/or other leaders from the church in England and France. I was tasked with leading Bible studies on these mission trips. However, occasionally I served as prayer and/or devotional lead minister in services. Not being a fluent French speaker, I ministered through an interpreter who was, again, sometimes my own blood sibling who is a fluent French speaker. She accompanied us on these trips as one of our interpreters and prior to the trip often translated all the event programs, liturgies, teaching plans, and songs into French for worship in both English and French.[3] My other biological sister—the twin of the linguist, and another person who was a congregant from the church in Cheshire who lead song-worship—also participated in one of these French mission trips. Some summers would be spent with the young adults of the congregation on a retreat.

Later in 2005, I again participated in an international multicultural conference in South Africa. I presented an academic paper which is now

---

2. I am now divorced since January 2005 and single. To be explored further in chapter 5.

3. Now married and raising her daughter, along with other commitments, my sister no longer engages in international missions but focuses more locally on missions and evangelism through an ecumenical community choir and her local congregation. Unfortunately, our close family-tie has waned overtime.

published[4] and chaired a few sessions at the conference. For a year, I was also appointed as the co-coordinator of the organization, the then International Association of Black Religions and Spiritualities (IABRS). On reflection, these mission trips to France, and church and academic visits elsewhere, were certainly the foundational outlets for exploring womanist spirituality at High Parish.

This chapter is similar to chapter 4 in that it draws on the findings of womanist spirituality of Loyal Sisters in the British church through the other case-study church, High Parish. Whilst there may be some overlap with discussions mention about Messa Pentecostal, this chapter is essentially about Loyal Sisters' spirituality at High Parish.

Data and my findings for this book are derived from the evidence and my experience of immersion and observation with individuals or groups of women in this congregation: through several social events at the church site before and after mainly Sunday services when the parish community meal occurred every week. I attended all of them until I left in 2022. Other times when I interacted with the women was at outside social gatherings and in a WhatsApp group. Due to strong cultural practices and beliefs of gender divisions in social places among some of the national/cultural groups, I met with most of the women in their woman-only places and through phone communications rather than face-to-face in gender inclusive environments, including church services and some social events. Sexism allowed men to be in public and mixed-gendered places but, due to their cultural sociality, some of the women felt prohibited from such spaces where gender mixing was present.

This data observation was not part of my original research project per se as stated above. I was engaged in ministry work at the time and data was gathered for that purpose. However some of that data has now also served the purposes of this book. At this church, I sometimes held a covert researcher role as most of the congregants would not be aware of my observation for spiritual reflection, at appropriate times, as part of my ministry role and neither was I always consciously observing everything which occurred in the service and in community activities. I was a worshiper and a congregant participant too whilst not going totally into native-research mode.

As a researcher and disciple-minister, I had to be very sensitive to the composition of the congregation in the sense that some of them were

---

4. McCalla, "Towards Greater Involvement of the British Black Church in the Secular Education of Black Youth," 245–61.

new and old arrivals to England, as asylum seekers and refugees. Care and attention was therefore required in my interaction with them. Whilst there are several countries where Christian and political repression occur and thus refugees flee to Britain from persecution, famine, and war in Middle Eastern countries such as Iran, Afghanistan, and Syria, most of the refugees in High Parish are Iranian citizens who started arriving at High Parish in 2017. At the time of research, no refugees came to High Parish from the other named countries. What follows is the period of investigation from 2019–2021 and small periods in 2022.

I commence with a contextual framework of High Parish and Loyal Sisters. Second, I focus on immigration and its impact on Loyal Sisters at High Parish. In the third section I explore the community and diversity of High Parish and its Loyal Sisters. Section four considers the general and spiritual lifestyle of High Parish Loyal Sisters. In section five I question and examine the extent to which womanist spirituality operates in High Parish given its all white ministerial leadership and the presence of patriarchy before my concluding section where I summarize the chapter.

High Parish and Loyal Sisters

High Parish is a Church of England (CoE) congregation and part of a Team Parish church of four congregations. The alias name is High Parish. The demographics consist of about 150 regular attendee congregants with others who are not regular attenders of the church. Whilst the Anglican Church and CoE is very diverse in terms of its church worship traditions, High Parish could be regarded as a pioneering congregation, that is, High Paris is atypical of many conventional Anglican congregations.

High Parish is an inclusive, multicultural/intercultural church of the catholic Anglican tradition.[5] At the time of writing, it was led by a full-time paid, heterosexual, married, white, male, middle-aged vicar. It was assisted by two white female ordained priests who were also paid; and two white female unpaid CoE lay ministers who were also all heterosexual and married. High Parish is located in a socially and economically deprived, urbanized, inner-city, residential area with a population of diverse races, cultures, nations, and religious faiths.

---

5. The acronym name, High Parish, is chosen to symbolize the high church tradition in the Anglican Church. The hierarchy in the Anglican Church is also noted in the type of church traditional with the Catholic tradition being High Church. Charismatic and progressive church traditions are known as Low Church.

High Parish females are generally Loyal Sisters. They are faithful congregants and parishioners due to their Christian spirituality and/or some of the social and economic support they get from High Parish and its partner organizations as I shall discussion below. Most of the support relates to their refugee and asylum-seeker statuses, without which, many of them would not get the necessary social and economic requirements to exist and gain the quality of life to survive. It is a place where Christian refugee and asylum-seeker females are now free to practice their faith. It is a place where female non-Christian refugee and asylum seekers can be referred for social and economic services they require to live in England whilst they process through the British immigration system even if they do not attend High Parish as congregants and/or worshipers. I shall focus mainly on the women's experiences of church- and community-life in Britain. Any issues that emerge about immigration shall be considered whilst engaging with issues about church and community at High Parish. I shall use this chapter and book to delve into some immigration policies and issues and the extent to which immigration effects on High Parish women of color. I now focus on that theme in the next section.

Loyal Sisters and Immigration

Alongside traditional, long-time, white British, and Black Caribbean (mainly Jamaican) migrant attendees of the Windrush Generation and some of their second-generation children, High Parish's congregation's demography now also consists mainly of Black and Asian refugee and asylum seekers. It also comprise of lesbian, gay, bisexual, transgender, queer (or those querying their gender identity or sexual orientation), and intersexual (LGBTQI+) communities. They all either come from the Continent of Africa, such as Nigeria, Ghana, and Cameron, and Middle Eastern/Southern Asian countries like Iran (the majority of them), Iraq, Pakistan, India, and Bangladesh. High Parish employs a part-time Iranian male to support the leadership with Middle-Eastern refugee and asylum-seeker congregants. They are therefore British diasporic Asians, Africans, and Caribbeans from numerous countries, and also native white British peoples.

A disproportion of asylum-seeker and refugee congregants first arrived at the church in 2017. The mobility is high as people find temporary settlement at High Parish, obtain their stay in the UK and then relocate to other parts of the UK for work and long-term or permanent residencies. Others remain at High Parish after their stay in the UK. Unfortunately, some people depart if their LTR in the UK is rejected by the Home Office. However, many African asylum seekers were in the country long before 2017.

Middle-Eastern Asian congregants fled their homeland for Britain because of either political and/or religious persecution and/or war. At High Parish there is also a large LGBTQI+ community from Africa who fled to the UK because of their nations' and the Anglican Communion's adverse stance on LGBTQI+ rights. The continent of Africa is still adverse to LGBTQI+ rights and this is reflected also in the Anglican Communion. Whilst same-sex marriages are still forbidden in the Anglican Church globally, same-sex blessings are now permitted after a General Synod agreement in February 2023.[6] However, whilst the agreement has been welcomed with joy by High Parish and other churches in England, with the exception of the Evangelical branch of the church, for some African Anglican Communion countries, the agreement has gone too far. In the African America church in the US, Kelly Brown Douglas also records the homophobic, hostile environment, which LGBTQ+ people, and notably Black women, experience due to their sexuality.[7] Nevertheless, High Parish remains a place of safety for asylum seekers fleeing from the African continent due to LGBTQI+ persecution.

Others left their homeland for economic reasons. For these refugees and asylum seekers, the community activities at High Parish also provides opportunities to discuss issues such as processing their immigration statuses, immigration tribunal hearings, and meetings with immigration lawyers. For some of them, obtaining proof for processing their immigration status is difficult since they left their country in a hurry and with only the clothes they were wearing. Some of them mention their difficulties with living in poor quality housing on arrival in the UK and how they are coping with that situation. Some talk about their time in detention centers prior to being housed, others about having no money, their reliance on the kind support of others and attempting to rebuild their lives in Britain. All refugees and asylum seekers often talk about missing their families back in their countries of origin, especially if they arrived in England as the only person in their family and/or the loss and

---

6. Church of England, "Prayers for God's Blessing for Same-Sex Couples."
7. Brown Douglas, *Sexuality and the Black Church*, 236.

sadness of family members who were killed in war or persecution in their homeland. Some of them converse about struggling with the English language although others are very fluent English-speakers.

It is important to know that all the immigrant women were subjected to the draconian measures of the 2014 and 2016 Immigration Acts which created a "hostile environment" for them and their families whilst they processed through the immigration system and even when their stay in the UK was obtained. These Acts forced every professional agency to heavily scrutinize the lives of refugee and asylum seekers due to threats of fines and imprisonment if these professionals failed to comply with immigration laws. Compliance included making the women's existence in Britain unbearable in terms of No Recourse to Public Funds (NRPF), such as limited and no access to housing, no healthcare, bank accounts, welfare benefits, and tax credits; presuming them to be illegal immigrants and having no rights in the UK. Many of these women only acknowledge their plights after family breakdowns, unemployment, health issues, and/or a housing crisis. This was particularly realized for single women with children who received extremely marginalized social security support. Single women without children were notably impacted with NRPF. The effects of these policies have forced affected women and their families into destitution and poverty.[8]

The hostile environment also revealed the "Windrush Scandal" where legal Black British citizens from mainly the Caribbean were suddenly oppressed by various State officials if they were unable to prove their rights to be in the UK. The Home Office destroyed landing cards and other immigration documents in 2010—the only evidence of citizenship rights in the UK for many Windrush Generation immigrants. In such cases, they mistakenly lost their jobs, houses, health, other state benefits, became destitute and, in some cases, were deported to foreign lands they had either never lived or left as a child since being in England for decades.[9] However, this study does not capture the experience

---

8. Goodfellow, *Hostile Environment*, 303. Umut, *Migrant Women Transforming Citizenship*, 230. Umut, "Saving and Reproducing the Nation," 173–82. Umut et al., "PAR: Resistance to Racist Migration Policies in the UK," 93–106. Flynn et al., "No Recourse to Public Funds' policy in UK immigration law." Isin, "Performative Citizenship," 500–523. Kaptani et al., "Methodological Innovation in Research," 68–81. O'Neill et al., "Borders, Risk and Belonging," 129–47. Reynolds et al., "Migrant Mothers," 365–82. Reynolds et al., "Practice Policy Briefing." Reynolds and Zontini. "Bringing Transnational Families from the Margins to the Centre," 251–68.

9. Gentleman, *Windrush Betrayal*, 320. Liberty, *Guide to the Hostile Environment*, 60.

of women involved in this "Scandal" from the Windrush Generation although many did experience oppression and discrimination for being Black females with a foreign accent.

Government records reveal Iranian citizens being the highest national claimants of asylum in the UK since 2016 with statistical evidence of 10752 in June 2022[10] but these figures do not reveal how many of these Iranian applications were granted LTR or other immigration statuses. For many Iranian women at High parish, their exodus to Britain from the states of Persia/Iran was their only option to escape oppression and repression from the elite, totalitarian, male, political, and religious Muslim Clerical regime and to find either political and/or religious safety.

The international reporting of the capture, imprisonment and eventual release of dual citizen, Iranian-British Nazanin Zaghari-Ratcliffe in Iran from April 3, 2016 to March 16, 2022[11] is a testament of the brutal Iranian regime. The killing of the Kurdish Iranian woman, Mahsa Amini, by Iranian so-called "morality police" in the capital city Tahrah for "bad hijab"-wearing is another case. It led to national public protests by woman and girls, and other protestors, including civic and professional groups.[12] The poisoning of school girls by the cruel system shocked the world. This is in addition to the imprisonment of male and female protesters. The Iranian protest in 2022 was different to former protests since it was not a protest of isolated rebellions but a national insurrection. Despite the murdering, maiming, imprisonment, and torture of dissidents, the insurrection in Iran and global support for the dissenters continues. This is despite the lack of a formal political and/or religious campaign leader or group. Nonetheless, awarding the 2023 Nobel Peace Prize to the imprisoned women and human rights activist, Narges Mohammadi, showed the Iranian regime that the world was united with the protestors for female and human freedom from oppression.[13] Many of the Iranian refugees at High Parish sought religious freedom due to their conversion to Christianity. Political liberty was also sought in Britain from the brutal Cleric regime for others whose departure from Iran was for political emancipation.

For many of the South Asian women, their departure from their homeland was a combination of either religious and/or cultural reasons, such as oppression due to seeking women's rights and opportunities.

10. Gov.UK, "How Many People Do We Grant Asylum or Protection to?"
11. Wikipedia, "Nazanin Zaghari-Ratcliffe."
12. The Observer, "Why Iran's Female-Led Revolt Fills Me With Hope."
13. BBC News, "Narges Mohammadi."

Arriving in Britain mainly from the Middle East these women arrived with only the clothes they wore and anything they could carry. Some had experienced treacherous sea- and land-crossings and through many national borders. Those from the African Continent fled for either economic and/or social reasons, such as better employment opportunities, due to economic impoverishment as orphans and/or emancipation from homophobic repression. They came through planned trips whereas others fled in a hurry to escape dangerous situations, such as experienced by some of their Asian female congregants. Some of these women fled their homeland alone whilst others departed with some or all of their families.

Although clearly strong and getting on with their lives very well, some of these female refugees and asylum seekers were demonstrably traumatized by their ordeal. I therefore tried not to deliberately ask any or very little questions about their experiences in arriving in this country and what they left behind in their birth homes/countries. I recognize that I am not a trained psychologist or therapist, and that those types of immigration questions are constantly being asked of them by immigration officials as they process through British migration to become citizens. I also acknowledged that, unfortunately, not all of them will qualify for British stay then citizenship. Instead, general ethnographic conversations provided quite a lot of the data and evidence from this congregation as they occasionally shared their stories without being prompted.

For the refugee and asylum-seeker women, some of whom are relatively new arrivals to the UK, High Parish is therefore a place and space of cultural association; a place to meet with other refugee and asylum-seeker nationals, and thus receive support and care, as well as a faith community to practice their Christianity. Lockdown was especially difficult for some of them but some of the African women sewed COVID-19, face masks which they gave to other congregants when lockdown restrictions were lifted. The African women are generally very resourceful in other ways too, such as plaiting each other's hair, cooking, sharing, and childcare for the whole African community and families. So for many of the women of color in High Parish, their loyalty to the church is out of social, economic, cultural, and spiritual necessity. Whilst some of the women, mainly the African women, also attend community womanist Sisterhoods[14] infrequently, which operate outside the confines of High Parish, attempting to create an environment of community in High Parish is extremely

---

14. McCalla, *Community Womanism*, forthcoming.

important to the well-being of all High Parish Loyal Sisters, congregants, and parishioners. I therefore turn my attention to this now.

Community, Multiculturalism, Diversity, Spirituality, and Loyal Sisters

Intercultural community theology is pervasive in High Parish. It is a community church. It is a diverse, inclusive church. Every week from Mondays to Saturdays a variety of community activities operate at High Parish. Many of these activities function in partnership with the City Council/local government, adult education services, and local partner community/charity groups and organizations. These services are free to High Parish congregants and parishioners but some are also provided at a low cost to the church. There are a number of life skills classes, workshops, and groups consisting of money saving, diet and mental health, healthy eating on a low budget, cash saving tips, how to save money on food bills, and supermarket budget-buying. There is a class on English for Speakers of Other Languages (ESOL), thus enabling congregants to participate in liturgical worship in song which is in English and often other languages too, other than for daily use in England. High Parish also operates general well-being sessions (stress reduction, motivation, confidence building, emotional resilience); crafts workshops; community cookery lessons; art and well-being workshops; a session on making the best use of your library; a sewing club; a surplus food market; yoga classes; a gardening group; a children's toy bank and a winter clothes bank to mention all the regular weekly community activities. High Parish partners with many local organizations where High Parish is able to make many referrals of congregants and parishioners to them when their support is required. High Parish also partners with immigration lawyers who provide free legal advice and representation to High Parish congregants.

Like other intercultural churches, High Parish discovered that one of the best ways to fellowship and break through barriers of culture is through food. This was done by the bringing-and-sharing of food from home or cooking-and-serving of food at church from different cultures and nationalities of High Parish congregants. The church's community center is the ideal setting for the weekly Sunday afternoon community lunch ("sharing bread" from their countries). This gathering is managed by the white male vicar who delegates cooking and food-bringing responsibilities to the congregation. Meals consist mainly of a variety of rice dishes, such as African jellof rice, Jamaican rice and peas, Asian basmati rice, and often either curried and/or spiced meat and/or vegetables. There is very rarely a potato in sight unless it is sweet potato, or when the occasional British Sunday roach-dinner is cooked. A variety of herbal hot teas, along with traditional English tea with milk, and soft drinks are consumed also. Meals are eaten with fork and knives, chopsticks, spoons, or even fingers; whatever is most culturally acceptable and comfortable for the congregation and parishioners who partake in the weekly community luncheon. In addition, High Parish is an eco-friendly church. The church makes active use of its large garden by growing its own fruit and vegetables in which its organic produce also contributes to the community luncheon and midweek meals and also sustains the food-requirements of its congregants and the parish population along with items in its weekly, Saturday, surplus-food market.

Another annual celebration at High Parish is the oldest Persian celebration of Shabe Yalda/Yalda Night, sometimes referred to as Shab-e Chelleh. It is another occasion at High Parish to fellowship and unite across nationalities, races, and cultures. Parish and congregants alike share in the festivity. It is also an opportunity to learn more about the Iranian culture. At High Parish, Yalda Night provides an opportunity for Iranian/Persian congregants to showcase their cultural talents. One such talent is the inscription of a person's name on gift cards; with messages of kindness and hope in the Farsi language which are then given to persons who request them. The card-inscriptions are an Iranian Yalda Night tradition.

Yalda Night is observed on December 21st by Iranians all over the world. It marks the winter solstice and longest night of the year, the end of autumn and the beginning of winter where days will again be longer and nights shorter. Yalda Night is a celebration with friends and family where a feast of Iranian chicken stew (Khoreshe Fesenjoon), rice with herbs and whitefish or smoked fish (Sabzi Polo Maahi), carrot rice usually served with chicken and saffron (Havij Polo), and/or rice and cabbage (Kalam Polo) are eaten, or other rice dishes with either walnuts and/or pomegranates since they are the traditional nut and fruit for Shabe Yalda. Almonds and watermelons are other fruits and nuts eaten on Yalda Night along with cakes and pastries. It is a night of poem-recitals, Iranian music-playing, singing and dancing, laughter, well-wishes, and merry conversations and as mentioned above, card inscriptions.[15]

15. "Yalsa Night: Longest Night of the Year."

High Parish church and community center is a very pivotal place for Middle-Eastern congregants and friends (mainly Iranians) to fellowship as well as to worship. It is especially a welcoming place at Christmas and Easter seasons for Middle-Eastern refugee and asylum-seeker congregants who would fellowship and celebrate Christmas in the church when white congregants and Black Africans would celebrate with their families at homes or in their temporary accommodations after the Christmas eucharistic service is completed. Most of the women and children are absent from these celebrations after the service, preferring to celebrate at home or when there are opportunities for only women to meet—again reminiscent of the Middle Eastern spiritual-cultural gendered divisions. In partnership with the local refugee center, out of town day trips are also organized for the congregation during summer holidays. At the time of writing this book, a day outing to Wales occurred.

Diverse Hulu Gems

The once-a-month Women's Group, Diverse Hulu Gems, provides a social and spiritual space for all women at High Parish although this group is heavily attended by Asian and African women and less so by white female congregants. Given the Middle Eastern culture of gender divisions, most of the Brown women attend this session regularly as some of them seldom worship or socialize with men in public and therefore very rarely attend other gatherings in which males are present, such as the main Sunday congregational worship or community lunch which follows it. Women assist as either Farsi, French, and/or Spanish interpreters in these congregational meetings which are conducted in English. The weekly women-only exercise session also accounts for the gendered culture of the Asian High Parish females also.

Diverse Hulu Gems is an ethnically diverse group of women of faith and no religious faith who meet to socialize and network. However, it is essentially for women and girls and their female friends and associates of High Parish. It comprises a large refugee and asylum-seeking population (although not all participants are immigrants) and thus I have not used the actual name of the group to protect the identity of the female participants.

Hulu is a pleasant, cute/sweet, female name. The group is not established for educational purposes even though learning is gleaned through interaction and immersion in it. Given the predominant composition of the group, its mission is for support and care of women through various social and faith activities, thus it is a multi-ethnic, multicultural, multinational, and multilingual group of Christian and non-Christian women who attempt to process through the British immigration system and resettle into a new life in Britain. The Diverse Hulu Gems worship sessions, which often consist of prayers, liturgies, and litanies, aim for cultural awareness of the women. For some of the women their loyalty is to this group and other female-only activities. It is not necessarily to High Parish generally whilst, for others, their faithfulness is to High Parish since it serves their cultural, social, and economic requirements.

Diverse Hulu Gems is led by a practicing white female priest and whilst a Black and Brown Sisterhood should ideally be led by Black and Brown females, the composition of this group essentially requires empowerment of the Brown and Black females to lead whilst they are very active participants. Apart from the monthly meetings this group also communicates through a WhatsApp group. Meetings ceased during lockdown but WhatsApp communications increased due to limited or no access to the internet by some of the females in the group to attend the online church services. Regular communication between meetings proved extremely invaluable to these women's psychological well-being given their immigration status. This was especially witnessed during lockdown when physical gatherings were impossible and thus demonstrates the importance of this group for pastoral care.

Finally, High Parish started to address the issue of domestic violence since 2020 when it came to light that several congregants and parishioners of color were experiencing domestic violence. The church now joins in the celebrations of the United Nations annual Orange Campaign Against Violence of Women and Girls which recurs for 16 days annually from November 25, International Day for the Elimination of Violence against Women, to December 10, International Human Rights Day. The assistant priest and leader of Diverse Hulu Gems is the church's safeguarding officer. The issue is now being taken seriously in High Parish and by the vicar too. Apart from serving the social and economic well-being of Loyal Sisters for their flourishing, I now turn to consider the Christian and spiritual lifestyle of Loyal Sisters at High Parish.

Spiritual Worship and Loyal Sisters

Being a liberal Catholic, diverse, and inclusive church of the Anglican tradition, High Parish's spirituality is also manifested through cultural and national religiosities. High Parish is not the first congregation in which intercultural worship[16] is familiar to me in the same Diocese. During my ministerial exploration in the Diocese I also spent some time in another intercultural but evangelical congregation of the Anglican tradition.

The sacrament of Holy Communion is a part of weekly Sunday worship at High Parish since the Eucharist is especially salvific in the Catholic tradition. The spiritual transformation of the bread and wine is symbolic of Jesus's body and blood after they are blessed in prayers by an ordained minister. For High Parish congregants, and notably Loyal Sisters, the Communion is particularly important as it is also regarded as Jesus's sharing in their suffering, that her presence is with them and it therefore reminds them that God cares about them.

At High Parish, the liturgy of the Sunday morning, eucharistic service is in three languages: English, Farsi, and French. Sometimes a Spanish translation of the liturgy is also provided. Translations are done by either paid, church–staff linguistics and/or a combination of congregational volunteers. A progressive, diverse, and traditional style of worship is conveyed through a combination of traditional hymns and charismatic songs from the countries from where the women originated and in which dancing and clapping occurs, accompanied by African drums and tambourines as well as the traditional Anglican pipe organ or piano. Examples of songs are "Amen siakudumisa/Amen, we praise your name, O God," "Jesu Tawa Pano/Jesus We Are Here," and "Ey Farzandane Nur/O Children of the Light."[17]

> Ey Frazandane nur, ای فرزندان نور
> gerde ham biyaeid, گرد هم بیایید
> Ba Shadi o Sorood, با شادی و سرود
> oo raa be saraeid. او را بسرایید.[18]

16. In Anglicanism, worship refers to the adoration to God throughout the whole service. A liturgy is often followed. It does not only mean singing as is often meant by worship in some Pentecostal services.

17. *Amen siakudumisa* is a South African song by Stephen C. Molefe. The English translated is "we praise your name, O God." "Jesu Tawa Pano" is a Shona African song by Patrick Matsikenyiri.

18. This is the first verse of a traditional Iranian/Persian hymn, "Ey Frazandane Nur," in Farsi. Composer, unknown. See the Further Reading for the English translation.

Apart from the planned leading of congregational singing by the group-songsters who are all Black, Brown, and white females, spontaneous leading of song by the white male vicar at High Parish is also commonplace in Sunday morning worship. His occasional impromptu of leading the congregation in song is also conventional to Pentecostal worship and is also apparent in Messa Pentecostal. The vicar at High Parish is a competent singer so he often sings the Scriptures and prayers in song in the various languages of the congregation.

The liturgy often also includes prayers from around the world. References to or quotations from famous people from various countries are also sometimes included in the liturgy especially from nations which represent the congregation; nationally, culturally, or racially. These prayers and references are usually also translated into Farsi, French, Spanish and English. For example, during my time at High Parish references to Martin Luther King Jr., Desmond Tutu, Howard Thurman, and Harriet Tubman were evidenced.

Amongst the other spiritual activities at High Parish is a separate Mohabbat[19] service which convenes on Sunday afternoons directly after the church community lunch mentioned above. It is held in the Farsi language with some English interpretations and, like the morning worship service, attended mainly by Persian/Iranian male worshipers but Iraqi, Pakistani, and Bangladeshi male worshipers too. The absence of many Brown Sisters has much to do with the cultural-sexual division which is interestingly still maintained by some of the Asian refugee and asylum-seeker congregants in the UK and in worship too. The females who attend this service do so as they flourish in their newfound liberation from misogynist repression which they endured in Iran whilst celebrating their salvific freedom in Jesus. They also seize every opportunity to actively participate in the service as readers, translators, and prayer leaders.

Separate congregational Bible studies are held during the week in the evenings for English, Farsi, and Spanish speakers. Whilst all African, Caribbean, and native Britons attend these Bible studies, the Asian females are underrepresented at the Bible studies due to gendered cultural reasons as mentioned above. Monday to Friday Morning Book of Common Prayers (BCP)[20] are open to the entire congregation but are mainly

---

19. Mohabbat translates as love in Farsi.

20. The Book of Common Prayer is the traditional prayer book of the Church of England since 1662.

clergy spaces where Black and Brown Loyal Sisters occasionally join them which is interesting since this is also a gender-inclusive space.

Apart from being an inclusive diverse community church, High Parish is also a climate change and ecology church. The month of September is dedicated to climate change and action in the CoE. High Parish celebrates Climate Sunday services every September and focuses its Bible studies on the climate also. All songs, Scriptures, prayers, and illustrations focuses on God and creation. In October, harvest is also practiced in which food donated to the church from community organizations is distributed to congregants. High parish certainly acknowledges God as creator of the universe and the importance of caring for and protecting God's environment and biodiversity. The presence of Loyal Sisters in the eco-spirituality of High Parish in September, October, and the church's community garden is notable. For some of them it is a reminder of their former rural existence and active participation in God's creation prior to their settlement in England. For other Loyal Sisters it is an opportunity to fellowship with like-minded females in the outdoors and engage in eco-Scriptures indoors.

Spiritual Womanism at High Parish?

High Parish is led by a white male vicar and associate, white female priests as mentioned above. It is not led by Brown or Black Sisters. Although High Parish has historically not always been a multicultural community church, but an Anglican traditional catholic congregation of mainly Anglo-Saxon whites and some Blacks from the Windrush Generation since the 1960s, as far as I am aware, it has always been led by a white male vicar. At High Parish Loyal Sisters are womanist in the sense that Black and Brown females find solidarity among themselves as kinship women and thus transcend oppression through their spirituality in a way they would not generally encounter elsewhere given their circumstances. This enables them to experience a certain degree of liberation. However, the absence of a Black or Brown female leader means that womanist theological leadership is not practiced at High Parish, although womanist spirituality and agency exists and is demonstrated in the lived-experiences of and solidarity among the Loyal Sisters.

Symbolism is very important in Anglo-Catholicism. The lighting of candles is commonly used for prayers and the wearing and signing of the cross represents Christ in the midst. Although being a liberal, Catholic, Anglican Church, where "bells and smells" is a common ritual of Sunday worship, High Parish does not practice prayers which invoke the presence of Mary, the mother of Jesus. However, High Parish has a Lady Chapel or place in the church for "Our Lady" in which an image of Jesus's mother Mary is present to symbolize the importance of her life in Christ's humanity and divinity and, for women, their importance too. Notwithstanding, leaders and congregants do not actively or formally recognize it in any services, liturgies, or church activities. The Lady Chapel therefore remains only as a latent symbol in the church and thus also demonstrates the leadership being a white man. Black and Brown Sisters are represented in some church positions such as on the church council/trustees (the Parish Church Council [PCC] and District Church Council [DCC]) but none of them lead in a department or ministry in the church. Black and Brown Sisters never preside over Sunday worship although they might lead worship alongside the president, since only ordained priests can preside over sacramental services in the Anglican tradition and at High Parish, morning eucharistic services are held every week. So in High Parish Sunday morning worship is led by the white ordained ministers. Brown and Black Sisters often participate in other roles in the services, such as reading Scriptures and prayers. They do not preach or are asked to do so. Brown and Black women do not lead the weekly Bible studies which are again led by white priests. They do not lead the Mohabbat service. This is led by Asian men. They do not lead the women's ministry. That meeting is led by a white female priest. They do not preside over Morning Prayers but may be asked to lead alongside the president. In High Parish, Black and Brown Sisters do not head anything.

Not being allowed to lead anything at High Parish as Brown and Black females is interesting given that, as a denomination, unlike Messa Pentecostal, the Anglican Church ordains females to the office of bishops. On November 30, 2017, the consecration of Iranian-British Guli Francis-Dehqani, the first, female bishop of Middle-Eastern Asian descent in the Church of England (CoE),[21] provides such a historic and significant case for acknowledgment. So too was the consecration of Rose Hudson-Wilkins, the first Caribbean British-Jamaican to be consecrated to the CoE Bishopric on November 19, 2019.[22] Bishop Dr. Francis-Dehqani was

21. Wikipedia, "Guli Francis-Dehqani."
22. Wikipedia, "Rose Hudson-Wilkin."

appointed as Lord Spiritual on November 1, 2021 in the House of Lords.[23] Bishop Rose Hudson-Wilkin is one of the most distinguished Black female ministers in the CoE; ordained since 1994, in 2008 she become the Chaplain to the Queen and, in 2010, priest-vicar of Westminster Abbey and the House of Commons Speaker.[24] The archdeacon, Ven. Dr. Rosemarie Mallett, became the second Black female bishop in the CoE on May 3, 2022. She is the bishop of Croydon.[25] On March 8, 2023, International Women's Day, Canon Smitha Prasadam, born in India and of South Asian origin, was named the new bishop of Huddersfield.[26] The appointment of these Black and Brown female bishops is a womanist step in the right direction so far as representation or actual figureheads. Dr. Guli's PhD thesis, completed in 1999 on religious feminism and Iranian missionaries in 1869–1934, demonstrates her knowledge of female oppression, resilience, and capacity to minister against adversity. In 2012 she became diocesan advisor on women's ministry in the Diocese of Peterborough. She has also served in multi-faith ministries in various roles.[27] Shai Linne's, "Triune Praise,"[28] is a fitting adoration to God for these females bishopric in the CoE. Notwithstanding, even with the appointment of Black and Asian bishops in the CoE, more remains to be done to significantly promote womanist theology and spirituality in the CoE.

Generally, apart from the rare occasions, the Black and Brown women at High Parish never complained about not being fully active in worship or leading anything since, for some of them, their own immigration status bars them from full civic engagement outside the church and some of them see this as a similar restriction to active participation in the church. They are just grateful to be in church, sing and fellowship with like-minded people as witnessed in churches by Kwoi Pui-lan's Asian women in Asia, although in that case their worship is in their native lands.[29] Similarly, they fought oppression and women's rights. Commu-

23. Wikipedia, "Guli Francis-Dehqani."
24. Wikipedia, "Rose Hudson-Wilkin."
25. Wikipedia, "Rosemarie Mallett."
26. Wikipedia, "Smitha Prasadam."
27. Wikipedia, "Guli Francis-Dehqani."
28. Shai Linne, "Triune Praise." I introduced this gospel rap song to High Parish for Trinity Sunday on June 7, 2020 for the online service music playlist under lockdown. Trinity Sunday occurs the following week after Pentecost Sunday in the Anglican seasonal calendar.
29. Pui-Lan, *Introducing Asian Feminist Theology*, 136. Pui-Lan, *Postcolonial Imagination and Feminist Theology*, 252.

nity spirituality is missional in High Parish. It is one of several churches in the Diocese[30] where community activities are extensive so most of the efforts of the Loyal Sisters are witnessed in social and community settings, although white priests rather than Black or Brown females lead these activities as well as the liturgy and worship.

For many of the Black and Brown Loyal Sisters, patriarchy and racism is not so much an issue for them at High Parish since High Parish is a community-oriented church attempting to meet their needs, albeit amidst white superiority where white priests are in charge. Secondly, for the refugee and asylum-seeking women High Parish is primarily a safer and friendlier place than general, British public life where they are sometimes treated inhumanly and are forced to heavily or totally rely on the basic generosity of charities for their sustenance for years if not decades whilst their refugee and asylum-seeker statuses are processed. Thirdly, for women fleeing persecution and/or abstract and absolute poverty in their homelands, the charitable donations meted out in England and High Parish is better than the persecution and poverty they escaped back home. Loyal Sisters could leave High Parish at any time. They are under no obligation to stay there. However, with nowhere else to go and no other nearby Anglican Church which could offer the specialized support to asylum seekers and refugees which they receive at High Parish and its partner organizations, they stay at High Parish until they are either granted LTR, ILTR, or immigration nationalization statuses or are deported. Being refugee and asylum seekers means they have no real choices where they worship or fellowship since wherever they go prior to obtaining their rights to remain in the UK, is likely to be either the same or worse than High Parish. Some of the Black and Brown women are therefore Loyal Sisters by immigration default. For this reason, they are succumbed to only ever support the white priestly leadership which, although not womanist, is better than many other alternatives available to them.

There is another issue concerning Black and Brown women and leadership at High Parish. Some of the Black and Asian woman are theologically and culturally socialized to believe that women should not lead. Men led the Farsi Sunday afternoon service with one of the Brown females being the interpreter and she sometimes participates in the reading

---

30. A Diocese is one of the CoE's decentralized, autonomous, self-governing regional areas of the national church and is headed by the most senior bishop in that region.

of Scriptures in the main Sunday morning service. However, in other cases, Black and Brown women are not empowered or enfranchised to lead through training or support. Through misinterpretation of Scriptures or cultural prohibitions, some of them do not believe they should lead in spiritual spaces and places. We see a similar situation in Acts 6:1–6 in the Bible. The Grecian widows were overlooked in the foodbank provision compared with the Hebrew widows. Attempting to respond to the racial discrimination in the social action program, the church's democratic reaction was gravely sexist. No women were chosen to lead the daily distribution of food. Seven male deacons were selected by the whole congregation. This clearly shows not only the extent of sexism which existed in the early church but why it persisted since the decision was unanimous. It was unchallenged and undisputed. This sexist decision in the church was a microcosm of sexism which existed in the entire early church community. It was democratic but was it theocratic? In such cases today, religious and theological education and training is required for women (and men) at High Parish and elsewhere to fully appreciate and accept female leadership.

Although patriarchy exists in High Parish and, as seen above in Messa Pentecostal, most and some of these females respectively serve in them because they are not oppressive places for some of them although they are patriarchal and therefore discriminatory. At Messa Pentecostal, the absence of oppression was experienced by females who were either themselves leaders and did so without restrictions to their leadership from senior hierarchical structures. At High Parish this did not apply as none of the Brown and Black women led anything. However at High Parish, whilst sex discrimination is apparent for those who may sense a calling or want to lead, feelings of oppression due to leadership-prevention, was absent for many Brown and Black women who did not sense a calling to leadership or wanted to lead in the church. Some of them were therefore content to serve the church as disciples and/or function under white leaders where oppressive or repressive requirements, rules, and doctrines were not required of them. My conversation on Mother's Day, after the pandemic lockdown, with an African High Parish Loyal Sister, recently separated through marriage and the biological mother of four children, sixteen years and under, and who recently got her ILTR in the UK and therefore paid employment also, illustrates this point:

> Me: Happy Mothers' Day. I hope your children treated you well today.
>
> Loyal Sister: I thank God... was busy doing the cooking for lunch in church today.
>
> Me: Although it is great to help out at church it would have been nice for you to have had a break from the kitchen for at least one day, for Mother's Day, as the parent of school-age children. It would have been nice for all mothers in similar situations. [I meant that the church men should have treated the church Sisters well by cooking and serving the meal to the females on Mothers' Day even if they were not mothers]. Anyway, God bless you.
>
> Loyal Sister: I honestly didn't mind doing it. It's over now. I'll rest in bed until late tomorrow. God bless you too.

What is apparent for some Loyal Sisters is that patriarchy, in and of itself, is acceptable and so is white rule as long as patriarchy and white leadership is absent of misogynoir and racism which is manifested in white male and female oppression and even if white leadership means Black and Brown loyal submission. Nicola Toulis's study of Black females at a Black church who conveniently submitted to Black male leadership therefore concurs with my observations of some Black and Brown women's compliance with racism and misogynoir at High Parish.

Conclusion

This chapter shows the womanist spirituality of Loyal Sisters at High Parish which is manifested by their camaraderie, solidarity, and agency for each other and in support of the community and worship at High Parish. It demonstrates the economic and social hardship of their daily living due to the refugee and asylum-seeking British statuses and their reliance on the community-spirituality of High Parish and its partnership with State and community organizations. It shows their tenacity and resilience against the odds and their fortitude to withstand hierarchical, racist, and patriarchal leadership. They have succumb to much turmoil in Britain due to their immigration statuses yet they stay at High parish since they recognize it allows them a marginal sustainability in a way they would not obtain elsewhere. Being at High Parish is better than returning to the countries they fled due to the repression and destitution many of them experienced. Furthermore, for many of the Iranian Loyal Sisters, they can never return to Iran since this would be a literal death sentence for them. A stay in Britain is the only option available to them to be free and flourish now. Andries Van Tonder's South African hymn in the Zulu language, Siyahamba ekukhanyen kwenkhos / "We Are Marching in the Light of God,"[31] is an encouragement to the congregation to go forth in the power of the Holy Spirit.

Questions

1. What do we learn about Christian Black and Brown females from the spirituality of Loyal Sisters at High Parish?
2. What does this chapter teach us about life as refugees and asylum seekers in Britain and especially as females?
3. Is womanist agency required at High Parish and why or why not?

Further Reading

This is the English translation of a Farsi hymn, "Ey Frazandane Nur/O Children of the Light."[32]

> O Children of the Light,
> O let your voices raise.
> With gladness and with song,
> O Sing Messiah's praise.

---

31. "Siyahamba ekukhanyen kwenkhos"/"We Are Marching in the Light of God" is composed by Andries Van Tonder.
32. Composer unknown.

5

Womanist Testimony Service

This is my story,
This is my song,
Praising my Savior,
All the day long.[1]

ORAL TRADITION IS THE medium through which Black and Brown church Sisters customarily and predominately demonstrate their spirituality and convey information. Black and Brown women often communicate their personal experiences, events, facts, and fiction, their happiness and woes, through story-telling, testimonies, sermons, prayers, songs, dance, and/or poetry. The African American, female gospel singer, Shirley Caesar often testifies in her songs. "Feel the Spirit"[2] is one example. When discussing the spirituality of Loyal Sistas at Messa Pentecostal in chapter 3, we learned about the importance of testimony services to Pentecostal and/or Black church traditions. My autobiography in this chapter is an example of that tradition from a womanist stance.

The testimony in this chapter is womanist because it is a story which demonstrates my praise and thanksgiving to God for her grace, protection, deliverance, guidance, and assurance in various times in my life as

1. Crosby, "Blessed Assurance."
2. Caesar, "Feel the Spirit."

a Christian Black woman. However, my testimony here is a book chapter rather than an audible, pneumatic, call-and-response, interaction in a congregational service-setting. Notwithstanding, I aim to keep the tone informal so as to remain as close as possible to a church testimony in person. It's a space for encouragement, empowerment, emancipation, and worship in congregations, at home, work, college, or elsewhere by Loyal Sisters, their allies, and all readers. It allows the reader the time for spiritual response as intended and preferred during or after reading it. My testimony can therefore advance our knowledge and understanding of spiritual storytelling for all.

Due to space and time this testimony focuses mainly on my church engagements and discipleship ministry. I will address community activities more closely elsewhere.[3] It is also epistemological for understanding and pedagogical. Similarly, I shall not discuss the extensive difficulties associated with ordination and women of color in this chapter. Some of this shall be explored further in chapter 6. What now follows is my womanist testimony.

My Womanist Testimony

Greetings in the might name of Jesus, to the Loyal Sisters and everyone.

At the time of writing, as an ecumenist Sister, I am embarking on one of the most interesting but also troubling times of my entire life. I am also an ally with Loyal Sisters. First, I shall tell you why my life is interesting.

Interesting Times

It is interesting because personal circumstances, which I narrate below and in other parts of the book, are shaping my thinking and rethinking about life, my purpose in it, and the fact that I was born a Black female in England in this moment in time. I believe that I was not born to simply exist then die as indicated in the biblical books of Proverbs and Ecclesiastes. To be in God's will has consistently concerned me throughout my life, and knowing my vocation and calling and fulfilling them in my Black female embodiment is more poignant now than ever before.

I am female and Black. I was born in Wolverhampton, England. I am a British citizen by birth under the British Nationality Act 1981 as I

---

3. See McCalla, *Community Womanism*, forthcoming.

was born in the UK before 1983, to Jamaican-born parents who are now deceased. They also became British citizens as mention in the British Nationality Act 1981.[4] My parents paid to become British citizens under the Immigration Act 1971 which required non-EU citizens to pay a fee for their citizenship. However, like many Jamaicans at the time, my parents did so reluctantly, seeing it as a "government, money-making scheme." This was because, at that time, for the Windrush Generation, they were already British Commonwealth citizens under both the 1948 British Nationality Act and 1962 Commonwealth Immigrants Act. On their arrival in the UK, Jamaica was and is still part of the Commonwealth and secondly, because they immigrated by Royal invitation to rebuild Britain's broken economy and social infrastructure after the Second World War. My parents therefore already had ILTR in the UK and British citizenship when they arrived in the late 1950s and early 1960s respectively and so did many Caribbeans at that time. I reside in England and am a second-generation, diasporic British woman with the same citizenship rights as any British-born white person of the same-age generation, that is, Generation X or above.[5]

I am a practicing Christian. I was raised in a Black-majority denomination which, for the purposes of this book, I shall not name but nevertheless, I know that some readers may already know the church, that is, those who are familiar with my story or know me from association with that denomination. By not naming the church it allows me to be candid about references to it throughout the book in relevant places, where both good and bad occurrences are manifested. In this, this Black-majority church is similar to other organizations. However, since I am an ecumenist and have therefore also visited or been a congregant of other Black-majority churches in different localities of England and the US, it should not be assumed that every reference I make in this book to Black-led or Black-majority churches I am referring to the Black-led denomination from which I originated.

I was christened at six months old. My conversion to Christianity occurred during my childhood. As far as children can sense God's presence, I was certainly aware of God from as early as between the ages of

---

4. British Nationality Act 1981, 2.2.1, Section 11 states which peoples are automatically British citizens if they are born before January 1, 1983.

5. Generation X were born from 1965 to 1980. See Table 1 in "Age Range by Generation."

two to five. So let me tell you another true story within my own story. This story has been told by the mother in it many times.

Over 50 years ago a mother returned home to nurse her two, newly-born babies. She already had two young children who were one and two years old respectively. In order to fall asleep, the one-year-old would sing church songs in bed until she got tired and fell asleep. One day the toddler started singing a song, "If You Know the Lord Is Keeping You,"[6] which originates from the Caribbean island of Jamaica.

Unknown to the infant as she sang, was the suffering of her mother who had mild systems of postnatal depression and anaemia. On hearing her daughter sing the mother trusted God for healing. This started the mother's journey to recovery and complete healing. Praise God! The mother in this story is my mother and the one year old singer is me—the now adult author of this book. I shall mention my mother, Dorothy McCalla, again below. She was a Loyal Sister but is now deceased since 2016. RIP and Rise in Glory!

I first spoke in tongues at age nine when I was "filled" with the Holy Ghost—a traditional experience of Pentecostal spirituality although not the only evidence of a pneumatic outpouring.[7] It was in a Sunday night altar service which occurs at the end of conventional Pentecostal worship. An immersion water baptism followed in the same year and the day after my baptism, I joined the church with the "hand of fellowship" as is customary in that denomination. It was then that I also started tithing my income/pocket money of 10p a week and when it increased to 25p, 50p, a £1, and so on. The then church treasurer informed my parents that she was both surprised and overjoyed when she opened the tithes envelop to see my 1p enclosed especially as no other children in the church were expected or tithed to the church. My parents informed her that it was my decision and not theirs and that every week I was also giving offerings to the church in the collection plate during services. Being an ecumenist now, my views on tithing have advanced considerably since my childhood. More practical giving and relevant and appropriate payments-in-kinds such as a tenth or donation of time and talents (volunteering/discipleship), are also my beliefs on tithing especially for people on very low-incomes and where financial hardship may prevent them from financially contributing to the church. However, whilst I regard these other types of

---

6. Alfred, "If You Know the Lord Is Keeping You." Gloria Alfred is a Jamaican gospel singer.

7. See Toulis, *Believing Identity*, 304. Stone, *Spirit and the Body*, 233.

giving as spiritual, I nonetheless acknowledge that they are more difficult to quantify and assess for the church than the orthodox one-tenth of one's financial increase as recorded in Lev 27:30 and elsewhere in the Bible. Aside, I have engaged in numerous fundraising activities throughout my lifetime apart from the obligatory membership tithes-paying.

From the age of two, I was singing as a soloist and then in the church choir. I preached my first church sermon at nine years old under the pastoral leadership of one of the founders and prominent leaders of the national Black-majority church in the West Midlands. He is now deceased. I preached and sang on Sundays quite regularly. From age 14 I became a lay leader in that congregation where I was the children's director serving children under 12 years, appointed by another pastor to that congregation at the time and who is now also deceased. At age 17, the same pastor who made my appointment to lead the children's ministry, appointed me to lead youth and young adults as director. I led and served a strong group of approximately 75 regular church-attending young people, aged from 12 to 35. Simultaneously, I became a women's ministry sub-group leader and worship song leader in other church departments. I served these roles in a voluntary capacity which was customary in the denomination for all lay leaders at that time.

At age 17, I also learnt to drive. My qualified driving instructor was the deacon of the church. My dad then bought me my first car. I loved that decrepit Ford Escort Mark 1 which was, even back then, an old car. I think I loved it because it was bought by my dad and was my first car. I was a young driver so my dad was conscious that the insurance would be high if he allowed me to drive a newer car. Besides, he said I could "practice" on it before getting a better one. That car served me well, my church ministry and my friends and family too.

At home, I moderated the family worship services when my dad (Galfymore) or mom (Dorothy)[8] were not leading them. My mother was sweet, quiet and, apart from heading pastoral, home cell groups at various times during my teen-years, she generally stayed in the background of church ministry; preferring to support the ministry of others. However, she was spiritually gifted to pray and was a mighty prayer warrior. She covered my siblings and me with powerful daily prayers until she became ill to death in 2015–2016 and could no longer pray.

---

8. These are the real names of my parents. They were legally married with the surname McCalla. My mom's maiden name was Baxter.

> If I could only hear my mother pray again.
> If I could only hear her tender voice as then.
> How happy I would be.
> [She] means so much to me.
> If I could hear my mother pray again.[9]

Both parents ensured that my siblings and I practiced daily prayers, accompanied with the Word (*the Logos*) through the Bible, by being examples of this themselves.

I did not do the activities of other children my own age at that time such as playing outside after school with friends as I was always either doing school homework or preparing for leadership at church or home worship. But I did not mind. I loved school as well as church. I stayed on at school into the sixth form and engaged in school politics as a student governor. I aspired to become a schoolteacher on leaving school since I was at primary school as I knew of two paternal aunts (my dad's sisters) in Jamaica who were then also schoolteachers. In some way, I also wanted to do ministry. All my life my parents served as congregational leaders and other members of my family were active ordained ministers. My parents were also upstanding in both the church and community so, at that time, at least, at church, my family was also the family everyone wanted to be.

I played my clarinet in the church band, school, and many bands and orchestras at then Graiseley Music School in Wolverhampton.[10] I also played the descant and treble recorders at school and Graiseley. Although I still have my clarinet and recorders, I don't play them anymore and have not done so since in my twenties. I also played the tambourine in church too. I like athletics so always participated in school sports days but I also liked hockey. In my spare time, I watched the news and documentaries on TV with my dad and sometimes went to the local spa and sauna with close church family friends in my late teenage years. Most of them were at least five to fifteen years older than me. That was probably because most of them were leaders in the church themselves or friends of leaders. I certainly preferred mature and experienced companions, or people who were more serious and responsible since those people tended to know when it was appropriate and sensible to laugh too. I really don't think much has changed now although younger people of the same type

---

9. Whitfield Vaughan, "If I Could Hear My Mother Pray Again."
10. Real name.

of personalities are the type of people I will befriend whilst, as always, I am generally open to general pleasantries with anyone.

I spent some summer school holidays at church camps in the countryside (Wales) where I also led worship services or Bible studies and was a national youth camp group leader. It was at one of these camps at age 13 that I met a dear friend from London and my now sister-in-law from Sheffield. My sister-in-law was then also 13 and my other friend was then 14 years. They were and still are also Christian Loyal Sisters. The separation of my friend's parents in London led to a toxic family relationship and she needed stability, peace, and love. From then onwards she would spend every summer, Christmas, and Easter holidays at our home in Wolverhampton. I seldom hear or communicate with her now as we've both moved on. However, back in the day and until my twenties, she was part of our family; such was the friendship we had forged with her and someone my family would definitely not have kept such a close bond if she was likely to have caused trouble for us, then and now. Well, as for the friend from Sheffield, she is now real family as she later married my biological brother. Although I do not share all their values and beliefs about everything, nonetheless, they are one of the most perfect examples of Christian love and marriage I have ever known. I really admire that about them.

Some summer holidays I stayed at the home of a senior maternal figure in my local congregation who, at the time of writing this book, has in 2023 died at 105 years old.

I cooked and baked some week days and every Saturday afternoon since I was a child. I also baked the Christmas cake every year; iced it too, and baked and iced one for my pastor who appointed me as youth director. No wonder my mom, Dorothy McCalla, nick-named me "mama" when I was a child. However, I never heard about Sojourner Truth, Harriet Tubman, or Alice Walker as a child and I don't think my mother did also as she never mentioned them. However, in the 1980s, I did watch the film *The Color Purple*[11] but then, never knew Alice Walker authored the book[12] from which the film emanated. My biological mother thought I was quite precocious and mature for my age when I was a preschool child and thereafter, as well as very industrious but, apart from that, generally quiet. The name stuck. The name "mama" was very endearing and showed my mother's affection and love for me, her daughter. The name

11. Spielberg, *Color Purple*.
12. Walker, *Color Purple*.

"mama" is now quite prophetic since neither my mother nor I knew that I would become a Black feminist-womanist scholar.

My mom also sometimes dressed me in red as a child whilst pink was her favorite color. I used to knit, crotchet, and sew too; sometimes I made my own clothes and a few items for friends. My biological sisters also did the same and my mom crocheted also. One year I knitted a red mohair jumper for an upcoming national winter/New Year church retreat. It received compliments from everyone. However, I did not tell them that I made it. The retreat director contrasted it with the camel's hair worn by John the Baptist. I jokingly informed him that it is evident that my ministry is very different to John the Baptist. I have less time to bake these days and do not knit, sew, or crotchet anymore.

I married a senior pastor in my early twenties. However, over a decade later in my thirties, we amicably divorced. During our separation, which we planned together, we required space and time for spiritual reflection and prayer about some issues we were experiencing. These issues related mainly to incidents of spiritual abuse I was then encountering in the church. It had detrimentally impacted our marital relationship. It also related to our personal coupling and did not include anyone else. My ex–husband remarried the woman he met in the first year of our two–year separation prior to our divorce. Although the timing of their coupling is spiritually controversial according to some church's doctrines on marriage and divorce, nonetheless, I hope now that at least one of us is in love and happily married.

At the time of writing, I am still single and available for remarriage to only Mr. Right. I only need one man. The right one. I am also still childless since my former husband and I had no children together. Although now ecumenical I have chosen to remain celibate until marriage since I originated from a Pentecostal Church where celibacy is fundamental to the church's doctrine. Similarly, since I have not yet found Mr. Right it is perhaps easier to maintain my celibacy than if I had found Mr. Right. Celibacy until marriage is also still a personal choice because marriage is still sacrosanct to me where my Mr. Right alone would have permission to all of me apart from God whose omnipotence enables her to know me completely. However, I realize that celibacy may not be the choice of everyone in any church or in the secular environment. This is because it is a very difficult and seemingly an abnormal human option for some people in loving pre-marital relationships. I was a virgin before I was married—a doctrine which I sometimes think borders on absurdity and cruelty for especially long-term singletons who prefer love and marriage but are struggling to find the right person and who are not cohabiting. However, it is a spiritual doctrine in some denominations. I therefore acknowledge that the opposite extreme is promiscuity which has its consequences too, especially for childbearing persons and notably for women of color. Secondly, I am now in my fifties and premenopausal and assuming I am biologically fertile until the menopause, I can have my own natal children if/when I find Mr. Right. Notwithstanding, thank God, there are other options available to childless females. I emphatically talk about them in my other book, *Community Womanism*, along with how Christian female singletons are perceived and treated by the British church and the difficulties for Black women to find love and marriage due to our race.[13] The issue of Black female singleness dates back to the Transatlantic Slave Trade.[14] This is not necessarily only an issue of sex but one of love and emotional intimacy, companionship and coupling, and even spiritual well-being, for Christian, Black, female singletons as we are holistic humans comprising of body, soul, and spirit.[15]

On marrying my then husband, I moved from Wolverhampton to Cheshire/Greater Manchester and held several local church appointments in the North West and national church until 2006 when I left England for an academic job in the US. I volunteered as Christian education (youth) and inter-church director in Birmingham and regional pastoral care director, Greater Manchester, where I pioneered several pastors,' ministers,' and regional leaders' cell groups along with the oversight and leadership of pastoral care in congregations in that region. Accompanying my then husband, I was associate pastor, assistant Sunday School principal, and church committee member in the local church in Cheshire. I served in executive youth missions teams in France in the summers and prison chaplaincy in Wolverhampton, before I moved to Cheshire, where I volunteered in prison chaplaincy in Manchester and Nottingham also. I worked as an academic in Nottingham at the time. Again I volunteered as choir member both locally and regionally in Greater Manchester and as national and regional convention steward. In my then Black Pentecostal Church, there were no requirements to be ordained to carry out the ministerial roles I held. However, ministerial doctrines for leadership

---

13. McCalla, *Community Womanism*, forthcoming.
14. Stewart, *Black Women, Black Love*, 356.
15. McCalla, *Community Womanism*, forthcoming.

have changed. I would most certainly be required to be ordained now to minister in many of these roles.

In my childhood, teens, and early twenties, for me, it was a time of immense emancipation in ministry. In these voluntary lay leadership roles, I produced my strategic ministry plans and, apart from my assistant leaders who were appointed by the senior pastor of the congregation, I could also appoint my own voluntary staff to support my leadership roles and others who also served occasionally as disciples in support of my ministry too. I was not micromanaged by the church senior pastor or any of the pastors. Once I was appointed I was left to run the ministry department. In those days, leaders generally received very little training for the roles and ministries they were appointed. There was an expectation that you could carry out the ministry based on your outward signs of spirituality and due to your previous volunteering experience and aptitude in the church. If training was given, it was limited and through meetings at the early stages of the appointment. You learnt to minister on the job and was instructed to undertake the standard denominational training courses. In my role, as I ministered and needed advice, I could seek it from the pastor and other assistant ordained and lay leaders. I was neither afraid nor supercilious to ask for advice since I was fortunate to have served under very supportive and friendly pastors and ministers, and therefore sought advice when it was required. However, I did not seek it frequently. For accountability purposes, I reported my ministry endeavors to the local church in quarterly, church business meetings. This report was then escalated to the national church for their records along with other ministry work in the congregation. Occasionally, my pastor would enquiry of me how I was doing and if I required any support with anything. I was therefore not left in isolation and alone to run the ministry. Having this amount of freedom to lead gave me autonomy and this autonomy and emancipation enabled me to serve God, the youth ministry, and the congregation wholeheartedly and to my fullest. My pastors recognized my calling to ministry from a very early age, so too did my family, family friends, some schoolteachers, and school friends also.

In the 1980s I was generally academically above average. I left school with O and A level qualifications which, at that time, given my race and gender as a Black female, was noteworthy. School reports always spoke of my studious dedication and hardworking ethic which saw me working in secular paid jobs as a civil servant for the Department of Environment and a credit controller for British Telecom after leaving school as

I continued in church ministry and before going to university where I excelled educationally. Incidentally, as a graduate, I again engaged in educational policy making on the graduate committee at the University of Manchester. However, it was in ministry that my vocation, gifts, and talents were realized given my years as a child, teenager, and early twenties. From those early years of my life it was apparent to those who cared about me that I was called into some type of Christian ministry. My pastor said I was mature beyond my years, especially spiritually. Schoolteachers said I was generally quiet until someone mentioned something to do with religion and I would either preach, teach, or debate about either God, love, justice, hope, and/or repentance and attempted to reference discussion with Scripture. I worked hard, and sometimes too much and too hard. However, I found time for quiet and deep contemplation, and sometimes space alone to rest, reflect, and evaluate my life and ministry which I believed was required for my flourishing and productivity for when it was time for activity. Even my school teachers realized that about me.

I was supported in ministry and at home and school. It appeared that I had the Midas touch. Everything I touched, God blessed and it turned to gold! People said I was born with a silver spoon in my mouth. I could do no wrong, and, for real, and in terms of upholding church doctrines and standards, I barely did anything wrong! I tried to practice all the church rules and creeds as far as possible. I was one of the model Pentecostal Christian girls then women. I was the "go to" Sister whenever anyone wanted to talk about God, church, and the Bible or required spiritual advice and/or pastoral help whether they were young or old; male or female. I had a circle of friends who were similarly spiritual and ecclesiastical too. I loved Jesus, I loved the church, and I loved my call to lay leadership.

This was a time in my life when anything was possible. I was not too Black, female, young/old, educated, religious/secular, or British (but sometimes considered an immigrant), to lead in the church. For me, there were no barriers to ministry and I was not suppressed. I was not Miss Goldilocks. I was Miss Dreadlocks or more precisely, Miss Ponytail-twists, but I was just right! Yes, there were some jealous persons but it was definitely not malicious or harmful. I was loved, appreciated, valued, and most of all, I was respected by seemingly everyone and everywhere.

In my late teens and early twenties I became an ecumenist as I became exposed to other denominations and became a congregant of other denominations overtime. Whilst I remained loyal to the churches

I became a congregant, ecumenism redefined my relationship with the church I was raised in and my association with other denominations. For me, the full Christian gospel is found in various churches and therefore no denomination possesses the full Christian faith. However, what was core to them all and me too is my faith in Jesus: the incarnation of God, impregnated by the Holy Spirit, born to the virgin Mary, was murdered, resurrected, and shall return in the rapture.

I traveled to the US in December 2006 for employment as an academic dean at a Bible college and also established a charity over there where I offered adult continual education in mainly retreat settings. I also served in ministerial activities in the National Baptist Convention as a then congregant in that denomination. My ecumenical engagement also continued in other denominations at that time such as in the Methodists, Assemblies of God, Cooperative Baptists, to mention some, as well as community activities.

Returning to the UK in November 2009, I served in the community and in further lay ministry pursuits in the Church of England since 2010 where I then became a congregant. Much of my involvement in church, academia, and community, since returning to England in November 2009, will be published elsewhere and beyond the scope of this book. However, for my entire life I have served in various roles as a lay leader and disciple in mainly a Black church but also the Church of England and a short time in the Baptist Church too. Nevertheless, being an ecumenist, I have been active in other denominations also as mentioned already. The other area of predominant, active service, since my twenties, has been as a higher education academic in the UK and a short time in the US. I also served in various community endeavors.

Like participants in this book I experienced patriarchy in the British church prior to my time in the US and when I returned to the UK. Examples of these incidences will be provided in relevant places in this book. I have documented more of my patriarchal experiences in my community womanism book.[16] Being an ecumenist, it is important to note that patriarchal and misogynist racism which I experiences were in various denominations rather than only in the case studies in this book or the denomination I was converted to Christianity.

Since a purposeful-life is important to me, where I am at peace and happy, I think that when I can no longer serve the world in a meaningful and purposeful way, where I am wasting my invaluable time and personal

---

16. McCalla, *Community Womanism,* forthcoming.

God-given talent and gifts, for me, it is a time to die. For the first time in my life, I am not afraid to die. I am more afraid to live without a purpose. It is in the midst of this quest to know and fulfill my purpose in life that data in the church, academia, and the community surfaced and the concept of Loyal Sisters in Britain was born.

I also experienced troubled times so my testimony continues with this:

Troubling Times

My life was troubled when I fell on hard times due to a prolonged period of unemployment (or more precisely, working without pay) after returning to my country of origin, England, in November 2009. Whilst discussing the economic deprivation, in this section I will only occasionally mention relevant incidents which occurred from my mid-20s to my late 30s which were not times of economic or social deprivation. Further explanations which led to the economic hardship, is also addressed in my *Community Womanism* book.[17]

At the point of writing, I experienced 15 years of unemployment or unpaid work. One of the reasons I attended a CoE congregation and eventually became a congregant there, was partly due to my economic crisis and thus my attempts to worship at a church which was geographically nearby. Directly prior to this time, I was a senior academic at a Bible college in the US. Before going to the US in December 2006, I was already divorced in 2005, and as mentioned already, to date of writing this account in 2023, I am still single, heterosexual, and available for remarriage. On returning to England, my once healthy and very active father in the church and community and secular work too, was then terminally ill. He had suffered a stroke which terminated his life in 2015. In 2016, seven months later, my mom, who was my father's primary carer during his illness, along with professional carers, also died from a sudden diagnose of bowel cancer. I lived with my parents for some of the time when I returned to England from America so I also supported them with caring responsibilities during their illness, as did my siblings and in-laws, through a rota system which we formulated to ease the caring-load of home, hospital, and residential care-visits. However, struggling to gain paid work and no family or substantial community support, I twice experienced relative

---

17. McCalla, *Community Womanism*, forthcoming.

homelessness. On the first occasion, at the end of 2015, I was housed in poor temporary accommodation for two months. On the other incident, in 2019, for nine months, I survived in a house of multiple occupations (HMO), where I lived in one room but shared the remainder of the house with complete strangers—all of whom I immediately discovered were of white ethnicity and existed as career criminals.[18] Apart from my impoverished lifestyle, their existence was so unlike my own reality where I have no criminal record. I would not be able to work in schools and with children with a criminal record. All of them were smokers and/or drug-takers. One of them constantly and confidently boosted about his deviant status and the fact that he had been a criminal from his childhood and comes from a family of criminals and drug-taking gangsters—often males. Their delinquency was evident. Most if not all of them were literally, educationally illiterate and all were benefit claimants and had no aspirations to change their lifestyles. Another argued that the prison rehabilitation program was worthless and so too was education. Similarly, another of them justified theft with an example of stealing from the rich for the poor due to inherited economic inequalities. I did not engage in a theological and/or philosophical discussion with them but the reader may now wish to engage in what some commentators would describe as a Robin Hood explanation of their larceny. Their conversations were often laced with swearing. This too was where they and I differed.

Although the residents of the HMO were all aged between 20 and 40 as revealed by a police officer, except for me, the cognitive and behavioural skills of some of them were closer to that of young children. Even though they were all younger than me, this was not always evident from their physical appearance. Some of them were physically and medically unhealthy. One of them seemed to have respiratory issues which was displayed by a persistent choking and chesty cough. Another appeared to be constantly confused and often did not know his location. Apart from drug-taking, their overall daily diets were poor and unbalanced with a daily consumption of alcohol, the occasional processed meals and/or white bread, and a lack of fruit and vegetables. We shared the kitchen in the HMO so I observed their food supplies every time I opened the fridge and/or cupboards to get supplies from my food-shelves which

---

18. Local authorities/Councils are required under the Homelessness Reduction Act 2017 to house homeless people regardless of priority need. However, local authorities may not have a vetting system to ensure residents are suitably matched in shared accommodations.

were limited as were theirs apart from their numerous cans of beer. Their food consumption contrasted with my attempt at a balanced diet "on a shoe-string" of fresh fruit and vegetables and wholemeal bread, which I never feared them pilfering as I knew they would never take the fruit and vegetables. However, they would often steal my occasional bottled water since I gave them no reason to steal alcohol as I never drink, and my protein choices of cheese,[19] milk, and fish. I kept other food items which did not require refrigeration in the room I occupied. The residential location was another indication of dereliction in which capital and/or social investment was definitely required to develop the whole environmental infrastructure of poor-quality, social, and private rented housing and streets. The area was a dumpster. But would an investment be economically effective, efficient, profitable and sensible even if it was arguably moral given the criminality of some of the residents and the likely effect of vandalism after the investment?

Whilst I failed to communicate with the other HMO dwellers since I could not help them from my position of deprivation and had nowhere to flee should anything happen to me, it was evident to them that I was different to them in many ways. They assumed or found out from someone or through their possible stalking of me, that I am "religious" and "go to church" as a few of them mentioned it and stated that they know little or nothing about religion as they never go to church and are not religious. Although I spent very little time at the house, when I was actually there, there was always a flurry of strangers and bedpartners who entered and exited it since the residents not only left their room doors unlocked but the two main house doors too. Police officers also frequented the house. I always kept the door locked to the room I occupied and never allowed anyone into that room. I also always locked the front and back doors when I left and re-entered the HMO. Apart from three times when my siblings and nieces visited, I had no guests.

Except for the food-thefts, their offences towards me were generally related to antisocial behavior such as excessive activities, noise, and loud music at night where the landing lights were nearly always on and/or their movement in and outside the HMO. There was a few potential incidents of crime: knife-throwing in the kitchen by one of them at me and secondly, their harassment in attempts to befriend me and my continual refusal to engage with them. I think they also thought I was a criminal

---

19. Being menopausal since 2020, cheese is no longer part of my regular diet. I continue to eat eggs.

too since they were all criminals and frequently conversed about that reality. One of them held out his hand for me to shake it and told me to get used to them as I am in the same position as them. I made him no more the wiser and I refused his handshake. I was called a "toff" by another of them and a "rabbit" and "paedo"/"paedophile" by another. Thank God, it was not any worse than that. Like Jesus in Matt 13:58 who could do very little to help the people in Nazareth because they dishonored her/him, I was unable to engage with the other HMO persons since their vulnerability in relations to mine was incompatible.

After being housed, I contacted the police and local politicians. With a few exceptions, my situation and safety was effectively monitored by both agencies. The police in that locality would repeatedly remove the criminals from the HMO for my general protection or because they committed criminal offenses or incidents whilst inhabiting it. The council attempted to respond to my reports of antisocial behavior. An email transaction between a local councillor/politician and a senior housing manager at the council in April 2019 demonstrates this. I was copied into the conversation:

> Politician: I had a telephone conversation with Professor Maccalla today. She is still very concerned about her housing situation, particularly being placed in a HMO sharing the house with known felons. Ms Maccalla feels very much at risk and spends her time locked in her room or out of the property. She is also very concerned about her academic papers having nowhere to store them. Ms Maccalla is currently preparing academic work for presentation at Keele and Wolverhampton universities. She really does need proper housing. Part of her inability to obtain private rented accommodation is due to her being a benefit claimant. I would be obliged if you could suggest any alternatives to her, to remove her from what she describes as a quite precarious situation. I am concerned at the risk factors here.
>
> Senior Housing Manager: I know this case and I know [name of colleague] is fully up to speed with this.

The political councillor, housing department, and police also made attempts but failed to find me alternative accommodation. I found suitable housing when my economic and employment situation changed prior to lockdown. If I had not found employment and left the HMO, the repercussions of being in the HMO during lockdown is often too frightening to ponder so I thank God he provided a way of departure.

The quick and positive reaction by the police in that locality contrasted with what appeared as the lack of effective response from West Midlands Police (WMP) where I lived previous to being housed in the HMO and after leaving it. Being out of paid work for so long impacted the housing I could affordably obtain even when I was not in the HMO. WMP seemed less helpful when it came to my reports of suspected offences, such as alleged stalking and harassment and since all the perpetrators were unknown to me, many of whom I would never allow into my life whilst I am generally friendly with everyone. It was times like these that I prayed that the good practices of escorting church females in groups in public spaces through bodyguards and/or the church sorority, which were effective in the WMB in the CoGoP in the 1950s to 1990s as I discussed in chapter 2, were still operating in the church now. Notwithstanding, WMP got its comeuppance in November 2023 when it was placed into special measures and therefore underwent extensive monitoring by the official police watchdog, His Majesty's Inspectorate of Constabulary (HMIC) for failing to investigate reported alleged crimes and therefore not protecting victims and vulnerable people, among several other grounds of failures. However, the HMIC report showed disproportionate criminal investigations when suspected criminals were people of color.[20] Thank God, the police appeared to have acted soon after this special measure in my situation and, apart from the rare incident, the suspected harassment by residential neighbors seemed to end. Nonetheless, the seemingly sexist complicity by WMP with perpetrators was also apparent in the Derbyshire Police Force[21] and similarly demonstrated in research findings of racism and misogyny in the London Metropolitan Police (LMP).[22] Whilst police officers are tasked with upholding the law with regards to crime, at this time it was apparent to me that they are also humans and therefore flawed like the rest of humanity and require God's salvific grace and direction in their lives too. It was obvious that the criminal system and existing law does not always enable them to effectively carry out their jobs, and when it does, some police officers hide their misogyny and/or racism behind their office, police uniforms, and

---

20. Sky News, "West Midlands Police Put Into Special Measures Over Poor Investigations." See the Further Reading for additional commenting on stalking and sexual harassment.

21. Sky News, "Gracie Spinks."

22. Casey, "Independent Review," 363.

authority positions until it surfaces in similar cases of supposed complicity with alleged harassers which I have mentioned.

My upbringing was not one of privilege and enormous wealth since my parents sometimes talked about their struggle to especially pay bills when we were children and occasionally to buy school uniforms every year as we grew. We were socioeconomically working-class and the biological offspring of parents with middle-class values such as a hardworking ethic for renumeration and community volunteerism, mainly in the church, and also educational aspirations for their children. This lead to our upward social and economic mobility. That being the case, the other residents in the HMO in 2019 were what Charles Murray would call the "underclass" given their persistent deviant lifestyles[23] as mentioned above. Alternatively, I now know, as a family of six with three other siblings—an elder brother and two younger twin sisters—we were possibly lower middle-class in our socioeconomic status and social lifestyle than working-class and poor which I originally thought until this never-experienced, over decade-and-a-half and at the time of writing this book in 2022-2023 and compared with other occupants of the HMO. Our lower middle-class status for parts of our childhood was the result of both my late parents' upward social mobility from being working-class individuals when they arrived in Britain from Jamaica during the time of the Windrush Generation in the late 1950s and early 1960s respectively. I was fortunate to visit the beautiful island of Jamaica thrice in my twenties but I have not returned there due to my recent misfortune.

By the time I left the HMO, I was in employment but on low income. For years, I struggled to afford the very basic essentials in life such as food and personal hygiene products, often sacrificing meals instead of hygiene products when I could not afford both. Never before have I experienced such economic and social hardship. Thankfully, my parents are resting in peace otherwise they would be turning in their graves and extremely sad by any awareness that their highly educated and hardworking daughter is forced to live economically and socially worse off than they did prior to their deaths and especially since they were also hardworking parents and never welfare benefit claimants.

My parents met in the church in Birmingham, England; fell in love, married, and relocated to Wolverhampton where they shared a privately-own house with several other church Black families who were known

---

23. Murray et al., *Charles Murray and the Underclass*, 188/196.

to them. I later discovered that that house was owned by my late uncle. When I and my siblings were toddlers and babies, respectively, my parents moved us into council housing. With the help of my late uncle, my parents purchased their own house when I was in primary school. My dad worked in full-time, paid jobs all of his adult life, apart from a short illness of pneumonia when I was at secondary school and he was off work for a brief period. He also volunteered in various leadership roles in the Church such as church trustee. He played his saxophone in church services and the band too. However, his role as local Sunday School superintendent saw him pioneer various children and community programs such as, parent-children home visits and the biscuit and tea club. My mom mainly worked part-time in paid employment all of her adult life until the government official age of retirement. My ex-husband was not only a church pastor, as mentioned briefly above, but he also worked as a middle-income, full-time professional in building surveying and, like myself, university educated with several degrees. Like my parents, from the beginning of our matrimony, we also owned our house. Until this time, I have therefore never experienced poor, rented, housing conditions in my life. Like my parents who supported me socially and economically from their employment incomes, whilst we may have had some issues in other areas of our lives, I can confidently say that my social and economic well-being was sufficiently secure through my ex-husband when we were married.

Reflecting on my family upbringing, I can also say with complete confidence that as children, my parents were also supported by some of my extended family and the local church community in the Black Pentecostal Church we belonged to at that time. This clearly verifies the experience of Pentecostal economic and social collectivism, which was operational in the Pentecostal Black Churches in England in the 1950s-1980s[24] and at Azusa Street when it started in 1906 and during the Revival Movement in the early 1900s.[25] Valentina Alexander, Nicole Toulis, and Keri Day demonstrate that the collectivism of the Pentecostal Black Churches and Azusa Street respectively contrasted with the racism of some of the mainstream churches in England and neoliberalism of many white churches in the US and thus resisted by British Black churches[26] and Azusa Street.[27]

---

24. Alexander, "Mouse in a Jungle," 85–106. McCalla, "Black Churches and Voluntary Action," 137–75. Toulis, *Believing Identity*, 304.

25. Day, *Azusa Reimagined*, 218.

26. Alexander, "Mouse in a Jungle," 85–106. Toulis, *Believing Identity*, 304.

27. Day, *Religious Resistance to Neoliberalism*, 227.

The support which was apparent in the Pentecostal Black Church was lacking in the CoE when I fell on hard times. However, does the values of collectivism, theocracy, and democracy still functioning now in the Pentecostal Black Church where I was raised? Would I have been supported by it when I fell on hard times since I am a woman? Alternatively, would I be offered suitable paid work so I could live if I was still a member in it since the best way to escape poverty as a principle of basic supply-side economics amidst socioeconomic demand, is through adequate and liveable, paid work? Although I rarely shared my experience with anyone, preferring not to burden anyone with my cares, I recall informing three members from that church about my situation with the hope they may be able to help me. Two of them preceded to tell me that they were once also unemployed for a short period and the other ignored my calls for help. However, none of them seemed to acknowledge the longevity of my unemployment and the impact of this reality on my general well-being. Neither did they recognize there was no direct comparison with my quandaries since they were all in loving marital relationships to spouses earning regular, middle, and high incomes, respectively. My experience enabled me to also realize that other women's cries for help in similar circumstances at that church may also be ignored. In addition, I later discovered that other Loyal Sisters in that church are overcomers of trauma themselves. For example, two Loyal Sisters lost biological sons through murder and suicide respectively. Only an affected church Sisterhood could have assisted us all since individually these Sisters may have been too incapacitated to assist anyone else in their troubles.

At the time of writing this book, I have no debts to any creditors. My issue is that I have no regular income and what I obtain is often low. I was also premenopausal for the duration of this time. Often I could not differentiate between the symptoms of the perimenopause and the emotional and psychological impact of the social and economic hardship I was experiencing. They meshed into one almighty trauma and tragedy! So if I didn't know God I would desert him for it would appear as if he had deserted me. However, I trust and confide in God. Many people would not do so in my situation even those who others would argue have brought their situation on themselves. I am saying this experience could be spiritual as I have done and am doing everything I was and am supposed to do so as not to have encountered such a torrid time. This seems like Job in the Bible, "I know my redeemer lives and that in the end

[s]he will stand on the earth" (Job 19:25). My faith in God was the only constant in those troubled times.

> I lift up my eyes to the mountains—where does my help come from? My help comes from God, the Maker of heaven and earth. S/He will not let your foot slip—s/he who watches over you will not slumber; indeed, s/he who watches over Israel will neither slumber nor sleep .(Ps 121:1–4 NIV)

Would congregational, social, and economic resources be redistributed to serve the requirements of the congregation? I was raised from a social justice, compassionate, ethical, and confidentiality stance.

Like the British Black churches in the UK in the 1950s-1980s[28] and Azusa Street,[29] collectivism amid individual recognition—that is, support for one and all[30]—and democracy is very much the intended practice of supportive communities and Sisterhoods. However, at the time of writing, my steadfast faith in God's grace and mercy, coupled with a resilience and, until now, a fortitude I never knew or imagined I possessed, is helping me to rebuild my life: "God *is* nigh unto all them that call upon him/[her], to all that call upon him/[her] in truth" (Ps 145:18–20). Let me pause for a moment to remind the reader that this book is not a novel. It is not a figment of my imagination. I am writing real accounts as a religionist and social analysis with also a personal Christian faith in the Triune God. Like Sojourner Truth, "when I cried out . . . none but Jesus heard me! And ain't I a woman?"[31]

> Be not far from me; for trouble *is* near; for *there is* none to help. (Ps 22:11)
>
> I sought God, and He answered me; He delivered me from all my fears. (Ps 34:4)
>
> This poor [wo]man called out, and God heard [her]; He saved [her] from all [her] troubles. (Ps 34:6)

God did help me in big and small ways as mentioned above. In addition, although my biological brother has his own share of medical ordeals as a kidney/renal casualty and living on daily dialysis which he has often publicly shared on social media and in person, nonetheless, he has helped

---

28. McCalla, "Black Churches and Voluntary Action," 137–75.
29. Day, "Azusa Reimagined," 218.
30. McCalla, *Theology of Social Justice and the Politics of Presence*, forthcoming.
31. Truth, *Narrative of Sojourner Truth*, 134.

me with the PersonalCare Bank—a project I established to support low-income families through their children in schools.[32] I did this when I was also unemployed, relatively homeless, and living in temporary accommodation, that is, a HMO. I was also a welfare-benefit claimant. So I can confidently say, God continues to be good all the time.

> God is beside you in your grief.
> God is beside you in your pain.
> God is beside you in your sorrow.
> God is beside you as you heal.
> Amen.[33]

My Allyship with Loyal Sisters

Being a participant observer in this project means that my persona and personification is extremely important to the data, analysis, and outcome of this project. I want the Loyal Sisters in this project, and those women outside of it, to acknowledge that I also share some of their joys and happiness mentioned in this book, but some of their sorrows and pain too. One of my reasons for discussing the time of economic and social difficulties is to position myself in solidarity with some of the Black and Brown women in this book who have encountered, and some are still facing, economic and social calamity. Writing this book meant mentally and educationally processing the calamitous circumstances of participants and my own situation too. Whilst I am not a refugee or asylum seeker as are many of the females at High Parish and some at Messa Pentecostal, I realize that many of those women came to the UK and experienced destitution after absolute or relative financial and social security prior to their departure from their homeland and refugee status in Britain. For economic migrants seeking a better life in the UK, I also side with them in my time of deprivation. It was at this time that my faith in God through womanist spiritual redemption and transcendence as mentioned in a later chapter, became my anchor; and some of which is also beyond the scope and remit of this book. It was then that I truly appreciated the firm faith foundations I had already established from my youth and young adulthood which I wished to share to help someone else. That said,

---

32. Period Power was another organization which supported the PersonalCare Bank.

33. See Further Reading on the "Poem-Prayer."

I would not wish for anyone to experience my plights of recent years neither would I like to relive any of those encounters. Whilst I give God thanks for her precious grace and mercy to have overcome such adversity, I also acknowledge that I am a highly educated and very experienced human-being with multiple gifts, skills, and talents. As a British citizen, born and residing in England, I believe that my British entitlement to paid work has been denied to me for over a decade-and-a-half. With the same qualifications, experience, and over the same timeframe, as far as I am aware, no British white male or female has faced a similar experience in Britain. Britain would never allow such calamity to happen to them yet it has allowed it to happen to me and why? I am Black and female. That is why! Discrimination, racism, misogynoir, and sexism, to mention only a few intersectionalities, are evident factors. This is hardly surprising since it is also important to note that my research on Black and Brown female academics, and others too, also reveal us repeatedly experiencing oppression, discrimination, and/or under-presentation in higher education.[34]

Loyal Sisters who still groan, I care! #prayingwithloyalsisters.

My testimony continues in an article in chapter 6, titled, Claimants Statement. Hopefully this book will shed further light on these issues. However for now, it is important to know that I am also a Christian Black woman who trusts God's presence beside me every day, tries to love all humanity in action as I strive for females' rights, and hope for a time when all women of color will be emancipated from oppression and discrimination and live in harmony and peace if not in this life, in the eschatology.

"Please pray for me as I pray for you, in Jesus' name."

Questions

1. Is anything in my testimony as a Christian Black female similar or dissimilar to your own testimony?
2. Reflecting on my womanist testimony, what do you think, feel about, and learn from it?

---

34. McCalla, "Theology of Social Justice and the Politics of Presence" forthcoming. McCalla, "Academic and the Community meet, 165–83. Arday and Mirza, *Dismantling Race in Higher Education*, 396. University and College Union, *Precarious Work in Higher Education*, 62. Mirza, "Decolonizing Higher Education," 1–12.

3. "Feel the Spirit" is a gospel song by Shirley Caesar. Who is Shirley Caesar and what do we learn about womanist spirituality from her life? Do you know any womanist spiritual songsters from the British diaspora or countries in the British colonization/decolonization?

Further Reading

Stalking and Sexual, Racist Harassment in the Police Force

Several official investigations have revealed experiences of sexism, misogyny, and racism by employees in the police force.[35] In fact other reports find the same in other emergency services.[36] I therefore have no doubt that some members of the wider public, including Christian Black and Brown females, are also being harassed by members of the public as police officers—professionals, who are supposed to protect us, are complicit when complaints of isms are reported to them by ordinary residents in the population. Instead, victims are sometimes accused of either being pretentious, mentally ill, and/or being gas-lighted by the police when they informally or formally report suspected harassment to them.

The Poem-Prayer

This prayer-poem was written on October 12, 2022—the third anniversary of my reconnection with a school friend on October 12, 2019 after over 25 years. This reconnection came after we reunited in our twenties since leaving school at 16 years. My school friend suddenly died in 2021 during the COVID-19 Pandemic but not from COVID-19. In 2019, I thought that my friend and I reunited at the right time. It was great sharing our Christianity and culture; her Pentecostal and Italian/Sicilian-British

---

35. Sky News, "West Midlands Police put into special measures over poor investigations." Sky News, "Gracie Spinks."

36. Association of Ambulance Chief Executives, "Reducing Misogyny and Improving Sexual Safety in the Ambulance Service." BBC News, "Misogyny and Sexism Rife in Dorset and Wiltshire Fire Service." BBC News, "South Wales Fire Service." Guardian, "London Fire Brigade Put Into Special Measures Over Misogyny and Racism." Independent, "Ambulance Staff Afraid to Speak Out Amid a Culture of Sexism Racism and Bullying." Independent, "Report Reveals Shocking Examples Racist, Sexist and Bullying Behaviour in England's Fire and Rescue Services." ITV News Wales, "Brave Whistleblower Speaks Out on 'Horrendous' Experience Exposing Sexual Harassment at Fire Service."

background and my Jamaican-British roots and ecumenical faith; our joys and my misfortune too. It was a wonderful day spent with her, her parents (at their home), her husband, and her husband's parents. That was indeed a very special and godly day. Rest in Peace and Rise in Glory!

In memory of my friend, a beautiful, godly, and generous woman, I wrote this prayer-poem for her husband in his time of grief and realized it was for me too. He received it prayerfully, gracefully, and thankfully.

6

BREAKING NEWS, January 18, 2023

CLAIMANT'S STATEMENT[1]

You better get right with God.
Come and do it now.
Under the cross of Jesus,
Lay your burden down.
You better get right with God.
Come and do it now.
Get right. Get right.
Get right with God.[2]

THIS IS A NEWS Statement in response to the outcome and conclusion of the Employment Tribunal Preliminary Hearing (PH) between Claimant, Professor Doreen W. McCalla and Respondents, Bishop of Lichfield and Lichfield Diocesan Board of Finance Inc., dated December 19–20, 2022.[3] It is a much

---

1. See the Further Reading on "Publishing This Statement."

2. A Jamaican gospel spiritual. Author unknown.

3. Professor D. McCalla v Lichfield Diocesan Board of Finance Inc. and Bishop of Lichfield: 1303655/2021—GOV.UK. https://www.gov.uk/employment-tribunal-decisions/professor-d-mccalla-v-lichfield-diocesan-board-of-finance-inc-and-bishop-of-lichfield-1303655-slash-2021. See also the Further Reading on "The Judgement."

expanded version of a very short statement I submitted to a legal reporter at Law360 who kindly requested my response to the Hearing for his news article dated January 18, 2023.[4] It also provides some background to the PH.

The PH was intended to establish if there was jurisdiction, that is, law under the Equality Act 2010, to proceed with my Discrimination Claims where, from 2016 to 2021, I entered into the Discernment Process (DP) in the named Diocese and Bishop's Office for ordained ministry.[5] Many chapters for this book were produced from data generated whilst going through this DP. High Parish, one of my case study churches, was also part of my exploration in this DP. The PH concluded that there was no jurisdiction, that is, the DP in the Diocese of Lichfield, is a spiritual process and not work or a vocation related to work, under the Equality Act 2010. It concluded that the Respondents were not acting as Service Providers, that is, an employer or personal office provider, to me when I was exploring ministry in the Diocese and Bishop's Office.

My journey to ordination was abruptly cancelled by the Sponsoring Bishop, Sarah Bullock, Bishop of Shewsbury, on June 2, 2021 in a nonfactual letter.[6] In my Claims, the Respondent was therefore directly responsible for this, that is, the Bishop of Lichfield, Michael Ipgrave, and the Diocesan Board of Finance Inc. They did not question Sarah Bullock's decision at the time and remained firm to that decision at the date of writing this Statement. However, the Archbishop of Canterbury certainly sympathized with me. Speaking on behalf of the Archbishop in an email on June 21, 2023, his spokeswomen at Lambert Palace said:

> I am sorry to hear about how painful this has been for you, and I completely understand why you would choose to write to the Archbishop of Canterbury about it . . . [and] that you contest this decision and have sought legal action.

The "letter" of the law won since the Judgement concluded that the DP was spiritual and the Respondents were not Service Providers in the DP. In this chapter, letter also means the letter by

---

4. Sareen, "Spiritual Calling Is Not A Job."

5. See the Further Reading on "A Summation of my Sense of Calling to Ordained Ministry."

6. See the Further Reading on "The Discrimination Claims and the DP."

Sarah Bullock. However, the irony and paradox is that the spirit of the law, that is, love and care as I see recorded in the biblical Scripture, 1 Cor 3:6, referring to the difference between grace and law, was greatly lacking in my DP by the Respondents and will be demonstrated in this Claimant's Statement. This lack of spiritual grace therefore begs the question that if the DP was not spiritual in my case, it was therefore questionably vocational under the Equality Act 2010 albeit abusive and discriminatory. With the assistance of a barrister (as I will explain below) and my evidence in this chapter and elsewhere, could that alternative conclusion have been proven? This Statement also allows more of the Claimant's side to be heard since the PH revealed that there was no jurisdiction. It is therefore also all the more important for the sake of womanism, religiosity, social justice, and Black and Brown females everywhere. Similarly, whilst some Sisters remain loyal to their churches after the curtailment of their genuine, ministerial vocation and/or their womanist ministry by the British church, this chapter also shows that the growth in community womanism[7] is partly due to spiritual abuse associated with the ministerial vocation of Christian, Black and Brown women.

Before I go further allow me to make some disclaimers:

Disclaimers

First, I am not commenting as a lawyer since I am not a lawyer but the Claimant in this case. This Statement is mine alone and, whilst I could have exercised my right to remain silent, I felt it was necessary to present the Claimant's side on the outcome of the Employment Tribunal PH as a Christian, middle-aged, Black female with protected characteristics under the Equality Act 2010 although, in this case, no law meant that I could not go any further with my legal Claim of discrimination under the Act. I wanted to provide a context to the legal Judgement and further clarity to others who seek it especially with regards to womanist rights, social justice and/or Christian social ethics.

Second, although I will use this time to make a Statement on some of the content of the Judgement and shall occasionally refer to the Order, as I am not a lawyer, this time will not be used as a means to respond directly to the Judgement or Order of the Employment Tribunal PH.

Third, similarly, I will also not use this opportunity to reply to the Law360 Reporter's news

---

7. McCalla, *Community Womanism*, forthcoming.

article[8] on the PH at the Employment Tribunal, as again, I am not a lawyer, and even lawyers are not required to do so.

Fourth, in addition, I will not use this time to talk extensively about any possible evidence of discrimination itself since this was not the point of the PH at this Employment Tribunal although this Statement will contain some examples of discrimination for further, written analysis on another occasion.

The Preliminary Hearing[9]

The date of the PH was agreed in a legal, Case Management Hearing on February 14, 2022. This Claim was the first of its kind, that is, under Employment Law, no one had previously made a Claim of Discrimination whilst in the DP. Under the Equality Act 2010 the certainty of jurisdiction for my Claims were questionable. For this reason, the PH was very important. The PH was therefore not about hearing the various discrimination issues of this Claim. I was not asked to produce my evidence of discrimination for the Hearing bundle[10] by my solicitor, a white male, or the Judge, also white and male,[11] before, during or after this Hearing. However, the various incidents of discrimination submitted to the Tribunal in my Witness Statement was a clear indication that I had evidence in support of those examples of discrimination. I produced that evidence from the start and throughout the Claim for use should it be required in a continued trial, that is, if the PH had concluded that there was legal grounds to Hear my Claim to full trial. Incidentally, the Respondent did produce evidence for the bundle. Their Response was different to my Claims. However, some of their evidence clearly appeared to either be from another Diocese or the National Ministry Team. Not all the evidence appeared to be from the Diocese of Lichfield. Some of these bundle-documents were unavailable to me during my DP. Although I asked to see it earlier, I saw the bundle for the first time on the morning of the PH when I arrived for the Hearing.

8. Sareen, "Spiritual Calling Is Not A Job."
9. See Further Reading on "Preliminary Hearing."
10. A legal bundle is a folder of court documents of evidence which may be needed in the Hearing.
11. Please note that I was the only Black person in this Claim. I acknowledge that I was operating in systems of predominant whiteness and maleness both in the Diocese of Lichfield and the judiciary as a whole as well as in Employment Law specifically even if there were other disproportionate levels of Black presence in this account.

Under cross-examination I was referred to some of these documents I had not previously seen. I was asked about my immigration status from a form I had not seen until the PH. I questioned the relevance of the question given that I am actually automatically British under the Nationality Act 1981 and my British status was already disclosed for the Hearing. Under cross-examination I was again referred to the same form I had not previously seen until the Hearing and quizzed about my marital status when, in fact, my divorced status was already known to the Hearing and cleared for ordination.

Jacques Algazy KC concluded that the DP in the Diocese of Lichfield is a "discernment of a spiritual vocation or calling to God and is not to be equated to a trade, occupation or personal office within the meaning of the Equality Act." He did, however, maintain that there are some similarities to employment but this "does not alter the fundamental nature of that process." However, Judge Algazy KC did go on to say this could be changed if a job or public office was obtained: "Similarly, the fact that a person undergoing the DP might at some stage become an employee or hold public office in the CoE does change the correct characterisation of the process of the discernment of a spiritual vocation, whatever may be the subjective desire of that person."[12]

The Tribunal dismissal occurred because there was no jurisdiction. In other words, given the evidence presented to the Tribunal, there was no legislation in which Employment Law could be applied in this situation. A full trial in which my Claims for Discrimination in an Employment Tribunal could have followed this Tribunal Hearing if there was jurisdiction. Inevitably, there is a possible need for legislative changes to enable the legality so that a Discrimination Claim of this type can be pursued. Existing law under the Equality Act 2010 does not allow such pursuit as concluded from the Employment Tribunal. So, from the point of a spiritual redemption, this Claim is certainly redeemable.

Achievements of the PH

Let me continue now by saying that the Employment Tribunal PH did achieve some significant milestones for future potential Claims in existing Employment Law:

First, by establishing the Respondents in the Order as the Bishop of Lichfield and the Lichfield Board of Finance, as far

---

12. See also the note titled PH in the Further Reading for this chapter.

as I am aware, it now means that anyone employed or in an Office by either or both Respondents can now pursue a Claim in the existing Employment Law under the existing Equality Act 2010.

Second, as far as I am aware, anyone going through the DP who has an actual job in either the Bishop's Office and/or Lichfield Board of Finance Inc. can also pursue a Claim in the existing Employment Law with the existing Equality Act 2010 since the Respondents are now known.

Third, as intended, the PH established whether there was any jurisdiction for a Claim of Discrimination in my situation. Under existing Employment Law, as the Judgement concluded, there is no jurisdiction in the existing Equality Act 2010 as the Respondents were not Service Providers. It means that legislative change would be required to pursue a Discrimination Claim under the same circumstances.

Fourth, we now know that with no jurisdiction under existing Employment Law and in the absence of legislative changes to the Equality Act 2010, which would have to take place in the UK parliament, all candidates who enter the DP in which the Respondents are not Service Providers, have no protection. This is particularly concerning for candidates who have protected characteristics under the Equality Act 2010, since they are more susceptible to discrimination and what I also regard as spiritual abuse.[13]

Fifth, what is indisputable for me even before the PH, is that lay or ordained ministry in the church is a spiritual vocation and that the DP is supposed to establish that vocation. However, even with this being confirmed by the Judgement at the Employment Tribunal, for me, it does not mean that all persons involved in attempting to discern another person's ministry is acting with/in benign spirituality simply because it is acknowledged that ministry in the church is a spiritual vocation. Spirituality can be malign and therefore abusive, as well as benign, that is, to serve God and the church. For this reason I recommend legislative reform to protect persons from discrimination who embark on training in religious settings who could also experience adversity in similar circumstances as did I.

Sixth, prior to pursuing this Claim I sought an employment barrister's advice—white male—through my solicitor. At that time I had no idea that there were no previous Claims of this type pursued under Employment Law. I was then simply attempting

---

13. See Oakley and Humphreys, *Escaping the Maze of Spiritual Abuse*, 179.

to seek justice for what I saw as an ungodly, evil inflicted on me through discrimination which culminated in stopping me from possibly being ordained and obtaining a future Office and/or employment under the guise of genuine, spiritual discernment—a wrong which I wanted to prevent others from encountering with a similar race, sex/(gender), age, and possibly religion also. Although the Diocese and Bishop's Office knew I am an ecumenist, my Christian life and association with a Pentecostal Black Church was an issue in my DP, hence the possible inclusion of religion as a protected characteristic in my Claims. I knew I was not the first person to be wronged in a similar but greater way in the CoE. I have heard of other adverse cases. However, my case was extreme in terms of what I regarded as spiritual abuse and discrimination.

On my initial approach to my solicitor and when less evidence was then presented to the barrister he estimated that there was less than 50 percent chance of success. Not being a lawyer, I was not entirely sure what that meant in practice. I had substantial evidence to prove that discrimination actually occurred and this was verified by my solicitor. However, being able to legally establish if the Respondent was acting as a Service Provider under the Equality Act 2010 and therefore a direct link between the DP and actual employment or an Office, was something I was legally unable to determine with any certainty and what that actually meant in law until the PH. It was only then that I understood why there was less than a 50 per cent chance of success. So, in retrospect, my pursuit was a bigger risk than I thought at the time—a risk I would possibly have calculated differently had I known exactly what was at stake and although I did intend to seek justice. However, as an academic, field researcher, I am familiar with venturing into uncharted territory although this risk was very different. At the time, I therefore decided to act on the advice of the barrister who advised that it was still worth a legal pursuit in order to establish if there was jurisdiction should I wished to do so. Similarly, as suggested by a funder who I approached for legal funds in the initial stages of the Claim, I could have again sought legal advise from the same barrister later in the Claim as to whether to continue my pursuit. However, as I mention below, my lack of funding prevented this option. So instead, I took this Claim to a PH with the support and advice of the solicitor, Mr Ennis of Rees Page Solicitors.[14]

14. See Further Reading on "No-Win, No-Fee."

I now know that "no jurisdiction" has proven as invaluable as if there was a legality. A jurisdiction would have meant that I could have pursued a Claim with my evidence/facts[15] of discrimination. Similarly, an illegality means the possibility for a new legislation to progress through UK Parliament either in or outside the Equally Act 2010 in which the rights, freedom and integrity of different groups and individuals, especially those with protected characteristics, can be balanced with the religious/spiritual values and beliefs of sacred organizations. This Claim thus serves a social justice objective.

Seventh, in addition to saying that a church ministry is spiritual does not mean that someone who occupies a secular role outside the church may not also be called by God to that vocation. In my encounters with various people, for many years, this has been established. Some people believe they are called by God to serve as medical doctors, teachers, academics, and even lawyers, to mention some examples.

Eighth, on a personal note, the aftermath of the Employment Tribunal, PH and the Employment Tribunal Appeal (EAT) enabled me to better understand the legal process regarding my Claims and therefore further appreciate and value the expertise of legal professionals especially those pertaining to my Claims.

"Trust the Process"[16]

When I started the DP in 2016 I was instructed to only "trust the process" and that everyone's Process is different. In her email dated October 19, 2016, the then acting Director of Vocations echoed what my mentor/Vocation's Advisor (VA) said in our many vocation meetings:

> It is essential at this early stage that you do not seek advice from too many people, but from those whom the diocese has asked to work with you on this stage of your journey...if you do talk to others, check out what they say with [name of VA], who is your guide and mentor at this stage...I hope you will feel able to trust the well-proven system and process.

---

15. Methodologically, I would generally favor the word reality or a similar word as a qualitative and/or ethnographic researcher rather than "fact." However, I use the word fact here since it is used in law.

16. See Further Reading on "Trust the Process."

Table 3, June 4, 2021. My Discernment Process			
Dates From–To	Name, Location and Business of Employer (if applicable)	Ministry and Responsibilites, Diocese of Lichfield, Church of England (January 2016–June 2021)
April 2019– June 2021	A Lichfield, Diocesan congregation	Leading worship as Deacon in Sunday Services; Online preaching during lockdown; Co-Leading online, morning and evening BCP; Leading my creative Intercessions in Sunday Worship; Solo singing during Communion in Sunday morning worship; Active participation in bible studies; OT, NT and Gospel readings in Sunday morning services; Leading in the Music and Singing Group for Sunday morning worship; A candidate's assessment of Leadership and Preaching for her Reader Training; Pastoral support for congregants as required.
2016– 2021	Diocesan Vocation training	Courses Completion: Safeguarding Basic awareness C0 (25/09/2020) and Safeguarding Foundation C1 (14/10/2020). Undertaking written responses to the criteria required for ordination: Criterion A: Vocation, Criterion B: Ministry within the Church of England, Criterion C: Spirituality, Criterion D: Personality and Character, Criterion E: Relationships, Criterion F: Leadership and Collaboration, Criterion G: Faith, Criterion H: Mission and Evangelism, Criterion I: Quality of Mind;[17] Assignments, written work on placements and Life Journals; attendance and participation at criteria seminars and Annual Selwyn Lectures; participation in regular, vocation meetings with three different Advisors and the Bishop's Director of Ordinands; Vocations Assessment by Independent Chaplain; preparation for Bishop's Advisory Panel (2016–2021). Vocations exploration meeting with Diocesan Vicar (October 18, 2018). Successful completion of the Bishop's Certificate, Living Faith (2017). Participation in the Interfaith workshop series (2016–2017). Attendance and participation in the BAME Vocation's Conference, Queen's Ecumenical College, Birmingham. Attendance at the Prayer Retreat, Shallowford House, Staffordshire; Privileged to meet and . My Discernment Process talk about vocation and gain invaluable insights about ministry from the experiences of the first, Black female priest in the CoE, (September 2016).

---

17. CoE, "Criteria for Selection for the Ordained Ministry in the Church of England," 16.

Table 3, June 4, 2021. My Discernment Process		
Dates From–To	Name, Location and Business of Employer (if applicable)	Ministry and Responsibilites, Diocese of Lichfield, Church of England (January 2016–June 2021)
2016–2021	Five Lichfield, Diocesan congregations	Placements and observations (Each between three weeks to two months) of: Baptisms at three congregations, plus two full-water, immersion Baptisms at two churches; Weddings at one congregation and five Confirmations at one congregation.
2016–2021	Vocational ministry and other ministry activities	Monthly online and face-to-face meetings with supporting CoE priests (2016–2021). Participation in three and four services respectively on Sundays at nine churches (2016–2021). Leading the PersonalCare Bank and Diversity and Inclusion work in Divine Ministries Education Enterprise (nonprofit) Ltd (my own not-for-profit organisation of which ministry was assessed)—2016–2021. My Confirmation. Although I was baptised and took the hand of fellowship in the Pentecostal Church at the age nine, on October 2020 I was confirmed in the CoE, the equivalent to the hand of fellowship in the Pentecostal Church as it is not part of the Anglican Communion. Confirmation in CoE was necessary for Ordination. Attendance at the Evensong, Installation Service at Manchester Cathedral of the first Black, female Archdeacon of Manchester (May 14, 2017). Active membership and participation in prayer teams, women's group, Bible studies and preaching at five congregations (March 2016–March 2019). Participating as an active congregant at a local church (December 2017–March 2018). Meetings with the Director of a Community Interest Company (CIC) in a local area in the Diocese for discussion about his work in supporting community projects and his small, group sessions in his partnership with the local college as recommended by a vicar in the Diocese (2017). Being a member and active participant in the Lichfield Diocese Minority Ethnic Christian Affairs (MECA) and one-to-one meetings with BAME and other priests in the Diocese (2016–2017). Deanery Annual Service at one congregation (August 2016). Active participant in the monthly, BAME socials (2016).

At a BAME Vocations Conference which I was instructed to attend in July 2016 as part of the DP (see Table 3), I picked up a small leaflet which was printed by the National Ministry Team. It briefly outlined that in order to be ordained I was expected to complete nine criteria (see Table 3). However, the pamphlet did not say anything about the methodological process and the necessary timeframe required in order to complete the nine criteria. I was given no instruction on how and what a prospective candidate for ordination was required to do to be ordained. I again spoke with the then acting Director of Vocations. She explained what she considered to be the Diocesan DP. In her email of October 19, 2016 she seemed to be giving suggestions and making recommendations based on ideas given to her by my then VA and others. She mentioned no official documentations or guidelines on the DP in the Diocese or in the Ministry Team in the Church of England:

> I have now had a chance to talk to the [name of VA] and one or two others about your journey of exploration and discernment, and we have reached some decisions about the best way forward at this time... You should expect to spend some time working with [name] as Vocations Adviser. At a point when he sees you as ready to move on, he will refer you to a DDO... You would then spend a very much longer time working with the DDO... in fact, whatever the DDO thinks you may need... to help discern whether in the eyes of the diocese you have a calling to ordained ministry and, if this is discerned, to prepare you for a Bishop's Advisory Panel [BAP]... Should all this go well, you would then be invited to attend a BAP for the wider Church to discern whether they believe you to meet the selection criteria for an ordained minister in the CofE. If recommended, you would then start training.

Lindsey Hall was the new Diocesan Director of Ordinands (DDO). I was requested to contact her by my then vicar at the start of the DP. On contacting her, she replied in an email on April 18,

2016: "I would love to meet with you and would be very happy to set that up." Although Lindsey was the DDO for the duration of my DP we have never met and neither has she ever encouraged my vocation whilst she planned meetings with others who were discerning their vocations. However, she did communicate with me in various letters and met in a group meeting with other Diocesan Officers when incidents of discrimination arose where the orchestration of them involved her. These incidents of discrimination are beyond the scope of this Statement/chapter.

In attempting to avoid discrimination and the susceptibility of spiritual abuse, it is clear to me that a workable programme, with a strategy (and timeframe), rules and the standardization for discerning ministerial and spiritual vocation in the Diocese of Lichfield, is required—one in which is designed, accredited and regulated by an independent body such as, the Common Awards. The Common Awards accredits courses of CoE and theological colleges through Durham University. I suggest that this body consists of both clergy and academics.

The third alarm bell rang when I enquired with previous candidates who had gone through the DP and either succeeded or failed it. I asked them what they did to succeed and what they failed to do which prevented them from succeeding. It was then that I discovered that no one could definitively say why they succeeded and others failed. Some curates said it was probably because they are spiritually mature and others were not, that is, they had grown spiritually and others had not. Another curate said she thought her friend would pass the BAP, that is, an assessment for ordained ministry at the end of successfully completing the DP, but her friend did not do so. However, she passed the BAP and could not say why this was the case. Someone else who had failed the BAP could not say why she failed the BAP and when she spoke with her priest in a debriefing and for encouragement thereafter, her priest only gave her possible reasons as to why she failed but there were no absolute answers. Apart from one, young, Black, female in the Diocese, all these candidates were all middle-aged, white females. I then witnessed a young, white male in his mid-thirties who preached extensively in his local church and who had accepted preaching invitations from priests in other local congregations. He clearly appeared to me to be a candidate for ministry. When I spoke with him about my discernment after he was ordained he confirmed to me that he had spoken with his priest prior to the commencement of his DP and about ordination for several years but nothing happened to progress him into the DP. Whilst he was happily married, he revealed that he cohabited with his now wife, prior to wedlock. Now, in reflection, I wondered if that was the preventable cause to the commencement of his ministerial exploration since the CoE punitively sanctions applicants or potential candidates for ministry if it perceives them to have erred or sinned in the area of marital or personal relationships. However, if that was the reason, this too would have been unfair to this young man since the church had not then ordained him. Celibacy until marriage is only an absolute requirement for ordained ministers in the CoE.[18] A few weeks after our conversation I was informed that the rector of another church intervened and within a year of our conversation this white, young man accepted an unconditional, theological-college offer for theological training. He had not got a theological degree. Notwithstanding, there was no mention of him having completed a BAP prior to going to theological college. A Black, female, divorced ordinand (that is, a ministerial candidate in the CoE) who was training at a nearby theological college, did not have a theology degree prior to ministerial training, and had no previous, practical experience of ministry, told me that her DP lasted for four years. She said that it was only when she spoke with a Cathedral Dean about her frustration as to how long the process was taking, was she then fast tracked to a BAP, successfully completed work for it in one year and then went on to theological college. This is a sample of some of our conversations:

August 4, 2019,

> It was great meeting and speaking with you today. Thank you for following the leading in your spirit to attend [name of church]. No coincidence that we have met again today. God! Doreen x.

Reply:

> Hi Doreen it was lovely seeing you too! Our paths needed to cross today—The struggle is real for us black woman! Gods got this! Just keep walking.

And August 9, 2019:

> Doreen: The death of Toni Morrison has

---

18. CoE, *Issues in Human Sexuality*, 48.

caused me to reflect on Black womanhood etc.

Reply:

Black female ordinand: I know I was the same this morning—it's a journey my friend—let's keep on walking—if they can—we should!

Reply:

Doreen: Amen!

And November 12, 2020:

Black female ordinand: I've been attending the international black clergy conference—with about 200 from Episcopalian churches [Anglican]. We were asked to put in the chat box how long our DP was and was it a loving experience. Put it this way—I say a lot of people was saying it took ten–fifteen years[19] and it wasn't affirming and that they perceived God had called them! We are not alone. Keep walking.

These examples were incidents in which everyone had completed a BAP except, to my knowledge, the one, white, male, person mentioned above. However, no one had their BAP cancelled once it was booked or after completing the DP.

With so many variations in individual's accounts and where there were no guidelines, no transparency, no strategy, no curriculum or means of establishing and verifying if aims and goals were met and targets and objectives achieved, it appeared to me that this DP was a bit of a lottery, but unlike the lottery, without any rules. It was only from 2020 that a typical timeframe for a discernment into ordination was recorded to take about 10–18 months. However, that was after a period where there is "no timeframe" in which some candidates informed me that it took them only one year from the start of the DP until they attended BAP after completing the nine criteria, whereas for others the Process was much longer. It seemed that the DP was difficult for most people I spoke with simply because there was no action-plan. However, I discovered that the DP was especially

---

19. The timeframe of 10 to 15 years from the start of the vocation exploration to being ordained as priest for Black people in the CoE was also confirmed to me by a Black, male vicar in another Diocese. This exceeds the normal timeframe for white applicants of between four to seven years from the commencement of the DP to ordination as a priest.

tough if you are either Black or Black and female simply because, in many cases, tasks were added and invented as candidates progressed through the Process and the timeframe was lengthened. An ordained minister in another denomination said a similar thing on hearing the accounts of people processing through the CoE DP:

> Over the years I have witnessed numerous non-white people who have spoken about the process of ordination and how it has sapped them of energy related to the many hurdles they have had to endure. When they are finally ordained, they are absolutely worn out with the process/experience... While I understand the need for discernment and enquiry, the process has been somewhat disempowering. On the other hand, I have met many people from the dominant group who have spoken about the process and the most difficult part has been the period of discernment. I am still unclear why this should be.

Not fully comprehending reasons for such ambiguity in the DP I thought, but this is the CoE. Surely the church should know what they are doing! I therefore continued to explore my vocation through the DP. Nevertheless, my trust was definitely not in a DP which did not provide any transparency and consistency between applicants and which was therefore prone to incidences of discrimination, spiritual abuse and even slavery. My trust was in God and therefore in the spirit, and not the letter of the law.

Placements

Whilst there was no standardization in the DP which made it hard for me to ascertain for certainty what was required as a reasonable amount of work of all applicants exploring a vocation to ordination and the general content of it, it was clear that completing the nine criteria was a normal requirement of all applicants. Nonetheless, even in attempting to complete the nine criteria there was no guidelines on how much work was required of every candidate to successfully complete each criterion. In addition some candidates served in their parish church, did a course within the Diocese and/or participated in a vocation conference. In my case, I did all the above as Table 3 shows, and much more than would normally be required of applicants in the DP. What was so wrong, ungodly and evil, was that I was ordered to carry out excessive amount of tasks as Table 3 shows. This was under the pretentious guise that these tasks were all necessary for BAP and ordination and part of the DP. Besides, no guidelines meant that it was extremely difficult to challenge the excessiveness of the work I was doing without recognizing and accessing it with others who were either going through the Process or had previously gone through the Process or with others training as curates for ordination. However, the full extent of discrimination is beyond the scope of this chapter which I shall address on another occasion.

My DP mandated that I carried out placements and these were assessed in writing by the Bishop's Director of Ordinands (BDO), Revd Romita Shrisunder, an Asian female priest, of the Diocese/Bishop's Office who required this from me along with other assignments.

> Easter has now past as we move towards Pentecost in these new, times of lockdown. Please find attached my paper which is a response to your questions since we met in January 2019. [NB. This paper and questions were not in response to the nine criteria. This was extra work]. I have copied it to my incumbent (Doreen's email to Romita, April 24, 2020).

Romita's response on April 27, 2020:

> Dear Doreen,
> Thank you very much for your email and for the written reflection.

And again an email to me from Romita on May 22, 2020:

> Dear Doreen,
> As it had been a while since we last met in January 2019 I invited you to reflect on the past year and also addressed your questions regarding the process and expectations [that is, referring to the written reflection—the paper—previously submitted].
> For our meeting I would like you to undertake the task attached to the email; [another additional written task]. When you have done this task please contact

me to schedule an appointment. At the next meeting we will go through the task that you have done and further explore your sense of vocation.
With best wishes,
Romita.

In an email to Romita dated April 6, 2021 and copied to Bishop of Shrewsbury, Sarah Bullock, a white female; the Bishop of Lichfield, Michael Ipgrave, a white male and others, I wrote:

> we have discussed these three papers in one of the several meetings we have had... I am concerned that I am doing a lot of work—much more than others—over these five years; a point that has been mentioned by others too. Whilst my Process is very different... can you not see why I, like others, are concerned that this Process has taken over five years? Concerned is the operative word here and yet, even now, I am required to produce more and more work. When will this end? This Process is becoming abusive if it is not that already.

Placements of the type which I was required to do, are normally done by curates and not in the DP, yet I was required to complete them and without pay and without the Office of a curate. I was required to produce written work. Although written work was required of curates, to produce it at a standard I would normally produce for academic publications, is not a requirement of any curate. To date, I have received no remuneration for my academic work. I also carried out deacon roles during the DP almost every week at my parish church and, again, without pay and/or the Office of a deacon. I worked on my own projects through my own not-for-profit organization, and my activities in my projects were also assessed during the DP. The DP consumed all my time. I was not paid or funded for my work, effort and spiritual commitment and received no formal Office as a curate or deacon by the Diocese. It was for these reasons, that is, that I was doing the work of a curate and deacon and therefore ministering in those Offices whilst ordered to work for at least the equivalent of part-time work that I believe, I should have been paid as a person who was not receiving a salary from elsewhere at the time. The Bishop and Diocese were very much aware of this, so at the PH

I therefore argued that the Respondent, that is, the Diocese and Bishop of Lichfield was a Service Provider under the Equality Act 2010. Without any remuneration for extensive commitment I also think this could also be liken to modern slavery. Again, in principle, this means that I could obtain a curacy directly after BAP if it was not cancelled and because I am already educationally qualified with a master's degree in theology. In addition, I had not entered the DP as someone who was totally oblivious to the requirements of ministerial training since I have also taught applicants for ordination myself at a Bible college albeit in a different denomination. Furthermore, if there was the jurisdiction to allow me to pursue the various, discrimination elements of my Claim, it would not have been unreasonable to Claim a compensation for my work and likely damages for the spiritual abuse and economic exploitation caused to me during the DP.

Age and Marital Status Factors

Notwithstanding that Holy Order is for life as stated in the Judgement of the PH, age is also a factor in the DP in that less time is normally given to older candidates for spiritual discernment.[20] I was in my 40s and premenopausal when I started the DP. I am now in my 50s and was also at the time the DP was brusquely ended by Sarah Bullock. The Respondents knew my age at the commencement of the DP as I had to declare it on all registration forms at the beginning and at least two other times during the DP. My age was also required on BAP application forms.

Commenting on my many paperwork, placements and ministry in my parish church in an email to Romita dated July 24, 2020, my white and male vicar, and an Oxbridge, CoE, seminary tutor of ordinands, said:

> I am aware that Doreen has seen you now twice. She has shown me the substantial material that she submitted to you for both those conversations that explore fully her own sense of vocation and her understanding of ministry and the church. I am also having ongoing conversations with her about this... The seriousness and the energy that Doreen is putting into her exploration

---

20. Ministry Division, *Sending Candidates to BAP*, 32.

is to my mind impressive . . . Given her age [referring to me] and the already long process she has undertaken including with advisors and placements, I hope it would be possible to outline a clear timetable that would mean if the diocese sponsored her for a BAP and the BAP affirmed her vocation that she would be able to start training in Autumn of 2021. This would probably require a decision by the diocese by early 2021. Given that you are meeting with her almost monthly and she has and is producing substantial material for you and also reflecting on ministry with others, this timescale does not seem unreasonable or impossible.

An applicant's marital status is a major factor in the consideration for ordination in the CoE. Being divorced requires full clearance to pursue ordination.[21] This was agreed from the commencement of my DP and prior to the BAP and therefore the PH. Under the CoE doctrine on human sexuality, if I was ordained I could also remarry a man who was either widowed or in a similarly divorced situation to myself;[22] therefore, for me, the same doctrine would apply as someone who has never married.

Ministerial experience

When I joined the Diocese of Lichfield, CoE in 2010 I already had extensive lay leadership experience in other denominations since I was a child. This was in addition to my ministry during the Diocesan DP. In my email to Romita on April 6, 2021 and copied to Sarah Bullock, Michael Ipgrave, and others, I said:

> I completed my PhD in three years, I have worked at a Bible college/seminary as academic dean so have worked with people undergoing ministerial training themselves. I have a master's degree in Bible and theology, and performed in lay ministry in the church for 40 years, that is since being a child, albeit from other denominations and

---

21. Ministry Division, *Sending Candidates to BAP*, 32.
22. Church of England, *Issues in Human Sexuality*, 48.

also serving in the CoE for 10 years since joining [in 2010].

If I was allowed to attend a BAP and it was successful, I would not be a long way from being ordained as a curate and priest; therefore eligible for an Office, and/or employment. This is because I have an accredited theology degree (a masters degree) which is a requirement for ordination or its equivalent, and also former ministerial training/formation. I obtained this in 2007 and a decade before my DP in the Diocese/Bishop's Office started. In fact, among other things, theology/religiosity, is one of my specialist areas. I was an academic dean (second in command after the Principal/President) at an accredited, American, Bible college in 2007, that is, involved with the spiritual and academic formation of candidates in ordained and lay ministry. These factors would again mean that I was familiar with processes of ordination for ministry albeit in another denomination. Had I been allowed to progress to and successfully complete the BAP, I would not be required to attend theological college.

References and Endorsements

All my referees endorsed me for ordination prior to the BAP and the Sponsorship meeting with Sarah Bullock; that is, all references required by the Diocese/Bishop prior to BAP. They were my vicar, a lay leader in my parish church who represented the congregation, an existing or previous work colleague and a person who could comment on my suitability for training. The incumbent/vicar's reference stated:

> Doreen is able to articulate clearly and passionately her own faith journey and the impact of her calling upon her life... Doreen has a strong prayer life that owes much to her upbringing in the Pentecostal tradition... Doreen has also displayed an openness to the more liturgical forms of prayer in our particular Anglican tradition. She became one of the small number of people who joined in our Zoom Morning [and Evening] prayers... Doreen has been around Christian Churches for her whole life... I

have also experienced Doreen working in a pastoral role with a member of the congregation in particular difficulties. She displayed a strong ability to take a practical approach, able to sign post to appropriate agencies and advice that would help her situation... Doreen has led in worship taking the subdeacon role in our liturgy... Our church is a diverse church with people coming from different cultures, countries and theological backgrounds... she worked well with others in this group... Doreen has a strong faith, is a very capable worship leader and displays a strong spirituality rooted in a very real prayer life. She also displays initiative and creativity and is clearly very capable academically (4th May 2021).

The lay leader's reference mentioned:

Doreen participates in leading worship with the incumbent, and participates in leading intercessions and doing the readings. She was active on the worship team, being involved with this nearly every week, and this included singing solo at times. She preached the Pentecost sermon last year for the online service. She has contributed to the weekly church bible studies and has helped out at the Open Church sessions held on weekdays. She attended Morning Prayer at times prior to the pandemic, and also led this on occasions... I have seen her respond to demands placed on her unexpectedly by a member of the congregation, offering pastoral care both in the moment and on an on-going basis. I have also seen her respond to the request for help of homeless visitors (mother and daughter) to the church, liaising with members of the leadership team to offer appropriate support... She enjoys collaborating, and has taken opportunities to lead prayer and worship. She shows initiative, is creative, and is a self-starter... She has been honest in my experience... Our church is extremely diverse both racially and socially, and I have seen Doreen relate well to many of these people in our weekly church lunches. The Church might be wise to accept this person to train for ordained ministry (16th April 2021).

The occupational referee said:

I knew the candidate as a volunteer worker... I was employed... I believe her to be a person of great integrity and honesty... She handled difficult situations with enormous discretion... Doreen was able to work with this mixture of people... Doreen is always respectful to people, polite and prepared to listen... When leading groups she was gentle, clear, and quick to respond to queries or problems. Her style was to accept that different people worked at different paces and she seemed able to understand that... Always cheerful, offering the best of herself and getting the best from those around her... Her organisational skills were well respected by her local colleagues. She was focussed on "the job in hand" but ready to think over the horizon to tasks and problems that could emerge in the future... Doreen and I did not immediately discuss our shared faith because we were in a secular environment, but... it just seemed obvious that she had a faith. She knows the times to speak up and the times to simply love and respect... I know of no reason the Church could not accept this person to train for ordained ministry and believe Doreen will be a credit to the church and a real witness for the Gospel. (April 23, 2021)

The educational referee noted,

Academic acumen and intellectually insightful. Highly sociable. I have no doubt about her ability and call for ministry. I know Doreen to be a person of integrity and honesty (April 26, 2021).

Furthermore, an External Examiner who was a Diocesan Director of Ordinands (DDO) in another Diocese in CoE and therefore outside the Diocese of Lichfield/Bishop's Office, was also instructed by the Diocese/Bishop to assess and discern my vocation for ordained ministry; something that is not required of everyone prior to BAP. The External Examiner too endorsed my vocation after examination of the nine criteria:

> I met with Doreen on Tuesday 23rd February 11am, 2021 via Zoom... I found that she realistically reflected on the demands and cost that ordained ministry brings... I was content that Doreen conveyed a good grasp of her own tradition and other traditions within the Church of England... Doreen strikes me as a person who desires to do the right thing by others with integrity... I would be of the mind that she proceeds towards a BAP.

In addition to these references, in an email, I was also endorsed for ordination by another mentor on July 19th, 2020, whom my incumbent mentioned in his reference:

> God is good. Let's keep on praying—the Lord's purpose will prevail (Proverbs 19:21). It must prevail. God is leading your journey and I look forward to seeing you on that day of Ordination and beyond.

BAP and Ordination

I applied for BAP, a date was agreed with the CoE, National Ministry Team and all necessary paperwork was submitted on time as demonstrates on February 19, March 25, May 8, and May 17, 2021 by email correspondences between the Diocesan vocation's administrator and me.

> Dear [name of administer],
> Thanks for confirming that you have

received my DBS[23] certificate [and that it shows that I have no criminal records].

And:

Dear Doreen,
I am pleased to inform you that you have been booked to attend a Bishops Advisory Panel during the week of 12th—15th July [2021]... Please find attached a number of documents for you to fill in prior to your Bishops' Advisory Panel. The Referee Nomination Form needs to reach me as soon as possible and certainly by **31st March 2021**... Registration Form, Statement of Financial Position, Ethnic Monitoring Form, need to reach me by **Monday 10th May 2021** at the latest... a full CV, including details of any experience of work with children and vulnerable adults (including any voluntary work), and evidence of an exploration of any gaps in employment from leaving school to date. This should be sent to me with the above documents by **10th May**... We will also need a digital photo of you (a head and shoulders shot) to send with your sponsoring papers... You will see that the Registration Form is a very detailed document and it is this that will present you to the BAP Advisers prior to the Panel. It is therefore important that you take care in writing it. It will take quite a bit of time to complete. I suggest that you put some time in your diary now in order to be able to do it... There are two pieces of work that you need to prepare in advance of the panel: A Written Reflection... and send it to me by **Monday 10th May.** A Presentation—Information about what is required... at the panel is also attached.

And on May 8, 2021:

---

23. DBS is an acronym for Disclosure and Barring Service. It is the British agency which carries out national and international, criminal checks on individuals and produces records for individuals and organisations on request.

BREAKING NEWS, January 18, 2023

Dear [name of administer],
Please find attached the last of the paperwork for BAP—my written reflection.
Kind regards,
Doreen

Reply:

Dear Doreen,
Many thanks for this—safely received.
Kind regards
[name of administer]

And 17th May 2021:

Dear Doreen,
Many thanks. I have all the paperwork from you that is needed.
Kind regards
[name of administer]

The Nonfactual and Libellous Letter[24]

The letter from Sarah Bullock, date June 2, 2021, which led to the cancellation of my BAP and stopped my vocation in the Diocese of Lichfield, is nonfactual. It is based on an individual's opinion, assumptions, excuses and some outright untruths with no supporting evidence to substantiate the discontinuation of my vocation and the BAP.[25] For these reasons questions of integrity and sincerity about Sarah Bullock's Office as Bishop exist. First, the zoom meeting with Sarah Bullock on May 24, 2021 was the first and only time Sarah and I met and from which she claimed to come to her conclusion to terminate my vocation in the Diocese of Lichfield. In her three-page letter Sarah Bullock mainly takes issue with my calling to ordained ministry because she does not think it is "obedient, informed and realistic." By this she generally means "Candidates calling should be confirmed by others." Sarah Bullock claims that my calling is not recognized or confirmed by others. This is extremely strange since she said that she read all my BAP papers. In them, all referees and the external examiner confirmed my vocation to ordained ministry. The BAP paperwork does not also include the same from many other people throughout my lifetime. Sarah Bullock did not accept the confirmations from the Black churches I congregated throughout my life. She named these churches in her letter. She also

---

24. See Further Reading in this chapter on "My General Response to Sarah Bullock on 21st August 2021."

25. Space here prevents me from unpacking the entire analysis of this letter in this chapter. However a summation of Sarah Bullock's letter will suffice.

questioned the reference from my church incumbent/vicar, whom she named because, she argued that my ministry was not confirmed by other vicars at churches I attended in the Diocese. For BAP, I only required the affirmation of my then current vocational minister. Notwithstanding, there were several incidents of discrimination which involved the other vicars which is beyond the scope of this Statement. Furthermore, Sarah Bullock also said she too could not see my vocation. If she had allowed my DP to proceed to BAP, as is customary, BAP advisors would have advised her on this matter.

My character was also concerning to Sarah Bullock. She falsely accused me of not attending courses and meetings arranged by the diocesan vocations department for candidates undertaking the DP; all of which I attended and was an active participant. I provided evidence of my attendances. The Diocese wanted access to my medical records—my personality assessment to be precise—without my full knowledge and consent and when this was not mandatory or required in the DP. The medical professionals refused the Diocese access to this information. Sarah Bullock blamed me for that. She accused me of criminality when she knew this was untrue since I was working in schools as part of my DP and she also knew I have a history of ecclesial activity. Whilst all the evidence of race and sex discriminations in the Diocese was not in my BAP paperwork, Sarah Bullock heard about some of them and flagged them up in our meeting. She then blamed me for their discrimination in her letter which, interestingly, was what slave masters did to slaves in the Transatlantic Slave Trade. They blamed the slaves for the slave masters' cruelty and wrongdoing towards the slaves. Sarah Bullock's blame also demonstrates discrimination itself and an abuse of power. I was also blamed for distrusting the Process. I was therefore told "to move on" to something else since she terminated my progression to BAP and ordination in the Diocese of Lichfield.

If I had tried and failed to proceed to ordination through a just and fair DP, like anyone who tried and was unsuccessful, I would be disappointed. However, it was the injustice, unfairness and unethical way the DP was conducted and my vocation ended that not only makes it, for me, a bitter pill to swallow which, unlike medicine which is designed to heal, my experience of the DP has to date, only brought me discomfort and has caused me to conclude that the Progress is spiritually abusive, cruel and wrong. The effects of a libellous reference or letter on the reputation of the ministry of anyone can be very damaging. This is especially poignant when Black and Brown women are already experiencing discrimination in the church, and as this book shows, specifically in the CoE. So when I describe the DP as evil and ungodly, specifically as it relates to my experience, these adjectives are no hyperbola. The letter by Sarah Bullock also posed a possible, separate Claim of Defamation, along with her perjurious outburst under cross-examination, a possible criminal offence, during the PH itself, in which she falsely accused me of being educationally unqualified for the Office and/or employment of ordained ministry because I am an academic.[26] I stated earlier that, since 2007, I have a master degree in theology comprising of spiritual formation.[27] Furthermore, the various rumors which she stated during the course of this PH and the DP, also amounts to alleged slander.

More cheerfully, this adverse experience can also be positively redemptive.[28] This study also shows that attempts to thwart and the actual thwarting of the ministerial vocation of Christian, women of color by British Black and mainstream churches is another reason for the growth in community womanism as Black and Brown Sisters seek alternative spaces and places to fulfill their callings. However, admittedly, not everyone who expresses or feels a calling to ministry is genuine and neither is ministry a right vocational option for everyone. A DP, or a similar process, is therefore legitimate. In the CoE, in practice, the discernment of ministerial vocation should be a collaborative decision with various persons from different groups, such as, the referees, the BAP, a person from the ministerial team and the individual concerned too. It should include a sense of God's calling on the candidate's life and their spiritual values. Whilst collaborative decision-making for discerning a person's vocation can produce an incorrect result, I think it should be exercised in every denomination in which transparency is evident and where social justice and theocracy are practiced. Collectivism seems to me to be a more sure method of discerning a person's vocation than a monocratic one.

---

26. See Further Reading on "A Claim for Defamation."

27. See Further Reading, "Formation and Academics."

28. See the Further Reading on "A Summation of My Sense of Calling to Ordained Ministry."

Sarah Bullock's decision to terminate my vocation was made by her alone. It was episcopal, Diocesan, top-down leadership decision making. That is what has led to the qualms surrounding it. Please note I am Black and female. However, under the British Nationality Act 1981 I am automatically a British citizen from my birth. Apart from a very short period working in the US, I have lived in my country of birth (England) for most of my life. Although I did not say it at the time, the DP did appear to me to be like a scam where people with protected characteristics under the Equality Act 2010 can be most susceptible to spiritual abuse. To quote from Oakley and Humphreys,[29] where they investigated spiritual abuse in the CoE, they say:

> The difference between spiritual abuse and other forms of abuse are the spiritual context in which spiritual abuse occurs and the ways in which people are controlled through . . . the notion of 'divine position' as giving unquestionable authority and the use of God to coerce and control.

The facts in this DP appear to fit this definition of spiritual abuse.

Spiritual abuse is an uglier side of spiritualizing. Over spiritualizing can lead to superstition, or a witch-hunt and therefore untruths about someone or something as in some of the false allegations about me in the DP which led the Bishop's Office to discern that I am uncalled to a spiritual vocation. Religious heresy is prone when spiritualizing leads to absolute falsehood. I am not here referring to mere idle gossiping and rumors which can also happen in churches since they are places in communities where everyone is welcomed and thus such gossiping can lead to untruths. I am speaking about claiming a holy–spirit affirmation on something which may be false whether or not gossiping is involved. According to Numbers 23:19 and Hebrews 6:18–19, God cannot lie. Pneumatic spiritualizing can often produce the illogicality, supposed impracticalities and unexplained outcomes since it engages with the paranormal as demonstrated in this book. Also, an example of a supernatural, pneumatic paranormal/mysticism is if, after prayer, someone was healed from an incurable diagnosis that experienced medics cannot explain:

---

29. See Oakley and Humphreys, *Escaping the Maze of Spiritual Abuse*, 29.

thus, a miracle. So, to avoid any erring, spiritual discernment must be questioned for truth and reality. It was the failure to do so and the reliance on assumptions alone which was so wrong and therefore unethical about my DP.

Disciplinary and Grievance Procedures in the Diocese of Lichfield?

Apart from producing an unfactual letter, cancelling the BAP and terminating my vocational journey, there was no operational Complaints or Disciplinary Procedures in the Diocese/Bishop of Lichfield's Office to which grievances could be heard and satisfactorily solved as verified by Michael Ipgrave in an email to me dated June 10, 2021:

> I have delegated my responsibility to the Bishop of Shrewsbury, and I have absolute confidence in the fairness, thoroughness and wisdom of her judgement ... I am not minded to investigate the matter further ... You also asked about the availability of a complaints or grievance procedure in a case like

this. I can confirm that there is no grievance or complaints step within the vocations pathway.

The system in the Diocese of Lichfield simply does not provide a platform to redress complaints and therefore the reason I had to seek redress through the judiciary. One of the recommendations I made to the Employment Tribunal during the PH was the implementation of a Disciplinary Procure in the Diocese of Lichfield. This request would have been heard by an Employment Tribunal Hearing if there was legal grounds to Hear my Discrimination Claims.

When I approached the Archbishop's Office on June 21, 2023 the Archbishop's spokesperson stated and suggested the following:

> I am sorry to say that the Archbishop is unable to intervene in your situation, since all discernment, training and ordination are arranged locally, as the Church of England is a decentralised body ... We can only advise that you revisit your contact with the diocese or that you write to your Bishop

suggesting that he address the matter locally.

Taking the Archbishop's spokesperson's advice since the church's rules prevented his intervention, I contacted Bishop Ipgrave who replied on July 6, 2023 with the following:

> I have been reflecting on how best to respond to the suggestion from Lambeth Palace that I should 'address the matter locally'. As I am not entirely clear what matter it is that needs to be addressed, I think it would be good if you could make arrangements to meet with my chaplain... It is clear to me that your process of discernment in this diocese has come to an end, and the purpose of a meeting would not be to reopen that question.

In responding to the Bishop on July 6, 2023 I said,

> For me, something needs to be done to rectify this situation since I did not stop the BAP and Sarah Bullock has provided no justifiable reason for doing so. That's clear and even the Archbishop's Office understands that as the reason for my unacceptance of the outcome in what was, for me, an already questionable DP. I am afraid this issue is not going away without a satisfactory resolution since, what was, until recently, unknown in the public domain, is now very much exposed. I am willing to meet with your chaplain. However, for me, there is no point in meeting with your chaplain or anyone regarding my ordination if that is not the premise and starting point of our meeting. The meeting must be about finding an amicable way of evolving the issue of ordination, given my age, work already done, support by four referees and an external Examiner and now the Archbishop's Office to revisit the matter with you. Only if we can agree with that request will I meet with your chaplain.

BREAKING NEWS, January 18, 2023

At the time of writing there is still inaction in pursuit of my ordination in the Diocese of Lichfield. Furthermore, to date, as far as I am aware, there is no apology, no remorse, no repentance, no feelings of guilt, no embarrassment, no humility and no contrition from the Diocese and Bishop's Office.

When further details of my DP was revealed directly before and after the PH, some people in the church of various denominations and in the secular arena called it a "con." A prominent leader from a British Black–majority church said that "it was God" who had prevented the progression to ordination because

> to be ordained there would have continued the control the Church wanted over you. The unnecessary scrutiny of your life and the watching of you like a hawk, would continue. What was done to you in the DP was only the start of that since the Anglican Church's links with the Transatlantic Slave Trade and the racism which still exists in it and because you are a woman. Now you are free again. You need to publish it.

Other prominent leaders from the Black church saw it differently and recognized that there was a worth, value and freedom to ordination in the CoE for me but definitely in another diocese. My incumbent who supported me for ordination, is still in shock. Personally, whilst I remain an ecumenist, my Diocesan home, if not my denomination, is now no longer in the Diocese of Lichfield because I do not believe Jesus called me to sit on the pews/warm the benches. Nevertheless, the ending of this whole Process in this way, also necessitates my humility, prayer and evaluation of what this means now in terms of God's will for my life and Christian Black and Brown females everywhere.

To Conclude

The PH at the Employment Tribunal accomplished my aim, which was to establish if there was jurisdiction for my Discrimination Claims. Under existing Employment Law the Tribunal found that there was no jurisdiction for me to pursue my Discrimination Claim. This does not mean that the issues of discrimination are invalid in the context of social justice more broadly—the area of one of my specialisms—simply because there is no legal premise at the moment. At an appropriate time and place, the discriminatory issues from which this Hearing emanated, can be heard to advance knowledge and/or change policy and practice also.[30]

Notwithstanding, the PH achieved so much more than only my aims whilst the objectives of the Claim (a compensation, Office and/or employment, independent accreditation of the DP and/or establishment of a Complaints Procedure) which were identified from the outset of the Claim, were not accomplished through the Employment Tribunal because there was no jurisdiction. First, there is perhaps a need for revision to existing legislation. Changes to the Equality Act 2010, to protect the characteristics of individuals is exposed by this Claim. Matters of race, gender and religion, which directly impact Christian, Black women, like me, the Claimant, and age, in my specific Claim, can be balanced by the specific requirements of the CoE and other religious organizations through reform to legislation. Social injustice prevailed in Britain more generally before the Race Relations Acts 1965 and 1976, the Sex Discrimination Act 1975 and the Equal Pay Act 1970. Along with other social policies, the amalgam of these Acts led to the Equality Act 2010. This PH shows that this current Equality Act 2010 also requires reformation and, currently, this can only be done through the UK parliament.

Second, what is fundamentally wrong about the DP and spiritual vocation in the Diocese of Lichfield is that it allows spiritual abuse and discrimination to take place. For example, there is no timeframe in which this discernment takes place, each applicant is asked to do tasks, and in my case, placements also with written work to a very high standard, which are determined by the Diocese/Bishop's Office and can be as much or as little as the Diocese/Bishop decides for each individual. Since it is the Diocese/Bishop's Office which decides who does what, when, how much and for how long and with or without pay, and then decides whether that individual is ordained for ministry or not, thus deciding if that person's vocation is spiritual or not, is, for me, undoubtedly a cause for concern with regards to persons with protected characteristics. In other words, there is no standardization, no rules, no plans, and an effective strategy in the process to prevent discrimination and spiritual abuse. What

---

30. One of the vital purposes of academic research is to advance knowledge and/or change policy and practice for the common good of the public and society.

was already a difficult situation, in my case, was made worse when a decision was made to terminate my vocation through the act of one Bishop. Furthermore, existing legislation does not allow a possible pursuant the jurisdiction for Claims of Discrimination. In addition to possibly assist in the change to legislation, discrimination issues in this case may also help to reform relevant, religious organizational policies and practices, no less in the Diocese/Bishop of Lichfield, the CoE more generally, and other religious organizations too.

Third, the rightful Respondents for future, potential, Employment Tribunal Claims under existing Employment Law were identified by this PH. Furthermore, aside from the Employment Tribunal, I entered the DP for ordination. The outcome of the Employment Tribunal does not mean that God has not called me to ordination neither does it mean I suddenly now do not sense a call of God to ordination or that all those who discerned and endorsed me for ordination were wrong. In other words, "the letter kills but the spirit gives life" (2 Cor 3:6). By concluding that the Respondent was not a "service provider" under the Equality Act 2010, in the case of my DP, is not saying that my calling to ministerial vocation is not of God, spiritual and that I am not entitled to an ordained ministerial Office and/or paid employment at some point. In contemplative prayer and humility, I put my trust in God.

Questions:

- Although this Statement does not focus on the various issues of discrimination which led to this pursuit for justice and was not intended to do so through the PH, drawing on womanist theology and spirituality, do you think the Claimant exercised her rights in this case study? If so, how? Should she have done so?

- Other than taking legal action, what else could have been done, assuming that some of your answers may have been considered and actioned by the Claimant before taking legal action?

- Theologically reflecting on this chapter, the Further Reading and related documentations, would you agree with the Judgement that the DP is spiritual?

- Do you know of any women-of-color who also sensed a ministerial calling from God and where it was officially confirmed by others, but she was prevented from pursuing her vocation? If you do, what happened?

Further Reading

Publishing this Statement

Publishing this Statement is in keeping with the tradition of many, activist Black feminists/womanists who published in various written forms other than essays. See Lorde, *Sister Outsider*,[31] who published her speeches. In the interest of authenticity, I shall retain the writing style of a news article/Statement and notably for a wider readership and legal audience. However, this Statement is longer than would generally be required for a newspaper. The research methodology is action research It developed as the project progressed. Data for this chapter emerged from immersion in the Discernment Process (DP). It was not part of a planned research project. At the start of the DP I had no idea that such evidence of discrimination would emerge from the process. However, this evidence now serves the purpose of advancing knowledge and possibly and hopefully also change policy and practice. For the purposes of this book, it is therefore important for the reader to reflect on womanism in the reading of this chapter. In this book it is the second testimony of sorts; the first being chapter 5.

The Judgment

The PH is open to the public and so is the Judgement and Order of the Employment Tribunal. It is known to my legal team that some publication would emanate from this Claim and as soon as possible after the PH. This is to advance knowledge and, perhaps, change policy and practice. Being a public Hearing, there are no legal restrictions to publish the PH or my investigation by researchers, journalists and/or other likeminded persons. The publication of this Statement is therefore in the public interest rather than merely of interest to the public. This is my early attempt to publish work from the PH. The actual names of persons in the PH will be used in this Statement since they are already in the public domain. However, although I can disclose the names of all persons not named in the PH and others related to this Claim, I have chosen to disclose some persons in this Statement

---

31. Lorde, *Sister Outsider* 187

since only those relevant to the PH were named in the Judgement. However all persons are known to the Employment Tribunal. Notwithstanding I recognize that unnamed persons can be disclosed by named persons and others who are aware of the Claims and the research project itself as can be the situation in any research project despite the great lengths taken by the researcher to conceal the identities of persons. I cannot therefore take responsibility for such disclosures and neither will others associated with the Claims or this publication be liable for such disclosures.

A Summation of my Sense of Calling to Ordained Ministry

Recording my journey here is proving to be liberating for me as I believe I am also helping others who have experienced or are experiencing a similar encounter. This account is therefore also redemptive. It is important that incidents like these are not used to allow others to define you and what they think God has called you to be and do when they do not know you. It is more significant to hope only in God.

I guess I have always sensed a call to ordained ministry of sorts from a child but never really knew what that would look like as I was given no clear support, mentoring or guidance into accepting a call to ordained ministry until I became an academic dean at a Bible college in the US. Besides, I was very active in lay leadership in a Pentecostal Black Church since I was 14 years old and served in a number of lay leadership positions from then on. I was already singing as a soloist from aged two and engaged in public church preaching since I was nine years old. My then pastor told my parents that I was destined for church leadership. In my teens another local pastor at my church then first allured to me that I should consider ordained ministry and he hoped it would happen. However, it was not until my early twenties that my first, substantial encouragement into ordained ministry occurred in a casual, telephone conversation with a friend from Wolverhampton whilst I was living in Sale, Cheshire, near Manchester. At the Sale congregation, a deacon also encouraged me to pursue licensed ministry. I was certainly giving it serious consideration. At this time, I really did not see the need to be ordained as no one explained to me the benefits of ordination over lay leadership in the church. Also, there seemed to be no barriers to my ministry as a lay person at that time. In addition, at the same time, there were also some issues surrounding the role of licensed women in the church which concerned me which I demonstrate in this book. I also sensed a call to academia and/or chaplaincy and I did not think the Black church then was focused on or sufficiently equipped to train and support persons in secular ministries. I think I was far more emancipated as a lay leader than I would have been as a female, ordained minister at that time and which I expressed to an experienced, ordained minister in a conversation:

> I sometimes think that I should have accepted the encouragement to be licensed when I was in my 20s from members in Wolverhampton and Sale. But no regrets since I felt the church climate did not seem right to then accommodate my calling. Besides, ordination in the CoE would still be required even if I was already ordained in the Pentecostal Church as this church is not a part of the Anglican Communion and therefore the CoE would require that I am ordained as an Anglican.

Notwithstanding, as an ordained minister of other denominations, it is still possible to perform ordination roles in the CoE, such as a Free Church minister, if a role does not stipulate a CoE ordination.

It was only when I went to America in December 2006 and, from January 2007, when I was in a senior role at a seminary/Bible college as academic dean, that ordination was now becoming a role I needed to pursue and obtain if I wanted to completely fulfill my sacramental calling. The church context in the US is different to the church I was raised and served in until this time. I thus started my exploration to ordained ministry in one of the congregations in the Progressive Baptist Convention in the US which I attended regularly until I returned to England in November 2009. I started my ministerial exploration for ordained ministry in February 2016 in the Diocese of Lichfield in the CoE.

The Discrimination Claims and the DP

The Claims of Race, Sex/(gender) and Age Discrimination, which I shall not discuss in this Statement, were for a series of occurrences during my DP in the Diocese of Lichfield Board of Finance/Bishops Office from 2016 to 2021.

Generally, the DP occurs in the CoE to discernment a person's spiritual calling to lay or ordained ministry. It occurs prior to a Bishops Advisory Panel (BAP) where a person's calling is assessed by persons in the CoE over a usual, three-day period. In my case, the DP was complete in early May 2021. However, the BAP was cancelled after meeting with the Sponsoring Bishop, Sarah Bullock, in a one-hour zoom meeting on May 24, 2021. A nonfactual letter dated June 2, 2021 followed.

If the BAP discerns a person's calling to ministry in collaboration with the candidate, it will advise the Bishop in that Diocese of the outcome of it. With all evidence presented to the BAP, including all references, the Bishop will then make a decision to further that person's training to ordination. If the candidate has not got a theology degree with formation/ministry experience and training (or the equivalent) s/he would advance to theological college. If the candidate has a theological degree with formation, s/he would normally progress to curacy training. Three year's curacy as a deacon and then a priest will usually follow a progress from college training. However, this can vary depending on the age of the candidate where it can be shorter than three years for older or longer for younger candidates. If successful, after curacy training, the candidate will be signed off as a fully-qualified, ordained priest.[32] Chris Goldsmith, the National Ministry Office in the CoE, did not go to college but did theological courses to qualify as a priest whilst working since he did not already have a theology degree. However, like me, he then had a PhD.[33]

Preliminary Hearing (PH)

Some commenters have noted that the content of the Judgement appeared to be biased in favor of the Respondent. However, for me, given the evidence at the Hearing, there was possibly no other outcome in terms of the Conclusion as the Conclusion was determined by evidence pertaining to legal jurisdiction under the Equality Act 2010 and not on evidence of other factors. An Appeal Report dated June 9, 2023 also clearly confirmed the Conclusion of the PH. The PH was not intended to address wider issues of Discrimination as mentioned already. It was therefore important to write the

32. Ministry Division, *Sending Candidates to BAP*, 32.
33. Wikipedia, "Chris Goldsmith."

Claimant's immediate response to the PH in this book.

"No-win, No fee."

I was represented only by my solicitor, Mr. Ennis from Rees Page Solicitors, at the PH as my legal costs were covered under the legal Firm's policy of a "no-win no-fee;" without which this civil Claim would not have been possible. For that I am extremely grateful to my solicitor and the Firm. A similar, legal, contractual arrangement could not be obtained with the barrister as his legal Chambers does not operate a similar policy. This was very unfortunate as the possible representation of a barrister would have most likely have changed the way my preparation was conducted directly before the PH, support was given during my cross-examination as a Claimant and, as my solicitor and I discussed in our debriefing directly after the PH, how the PH proceeded. This was especially noted when it came to the cross-examination of Respondents and the Summation for the Claimant which would have been more robust and fierce if it was conducted by a barrister rather than my solicitor in the absence of a barrister, even if the Conclusion of the PH was unchanged. With a very different preparation, support during my cross-examination, a barrister's cross-examination of Respondents and a barrister's Summation for the Claimant, this may have also changed the writing of the Judgement and thus the reading of it although the Order would have been the same.

Trust the Process

Referring specifically to theological education in her book titled, *Trust in Theological Education*,[34] Eve Parker demonstrates that due to a culture of systemic elitism, sexism, racism and homophobia in British theological colleges trust in them has eroded. Through a pedagogical theology of liberation to deconstruct "trustworthiness" her work attempts to restore hope in theological education for all candidates in ministerial training. It is this same hope which needs to be regained in the DP. However, it cannot be done when transparency in the Process is lacking and when the Process fails to account for all groups of diverse people who enter it. Deliberately creating barriers of injustices for marginalized groups only fuels distrust in the DP. Cancelling candidates' progress to its completion at any

---

34. Parker, *Trust in Theological Education*, 206.

time during the Process, without any justification or reason, does the same.

My general response to Sarah Bullock on August 21, 2021 through my lawyer who, through her lawyer, claimed that her decision to stop my ministerial vocation was spiritual and therefore cannot be contested.

1. Spiritual experiences are not solely subjective. Sarah Bullock should know this as a Bishop in the CoE. Many spiritual encounters can be observed by others and are therefore objective evidence of spiritual encounters such as, the reactions of someone's conversion to Christianity, prayers, bible readings, songs, "speaking in tongues," dreams, visions, prophecies, mystical and/or supernatural happenings that cannot easily be explained and so forth. The conversion of Nicodemus in the Bible in John 3 is an example. Sarah does not mention any of these factors as confirmations of her decision in her letter of June 2, 2021.

2. The fact that Sarah does not mention any spiritual factors in her letter leads me to believe that her decision was not spiritual, as I mentioned before. Besides, I can provide spiritual evidence that support my reason for believing that I am called to be ordained. They are the BAP application: the references, the eternal chaplains report, even Romita's account to BAP, my own information of my experiences and so on; plus other documentation prior to the BAP application.

3. Sarah maintains that her decision was spiritual although she provides no evidence of it. I would therefore give her the benefit of the doubt and say it was, at least spiritual but not Godly. I say this for two reasons:

   First, I do believe that race and sex discriminations are evident in Sarah's decision along with other evidence of racism and sexism in the DP, and the facts will speak for themselves. If we are to believe that racism and sexism are sins, and the CoE has now accepted that racism is a sin in its latest report on racism, *Lament to Action*,[35]

---

35. CoE, *From Lament to Action*, 71.

although I have maintained this as a fact from my studies of Black theology for years, then Sarah's decision cannot be of God as God cannot sin. Second, Sarah's comments in her letter clearly demonstrate abuse and slander. They undermine me. They are patronising, condescending, harassing, victimizing and discriminatory—all evidence of spiritual abuse according to Oakley and Humphreys in their book, *Escaping the Maze of Spiritual Abuse*.[36] Similarly, the fact that Sarah has tried to shut down the legal process by claiming that her decision is spiritual and therefore cannot be challenged is also another example of spiritual abuse. Third, the fact that I have been blamed for this present situation in which I have not been put forward for BAP and thus the possibility of ordination and employment by the Respondent, is yet another example of spiritual abuse. The Respondent's solicitor is completely wrong by saying I am no way close to ordination. My theological and church experiences and educational qualification, clearly demonstrate that I was more closer to ordination than most people entering the DP from the start of my DP in February 2016.

Sarah's decision is spiritual if she so wants to say so. However, it is spiritual abuse.

4. Sharah Bullock also abuses her power by using her position as a Bishop to stop my BAP without any cause which also questions her actions being Godly and spiritual.

A Claim for Defamation

I investigated the possibility of a separate Defamation Claim directly against Sarah Bullock on November 25, 2021 as I had sufficient evidence for such a Claim. However, after the initial, free consultation, I did not pursue the Claim for financial reasons. The Defamation solicitor informed me that "No-win, No-fee" offers are seldom given in Defamation Claims as legal costs often outstrip the compensation awarded for such Claims. Defamation Claims therefore aim to restore any likely reputational damage caused by the defamation. Besides, I noted that my then current Claims for

---

36. See Oakley and Humphreys, *Escaping the Maze of Spiritual Abuse*, 29.

Discrimination were also intended to address some of the same issues of Defamation if there was the jurisdiction for full pursuit of my Discrimination Claims. Additionally, at the time of writing, a Claim for Defamation was then now legally out of time, that is, more than the six months since the last incident of defamation.

Formation and Academics

Other church leaders and congregants have also falsely accused all academics of being unspiritual and thus unqualified for church discipleship and/or lay or ordained ministry in many denominations simply because we are experts in our fields. It is thus assumed we only apply our intellect and not the Holy Spirit when we serve in a spiritual capacity. Lay or ordained ministry is therefore important in these cases in order to be fulfilled in ministerial vocation.

7

Sermon Reflection on Pentecost Sunday[1]

What Does This Mean?

> Sweep over my soul,
> Sweep over my soul,
> Sweet Spirit sweep over my soul;
> My rest is complete,
> While I sit at Your feet;
> Sweet Spirit, sweep over my soul.[2]

IMAGINE BEING IN CHURCH before lockdown where we are all gathered for our eucharistic morning service or, if you prefer, we are online for our Spiritual Communion as we are now in this lockdown because of the coronavirus pandemic. We pause to listen and reflect on the hymn, "Envía tu Espíritu."[3]

---

1. This is a womanist sermon for reflection which I preached online under lockdown on Pentecost Sunday, May 31, 2020. It was originally for High Parish congregation but went viral on other social media platforms. In this book I have retained the sermon in its written, presentational form for delivery to a congregation from the pulpit; that is a presentation with short paragraphs which is sometimes used by speech-makers as well as preachers.

2. Anonymous, "Sweep Over My Soul."

3. Hurd, "Envia tu Espiritu." A recording of the hymn is played to the congregation.

We now come to the part of the service where we offer the Peace.[4] But instead of communicating in our mother tongue we all speak in foreign languages we were never taught (*xenolalia*).

After the Peace we all return to our seats to continue the remainder of the service but a little confused and somewhat bemused by what has just happened.

After the service we then gather for coffee and tea and biscuits and cakes.

Again a non-speaking Farsi congregant has a conversation, in Farsi, with a Farsi-speaking congregant. At the same time while this Farsi conversation is taking place, an English-only speaker happily and fluently communicates in Swahili with a Swahili-speaking South African congregant and the English speaker also understands everything.

In the congregation this is what is taking place between the conversations of everyone during the coffee and tea social.[5]

Again, everyone is bewildered and says words like, I didn't know you could speak Farsi or Swahili or French or Urdu or Italian or Berber or Romanian or Falani or Latin or Yoruba or Spanish or Jamaican Patois or German or Igbo and so on. Questions like, when did you learn French, Swahili, Farsi, etc., are asked?

Now this is the situation observed in our New Testament reading in Acts 2:1–13 and what is depicted in the Jamaican spiritual, "The Holy Ghost Power is movin' just like a magnet."[6]

At Pentecost, 50 days after the Jewish Passover, the Jewish feast of Shavuot (in the Greek language) is celebrated.

However, on this particular Pentecost in our Scripture reading, the Holy Ghost (*Pneuma*) descended on the disciples in Jerusalem. They spoke in fluent human tongues, that is, foreign languages so that everyone presence understood what was said in their native language.

The surprise of the crowd causes the apostle Peter, in Acts 2:14–21, to address them with reference to the fulfillment of prophecy and the

---

The English Translation of Spanish is "Send out your Spirit " or "Come Holy Spirit …"

4. In the Anglican liturgical tradition, the Peace is an opportunity in the service for congregants to shake hands with others or show each other a sign of peace, that is, the praying hands, and utter the words, "Peace unto you." The Peace usually occurs prior to the collection of the offering and the sermon in the service.

5. See "The Social" in the Further Reading.

6. In Grace Thrillers, "Holy Ghost Power Medley."

baptismal outpouring of the Holy Spirit as recorded in Joel 2:28–32 and Psalm 16. Peter thus responds to their question, what does this mean?

For Christians today, Pentecost is also known as WhitSun or Whit Sunday. It is 50 days after Easter.

For us, when our Day of Pentecost comes, we will hear God speak to us anew and accept God into our lives because the Holy Ghost is presence in our conversion. The Holy Ghost is the third person of the Godhead.

Secondly, when the Spirit of God baptizes us we will understand her speaking in our language whether that is our literal native tongue, metaphorically, or in another way.

Another way could be, God speaking through us in a heavenly tongue in which we sense God's presence whilst speaking in an unknown language (*glossolalia*).

This experience is very different from when the Holy Ghost spoke to us in our conversion to Christianity as seen in Acts 19:1–7, where twelve Ephesian Christians were baptized with the Holy Ghost and immediately spoke in tongues and prophesied.

For when the Holy Spirit descends and "shows wonders in the heaven" something miraculous and remarkable takes place like light, heat, and warmth of "fire and billows of smoke" because we receive a fresh anointing which endows us with power and might from that spiritual presence.

When the Holy Ghost comes, prophecy is fulfilled. "Your sons and daughter will prophecy" (Joel 2:28).

I believe that is what happened when on November 30, 2017. Guli Francis-Dehqani, an Iranian-born Britain, was consecrated in the CoE as the first woman of Asian or Brown descent to the Bishopric. The same occurred for Rose Hudson-Wilkins, on November 19, 2019, a Jamaican-born British woman of Caribbean or Black origin. The Jamaican spiritual, "Fire, Fire, Fire, Fire"[7] will fall on me, composed by the Grace Thrillers, attests to such moments of supernatural transformations.

So what are we asking the Holy Spirit to do for us today? Or what is the Holy Spirit asking of us today?

Is she asking us to prophesy (or speak out) as mentioned in today's readings in Acts 2:14–21 and Num 11:24–30?

What is happening in our lives, homes, churches, communities, nation, and world concerning this COVID-19 pandemic? A pandemic like

---

7. Grace Thrillers, "Holy Ghost Power (Medley)."

this does not just happen without God knowing about it and therefore must be saying something to us. So what is the Holy Spirit saying?

How do we respond to the poorest and peoples of Black and Brown lives who are disproportionately affected by coronavirus?

What about the lives of Black and Brown females? Do we not matter to God?

Do we offer acts of kindness, such as, food parcels, hygiene personal care donations, and menstruation products or other supplies?

Is God asking you to "speak truth to power," like the American activist and Black feminist academic, Angela Y. Davis, who refuses to succumb to oppressive pressures which forbid her from activism against racism, sexism, and exploitative capitalism in the US and globally.[8]

So is the Holy Spirit saying to prophesy about the injustice of limited personal protective equipment (PPE) for frontline staff and keyworkers or maybe She is asking you to clap for them every Thursday?

What about the timing to reopen of our schools, workplaces, businesses, organizations and places of worship to the public and what does that mean for our health and safety?

Do you feel an overwhelming call to daily, intercessory prayers during this unprecedented time? Can we hear the Holy Spirit saying, "Peace be with You" as she did in our Gospel reading, John 30:19–31, for his disciples when she appeared to them after Jesus's death and ascension, and when Thomas doubted God's presence as do some of us especially in the midst of anxiety and fear?

"You [God] asked for faith and trust; we demanded proof and certainty.

Lord have mercy."[9]

Are we supportive and helpful rather than maliciously, envious and jealous of others as seen in our Old Testament reading, Num 11:24–30. Thankfully, godliness, wisdom, and pardon were also practiced in this Scripture.

"[God's] love was stronger than death; we built tombs around our hearts.

Christ have mercy.

You sent us into the world with a message of hope; we lingered in comfortable despair.

---

8. Davis, *Women, Race and Class*, 256.
9. High Parish, "Order of Holy Communion for Pentecost Sunday."

Lord have mercy."[10]

So to answer the question, what does this mean? Well, first, the Holy Ghost is for everyone who says sorry for (or truly repents of) anything that is against God and opens our hearts and minds to receive God, thus, on this occasion, she speaks with us in a language or way that we can understand, although at other times, she may speak to us in an unknown tongue.

The Holy Spirit is for all today and not just a selective nation or group!

Second, when the Spirit of God appears we will better understand the will of God for others and our lives.

We will be comforted, find joy, have life, be protected, change, know peace, tell the truth, prophesy, find courage, forgive, love everyone, and may even speak in unknown, heavenly, and/or earthly tongues.

In the name of the Father/Mother, Son/Daughter, and Holy Spirit. Hallelujah! Hallelujah!

Reflection Questions

1. What do we learn about the Holy Spirit (*Pneuma*) from this sermon?
2. With reference to the biblical texts in this sermon, how can they be effective in advancing womanism? They are Num 11:24–30, Psalm 16, Joel 2:28–32, John 30:19–31, Acts 2:1–21, Acts 19:1–7.
3. Is speaking in tongues the only evidence of the indwelling of the Holy Spirit in the lives of practicing Christians?

Further Reading

The Social

The social is a normal practice after Sunday worship services in the UK, Anglican tradition. It is an opportunity to fellowship with congregants and visitors who attend the service and is often regarded as an extension to the service rather than an optional activity. Free to all attendees at services is the refreshments of tea/coffee and cakes/biscuits after the service.

10. High Parish, "Order of Holy Communion for Pentecost Sunday."

Sometimes fruits are also offered. On special occasions other food items may also be served such as mulled wine and mince pies at Christmas and Easter eggs and hot cross buns at Easter. At High Parish, sweets, cakes, and savories from the countries of congregants are often served during the after-service social. Indian samosa is a particular favorite by all congregants.

8

Loving Race and Accepting Self

I shall Love me!
I love God. God loves me.
I love others. Some love me.
I love you. You love me.
And I love me[1]

HAVING CONSIDERED THE IMPORTANCE of the Holy Spirit at Pentecost in chapter 7, this chapter focuses on racial self-love and self-acceptance made possible through the pneumatic love.

I come to this chapter from a position of never being in a position of unloving my racial embodiment. However, I have always had an issue of body-size although I have never experienced issues relating to colorism or racial dislike or hate. Growing up I was a chubby child and therefore was sometimes teased for being overweight in conversations at church, school, and among family and friends. I was sometimes also instructed on how I should then lose weight. Being emotionally sensitive in my childhood more generally, and especially to comments relating to my weight, as a teenager I would eat as little as possible in order to maintain a normal weight even if this was not physically healthy. The

---

1. This is my poem about inclusion and social justice. I wrote it on February 14, 2017. It was inspired by a meditative note I saw in Thurman, "Thou Shalt Love," 46.

impact of these comments and an encounter in which my mom had to purchase a UK size 12 dress for me when we once went clothes-shopping because I could not fit into a size 10 dress, led me to be on constant diets. I even experienced years of being grossly underweight; so much so that my parents thought I was suffering from anorexia nervosa. Discovering the effects of anorexia nervosa on the lives of individuals and groups, especially females, and their loved ones, and therefore unwilling to succumb to the illness myself, in my twenties I was able to overcome my obsession with body-size, food and weight. However, for me, maintaining a healthy weight through a balanced diet will always be an issue in my life since my bodily metabolism operates in a way in which I am prone to being overweight. Furthermore, since I am now menopausal I have again changed my diet and exercise regime in order to maintain a healthy weight-balance and also to cope with the symptoms of the menopause as prescribed by my medical general practitioner. Hormone Replacement Therapy (HRT) was not prescribed. The diet-changes are relieving my menopausal symptoms and a satisfactory weight level also.[2]

Although not exactly the same issue as general, racial. dislike of self nevertheless, I have some experience of racial self-dislike in terms of embodiment and the repercussions of this on my overall well-being. This is especially because this relates to being a Black woman in Europe and Britain where slimness is generally and stereotypically accepted as beautiful rather than roundness, which is considered more attractive and beautiful in Africa and the Caribbean. Being able to accept my curviness and voluptuousness as normal and beautiful is liberating and empowering since it has allowed me to accept and fully love myself unconditionally. This self-love and acceptance has also enabled me to maintain my psychological, emotional and spiritual well-being and love other females who look racially and physically like me. I am loved by God as a Black female so I love other Black and Brown females too. Loving God and myself has also enabled me to love all humanity also. I learnt the following song as a teenager at a church youth camp. It epitomizes my aspirations:

> More like you.
> I want to be more like you.
> When I look into my life,
> Many things don't seem quite right.

---

2. I am referring to literal body weight rather than being called "fat" in a metaphorical sense as used by some people when they are attempting to undermine me in contexts of spiritual abuse or by falsely accusing me of arrogance.

> But I pray each day,
> That you draw me closer to that place,
> As long as you guide me,
> I know that I can be.
> [God] I want to be more like you.[3]

Through my church and community engagement it has emerged that self-love is an issue of concern for some Black and Brown females. This chapter starts with a serious self-reflection and examination of self. It examines how the analysis of Black and Asian ethnic groups of women relates to identity, self-love, and self-acceptance for the development of Loyal Sisterhoods and discussions on British diasporic women as previously discussed in former chapters.

This chapter shall address race as it intersects with the concept of women. I shall connect race to the significance of it for women of color in terms of our/their personal, racial, ethnic, national, and cultural identities, and self-love and self-acceptance. So this chapter discusses the importance of loving and accepting oneself as Black and Brown women and girls. Secondly, this chapter shall develop the preamble of what it means to be Brown and Black as used in the UK as mentioned in other chapters of this book and its relations to self-love and self-acceptance. Having addressed race and ethnicity in chapter 1, I shall now focus on the extent of self-loathing and self-unacceptance of Black and Brown females in section 2. Section 3 shows that the products of failing to self-love and self-accept, which is harmful to self and others, is due to historical, current, and demographical contexts where self-hate and self-unacceptance of culture, race, and ethnicity are normalized for British females of color. Finally, the chapter concludes with a summation of the entire discussion of self-love, self-acceptance, and the Sisterhood in the British diaspora.

Self-Love and Acceptance of Self

Womanism values "love" as a central theme and practice in all its attributes. We get a sense from womanist theological and spiritual writings on love that *agape* (God's love, the highest form of love) is an expectation of Christian faith. Agape is a tall order but that is love. However, beyond this love, womanism values *philo* (brotherly/sisterly love, which

---

3. Smith and Bailey, "More Like You." The composers and musicians are congregants of a nationalized Black church in London. I changed the word "Lord" to God in the last line only for the purposes of this book on women.

is one we have among friends, community, and associates). Both of these "loves" I shall address in this book. This chapter shall focus on self-love and self-acceptance and demonstrate how integral it is to self/person and therefore for being comfortable in one's skin and self.

Alice Walker says that a womanist

> Loves music. Loves dance. Loves the moon. Loves the Spirit. Loves love and food and roundness. Loves struggle. Loves the Folk. Loves herself. Regardless.[4]

It is to the notion of "Loves herself. Regardless" which this chapter shall address.

One way Sisters affirm themselves is through loving self. This kind of self-love is not about egoism, narcissism, selfishness, or self-righteousness. Womanist spirituality endorses this self-love conceptualization. God loves us. She expects us also to love self collectively as women of color for we are "fearfully and wonderfully made" (Ps 139:14). Self-love is an important attribute to possess in the lives of Loyal Sisters since western society often defines beauty and worth in terms of whiteness and all that is associated with it. So the closer a Sister can be defined and seen to being white, the more she will be seen as beautiful and worthy in some circles in western society, no less the British context. The more one lives in a predominantly white populated country such as the UK, the land of previous slave masters, the bedrock of former colonialization, the home of former reigning empire, amid the pervasiveness of racism and sexism and the Brexit continent of Europe, the more significant it is for Loyal Sisters to love self.

Loving self as Christian Brown and Black women means accepting our Black and Brown darker skins (blackberry, bright, or tan) and our natural Black and Brown physics as beautiful, that is, loving our bodies whether fat, thin, tall, short. For women of Afro descent that is, to generalize, to love our hair texture and length (wavy and long or coarse and short), full lips, broad noses, big buttocks, and large hips. For those of Asian origin, it is about loving our dark hair, brown eyes, and thick eyebrows. It is about accepting that whilst the public may define beauty from a white European or North American embodiment, God loves and appreciates us as She made us ("[S]He has made everything beautiful in [Her] time" [Eccl 3: 11a]). We do not have to be enslaved by dominant

---

4. Walker, *In Search of Our Mother's Gardens*, xi–xii.

images and myths of beauty[5] as Black and Brown females but can deconstruct such images to reconstruct acceptable and realistic Brown and Black beauties. In my encouragement to Sisters of faith I instruct them to chant to themselves, with confidence and belief, often, if not every day, the phrase, *Beautiful me! I love me! God loves me!* We are all required to love self because we are all created in the image of God (*imago Dei*). We are all equal and all valued and all important. It is in the *imago Dei* we are all created and in whom Chine McDonald has profoundly demonstrated in her autobiographical book, *God Is Not a White Man*[6] and also Angela N. Parker, from womanist, biblical hermeneutics, in hers, *If God Still Breathes, Why Can't I?*[7]

Mukti Barton is the first in a British context to address and challenge British diasporic, Christian Black and Asian women to see the *imago Dei* in relations to gender, race, age, and divinity as *Chokmah* (divine Wisdom) and *Ruach* (divine Spirit) where we are loved by God. As a Christian Asian female, theologian and priest in the CoE, she often shares her own experience of self and how this is sometimes unloved by the British church. Notwithstanding, through the adoption of biblical hermeneutics, Barton accepts that she is loved by God and has learnt to love herself.[8] In her paper[9] the central arguments are that the transcendent God is a gendered God who is both masculine and feminine and neither, and can be depicted in the traditional Euro-American Christianity as an old white man but must also be seen as Black or Brown, young and female. Other rejections of western portraits of only white beauty is also demonstrated by Barton.[10] More than an autobiographical narrative, social commentary, and, I would suggest, from a "third wave religious thought" in its approach as discussed in *Community Womanism*,[11] Chine McDonald's, *God Is Not a White Man*[12] is profoundly provocative but deeply honest about the racialized sexism of Black women's lives in the British church and public. Chine McDonald, like Mukti Barton,[13] reminds us that Black

---

5. Wolf, *Beauty Myth*, 352.
6. McDonald, *God Is Not a White Man*, 239.
7. Parker, *If God Still Breathes, Why Can't I?*, 133.
8. Barton, "I am Black and Beautiful," 167–87.
9. Barton, "Gender-Bender God," 142–66.
10. Barton, "Skin of Miriam Became as White as Snow," 68–80; 158–68.
11. McCalla, *Community Womanism*.
12. McDonald, *God Is Not a White Man*, 239.
13. Barton, "Gender-Bender God," 142–66.

Loving Race and Accepting Self

and Brown women are created in God's image (*imago Dei*) and thus are worthy of value and praise. In McDonald's book we meet a God who is not a Euro-British white male but a Nigerian-British female growing up in England as a practicing Christian and congregant of the CoE who fully understands her own experiences as a Christian Black woman with all its achievements and complexities.[14]

In the church and community, Black women's unique characteristics personify both a feminine and Black Christ-likeness; a Christian womanist ontology of being human. Through them we acknowledge the gendered, racialized, and intergenerational Jesus who is not just male and white, as commonly perceived and often caricatured in church and community, but also Black, young and old. Thus they remind us that we are created in the Divine image of God (*imago Dei*)—as echoed by McDonald in her book, *God is not a White Man*[15]—"male and female created He them" (Gen 1:27). Through Loyal Sisters we see the classless and statusless Jesus who cares especially for poor and suffering Black and Brown women and those whom an ungodly world has under-classed, devalued, rejected, and/or marginalized; sometimes through highly structured and systemic regimes and institutions and often because of their combined race, gender, and class and other forms of social intersections such as religion, culture, colonization, belief, age, and other types of intersectionalities.[16] Through examining the lives of Loyal Sisters we get an insight into the global Christ. He is Jesus to Black and Brown women in Africa, Asia, the Caribbean, Australasia, the Americas, and Europe. Jesus belongs to Black and Brown women all over the world. So loving our race and womanhood is vital to acceptance of self.

This appeal to self-love is premised on its relationship to racial, ethnic, and cultural identifications. Being able to identify ourselves racially, ethnically, and culturally we can truly love and accept ourselves. It is in this context that self-love is defined. Having addressed race and ethnicity I shall now focus on the extent of self-loathing and self-unacceptance of Black and Brown females.

---

14. McDonald, *God Is Not a White Man*, 239.

15. McDonald, *God Is Not a White Man*, 239.

16. Crenshaw, "Demarginalizing the Intersection of Race and Sex," 138–67. Crenshaw, "Mapping the Margins," 1241–99. Cho et al., "Toward a Field of Intersectionality Studies," 785–810.

Self-Loathing and Self-Unacceptance

It was apparent from my observations and conversations with Christian Black and Brown females, Brown and Black women and girls of others faiths and no religious faith, and Black and Brown females in various communities that some Black and Brown women and girls struggled with self-ownership. Secondly, this self-disowning impacts their ability to also appreciate the Black and Brown ethnicities of women and girls who look like them. Instead, they accept Black and/or Brown, female inferiority whilst appreciating white and/or male superiority. For some of the refugee and asylum seeker, Brown and Black women at High Parish, the issue of identity becomes especially important when faced with issues of immigration. Not only must they be able to speak English to qualify for British immigration status but under Immigration Acts 2014 and 2016, where a hostile environment is created for them as foreigners, they must also be able to support themselves socially and economically. Similarly, some of these women perceive that they must be as British as possible thus losing their national, cultural, and personal/racial identities entirely in order to qualify as British nationals which in turn sometimes leaves some of them facing an identity crisis.

At High Parish, I recount also recently witnessing an incident of colorism and a racial identity crisis. A highly attractive, professional, middle-aged, Asian woman of Middle-Eastern descent said to a British white woman that she was "very beautiful because of your blue eyes, thick, blond hair and white skin." Suspecting that the admiration of the white woman stemmed from this Asian woman's self-loathing because she was not white-skinned, blue-eyed, and blond-haired but instead, was dark-haired, dark-complexioned and brown-eyed, I politely asked her if she also thought she was beautiful, to which she answered with no hesitation, "No!" Of course, I immediately asked her why she didn't think she was beautiful and her answer confirmed my suspicion. She went on to say that she has a cousin who is beautiful because her cousin has green eyes, pale brown skin which looks white, and that her cousin also has light brown hair. Needless to say, I spent a few moments trying to affirm this woman's beauty by informing her that as a woman who self-identifies as Asian, she should also regard her appearance as beautiful and that the world is a much better place for its ethnic diversity of peoples just like her. Alice Walker also says it well. The daughter asks, "Why are we brown, pink and yellow, and our cousins are white, beige and black?" and the mother replies, "Well you know the colored race is just like a flowered garden, with every color flower represented."[17] The daughter thus does not see herself as inferior as there is no hierarchy, but equality, of all races as defined by her mother through the flowers-garden.[18]

During my time at High Parish I met other Asian females who had dyed their hair blond soon after arriving and living in the UK. Whilst I have no objections to this, in and of itself, I wondered if dying their hair had anything to do with their rejection of their racial identity. Was dying their hair blond a "mask" for self-rejection? My enquiries revealed that some of them wanted "to fit into British society," "be British," "be accepted" and to show they are making every effort to meet the requirements to stay in the UK. However, other than for this reason, they were absolutely happy being Asian. For these women, it was about cultural belonging in their host country. Other enquiries revealed that dying their hair blond was about womanist resistance against and protest and liberation from their once repressive Iranian lifestyle where wearing the hijab (and other attire) was obligatory for Iranian females in Iran. It was used as the regime's control and power over them. For me, the wearing of traditional, cultural attire should always be about choice but these women's choices had been obliterated in Iran where Iranian females have no choice as to what they wear. Other enquiries showed colorism as the reason for the hair-dying since fitting into British society meant no longer loving their appearance as Asian women or practicing their national cultures. Incidentally, I also know Black females who have done the same for similar reasons to the ones mentioned here, while for others, it is a fashion and brand statement. In addition, one of the white female priests at High Parish also dyed her hair blond and straightened it from her natural curly dark brown hair. Their motives can all be varied: from womanist resistance, branding; following a fan-base; cultural association; or self-loathing and/or belonging. In the case of the white female priest, who is from a working-class background, it is about class-identification and belonging since Anglican priests traditionally identify as middle and upper classes. Whilst this book is about women of color, it is clear that self-hate and an identity crisis can affect all women (and men too) for different reasons if they do not fit the dominant cultures of beauty in colonized Britain.

17. Walker, "Womanist," 19.
18. Walker, "Womanist," 19.

For women of color, it is the acceptance of self-inferiority which, without recognition, healing, and change, has led to self-loathing and hate of others who look like us instead of self-love and love of others who resemble us. Systems of racism and sexism can lead Black and Brown females to self-hate and hate other Black and Brown females too. Institutional racism and sexist patriarchy can also lead to sexist and racist oppression and discrimination towards Black and Brown females by Black and Brown females. I discovered this when a Black woman minister in the Anglican Church admitted that the decolonization of the CoE liturgy was necessary but later took advantage of the kindness of a Black female professional who she sought for professional advice to assist in the decolonization of the liturgy. So the intersectionality of sexism and racism can lead to the dysfunctionality of self and in terms of Blackness and Brownness, it can also lead to racial inferior complexes with regards to other females who look like you.

In secular studies, Debbie Weekes also discovered colorism to be an issue among Black females.[19] Notwithstanding in her ground-breaking book, *Living While Black*, radical psychotherapist Guilaine Kinouani draws on and develops Joy Degruy's work on Post Traumatic Slave Syndrome (PTSS) to demonstrate that apart from everyday racism and microaggressions, Black people experience other racial traumas which are undoubtedly causal factors of racial inferiority complex. Kinouani shows that Black people internalize colonial socialization from generation to generation ("intergenerational trauma").[20] In *A Redemption Song*,[21] Delroy Hall also demonstrates the same from a perspective of Black British culture and pastoral theology when examining Black people generally and, specially, Black males. Kinouani and Hall demonstrate that a racial identity crisis and its links to self-hate can be deeper than sociological colorism. For them it is psychological and historical, what I call here psycho-historical trauma. To add, I would say that trauma could also be responsible for failure to accept and appreciate your own people—that is, those who look like ourselves. Under the Transatlantic Slave Trade, slaves learnt not to agree with the praise from slave masters/mistresses for their good performance or that of their biological relatives since this could

---

19. Weekes, "Shades of Blackness," 113–26.
20. Kinouani, *Living While Black*, 27–49.
21. Hall, *Redemption Song*, 183. On the issue of psychological therapeutic self-care for healing from racism, Bob Marley's "Redemption Song" reminds Black people "to free our minds from mental slavery."

lead to the separation of families in which families would never again be reunited. For example, if the slave master told a mother that her daughter Nelly was a good cotton-picker, the mother would possibly reply with something like, I think she could do much better. Enslaved women learnt not to say anything like, Oh yes sir. Nelly is very good.

Neither Kinouani and Hall write from the position of Brown/Asian people nor women respectively, but much of what they say as psychotherapists is useful as a basis for developing our epistemology on trauma for all people of color generally, and specifically, women of color. However, the combination of psycho-historical trauma and patriarchal oppression could also be responsible for racialized and socialized, misogynistic self-loathing by some Black and Brown females since patriarchal racism was also prevalent during slavery. I believed that the impact of the slave syndrome was apparent when I joined a local Baptist Church's women's gym on returning from the US in November 2009, only to later experience jealous mistreatment in the step-aerobics sessions from some of the Boomers and Post World War women of Jamaican origin because I was then quite fit and it showed. Similarly, in order to support their businesses, many professional and/or educated Christian Black females attended the salons of mainly Generation X and Boomer Christian Black female hairdressers in a certain city but later complained of being mistreated by them. Examples ranged from being deliberately burnt with curling tongs to cutting their hair too short when they required a trim. They are excessively over-charged since there is sometimes a wrongful assumption that these professionals and educated women are extremely wealthy. Pouring a whole sink of dirty water over them in front of other customers after a rinse, is another example.

When the Windrush Generation traveled to England and parents left their children in Jamaica with relatives, usually grandparents, with the hope of returning in five years' time but did not, this too led to trauma for some parents and children affected. Many of the Windrush Generation who lived in the UK were unable to return to Jamaica after five years as some of them could not afford to do so and/or their UK settlement, home, work, and/or church lifestyles prevented their return. However, they saved their often low incomes over years through partner schemes to "send"/pay for their children to be reunited in England. Apart from the pictures these children received from their parents in the barrels of food, clothing, and other useful items which their parents posted to their children in Jamaica every Christmas after they arrived in England, on meeting, these families found themselves reuniting with complete strangers.[22] A recent television and YouTube documentary, *Barrel Children*, captures this experience.[23] A minister of a Black church recently described the reaction of a relative who was left behind in Jamaica as "bitter." Whilst I accept that his intentions were pure towards his relative, I nonetheless thought his word-choice seemingly demonstrated the often misunderstanding regarding the adverse emotional impact of trauma this separation of parent from child can have on both parents and children even when these children are now adults and even when parents have expressed their unintentional desires to depart from Jamaica to England without their children. In many instances their then limited economic resources was the sole factor for their decision. The experience of trauma is perhaps similar to a child who badly reacts to the knowledge of being abandoned by their biological parents at birth only to be placed into institutional state or private residential care, fostered, and/or adopted. For some people the pain still exists when they are in happy homes and with loving foster or adopted parents whereas for other children, the gratitude of having loving and caring foster or adopted parents is sobering enough for them.

Kinouani and Hall point out that the effects of everyday and institutional racisms, slavery, and colonization may still be in Black people's DNA and has led to trauma and self-hate.[24] The trauma of Persian oppression on Iranian females (and males) who fled persecution and are congregants at High Parish at the time of this study, and then the daily suffering of knowing that they will never return to their homeland in person ever again to see their relatives whom they left behind, was noticeable. They often talked about "missing [their] parents," "not being able to hug my son. I only see him on Skype," "leaving their business," "leaving their house" and having "bank accounts frozen" in Iran and therefore losing all their wealth and having to start afresh in England. However, for all of them, the rebuilding of their lives begins when they receive their LTR immigration statuses which can often take years to process. Until then, these women are totally dependent on the generosity of others, charities, and High Parish in order to survive. The traumatic repercussions of asylum seekers and refugees at High Parish were/are great.

To add, Kinouani states that mass immigration in recent historical times, from the 1950s and 1960s, on the Windrush Generation and

22. Wikipedia, "Barrel Children."
23. White, *Barrel Children*.
24. Kinouani, *Living While Black*, 248. Hall, *Redemption Song*, 183.

their descendants, especially for those caught-up in the fallout of this due to recent Home Office errors of the labeling of British citizens as illegal through notions of the "hostile environment," is traumatically impacting on the psyche of Black people[25] of which women are included. It therefore also follows that Black and Brown women in the UK are also psychologically traumatized by migration too and thus affected by self-dislike if not complete self-hate. In addition, I believe the effects of the recent 2014 and 2016 Immigration Acts and ensuing immigration policies on all refugees and asylum seekers, including Black and Brown females, can also be detrimental to their mental well-being and lead to self-hate due to the absence of belonging and settlement. Furthermore, even successful economic migrants can also experience trauma which leads to self-hate especially for women of color.

In meeting diasporic Christian women who self-identify as Asian I observe something which is common to all of their experiences despite their ethnicities and that is, they have all fled or escaped from someone or something. They are either a convert to Christianity from another religious faith and have undergone immense trauma after the conversion such as the severing of family-ties and the impacts of abandonment which this experience has left them. Other examples are of Asian women who have fled their native lands through persecution for their Christian faith when other faiths are the national and cultural norm, political beliefs, or war and such like, and thus arrive in the UK as refugees and/or asylum seekers. There are others who flee domestic abuse and violence, threats of honor-killings and related issues from abroad and in the UK. Yet still, there are others who arrive in the UK for economic reasons, that is, to either find work or due to a work opportunity as economic migrants. In all cases, these Christian, Asian/Brown women find themselves having to navigate the new context of either country and/or the British church which is often unfamiliar and with people who are new and often different from the people they were previously acquainted. These experiences can inevitably lead to emotional and psychological trauma.

In addition to the trauma of displacement and unfamiliarity, when sexualized racism and racialized sexism and/or misogynoir are part of faith and spiritual systems and structures, such as the British church, this is even harder for Black and Brown females to accept since it is in these places where Black and Brown women expect and assume to find

---

25. Kinouani, *Living While Black*, 248.

acceptance and be loved, appreciated, and valued for who they are, that is, women of color who are created in the image of God. Both High Parish and Messa Pentecostal are part of denominations which have direct links to either the Transatlantic Slave Trade, such as the CoE, or white Holiness Movements in the US where racism was/still is rooted in the theology, as in some Pentecostal Black Churches. Brown and Black women and girls assume equality with other ethnic humans in Christianity and therefore expect pastoral care in places of faith. The absence of dignity and respect for Black and Brown women in the British church and associated communities can also lead to trauma and self-hate.

Having now established the scale of the problem of self-loathing as Black and Brown Sisters, I shall now explore the importance of self-love in terms of our well-being as Black and Brown Sisters since, by doing this, we are empowered and function as whole human beings, individually and collectively. Besides, as mentioned earlier, Black and Brown females are to love self regardless even when the church does not love us. Racial, ethnic, and cultural self-identifications in the context of self-love and self-care is the focus of the next section.

Self-Love and Self-Care

Prior to concluding this chapter I wish to focus on the issues of self-love, self-healing, and self-care for Black and Brown Sisters. It is vitally important to love self regardless as Black and Brown women who suffer patriarchy and the combination of sexual and racial discrimination in the world.[26] Self-love is essential even when something has gone wrong in our lives, or if you have experienced abuse or violation of whatever form. The impacts of the Transatlantic Slave Trade for many diasporic Black peoples, and/or colonialism for both Black and Brown peoples, means that racial purity is less likely since many of our ancestral mothers would have been forcibly impregnated by their slave masters and/or their male colonizers. Even with this knowledge we are to love ourselves as Black and Brown females. If "God demonstrates His own love for us in this: whilst we were still sinners, Christ died for us" (Rom 5:8 NIV) and continues to love us irrespective of our circumstances, as Brown and Black females, we deserve and are worthy of self-love. We cannot stop loving self!

---

26. hooks, *Sisters of the Yam*, 187.

For women of Asian origin who are generalized as sexually passive and docile in the British context, especially Muslim females where the seclusion of the veil, purdah, and harem reinforces these stereotypes, self-love is significant in your whole embodiment. For women of African and the Caribbean descendants who are stereotyped as, at best, flirtatious and, at worst, promiscuous, a "Sable Venus," sexual temptress, "she devil," and the "mule ah de world,"[27] it is important for us to love self for possessing real sensual feelings and expressing sexual affection without being ashamed or guilty of one's sexuality. God gave us those feelings to be used appropriately and responsibly in loving relationships and not to be repressed. With regards to women of faith, on the stereotypical point of promiscuous and flirtatious women of African and Caribbean descent, this negative stereotype is definitely untrue—a point I shall return to in *Community Womanism* when addressing the issue of Black female love.[28]

When compliments of others are granted, loving self also means accepting the genuine and generous compliments with regards to self. Furthermore, loving self means appreciating our personal or collective achievements. It means that as Black and Brown females we may, at times, have to "sing our own praises," that is, encourage ourselves, as others may not do so, so as to build our own self-confidence, self-esteem and value, in the hope that our worth will be recognized by church, faith communities, and wider societal communities. Accepting self must also recur even when validation and praise is not forthcoming from these systems. The discrimination of Black and Brown women means that we sometimes have to find the courage "to blow our own trumpets" and love and respect ourselves enough to do so. Whilst praising and thanking God, which Loyal Sisters will first accord to God, it is unsurprising to find Sisters of faith recognizing successes of others too. It is in the characteristics and nature of Loyal Sisters to do this:

To be a Better Human
I can never be like some humans
Because I am me.
Yet I admire the good in other humans,
I can never be,
And aspire to attain those good qualities
To be a better me.
So why should not I also try to possess

27. Bush, "Sable Venus,' 'She Devil' or 'Drudge,'?" 761–89.
28. McCalla, *Community Womanism*, forthcoming.

> As much of God as is possible,
> By Her grace,
> To be a better human?[29]

In addition, professional support, such as therapy and counseling, may be required to heal from the effects of racism as Kinouani and Hall[30] mention. I believe that in the case of Black and Brown women, professional therapy may also be required to overcome the impacts of sexism too and other connected intersectionalities. However, I note that professional help is often financially costly and may be out of the economic-reach for some Black and Brown females who are most likely to require its services since psychotherapy and similar services are often offered in the private healthcare sector and not the NHS apart from the basic provision which is free. Notwithstanding, self-care or self-help is also recommended by Kinouani such as "homeness" that is, as far as possible, to make your epistemic (body and mind), physical and cultural places and spaces welcoming, comfortable, and liveable so as to reduce stress and anxiety[31] which leads to trauma and thus self-unacceptance. Kinouani acknowledges that Christianity has led to trauma for some Black people due to its own oppressive systems of racism.[32]

In Robert Beckford's film documentary, *After the Flood*,[33] he acknowledges that racism can only be eradicated when the reconciliation between the British establishment and the British church and Black people, happens. He argues that Black people need to forgive the British church and the British establishment for the wrong done to us in the past, and especially during slavery. However, for Beckford, the church and establishment also have a responsibility to dismantle racism if the reconciliation is to ever occur. Whilst I accept that the British church and the establishment have a responsibility to eradicate racism, I acknowledge that this is very unlikely to happen until the British church and establishment first recognize the existence of racism in its institutions, and since institutional sexism and patriarchy also exists in the church too. These are oppressions which the church needs to acknowledge and then repent of them. Only then can the British church move from racial and sexist

---

29. I wrote this poem on October 10, 2010.
30. Kinouani, *Living While Black*, 248. Hall, *Redemption Song*, 183.
31. Guilaine Kinouani, *Living While Black*, 246.
32. Guilaine Kinouani, *Living While Black*, 246.
33. Beckford, *After the Flood*.

denial to racial and sexist acceptance which is required for repentance and change in it. Similarly, I also agree with Beckford that in order for change to happen, Black people must also reconcile with the British church through forgiving the church's sins of racism. However, for me, forgiveness of wrongs done to people of color by the British church is highly problematic for Black and Brown females if they are struggling to love their own Black and Brown selves.[34] The struggle to combat racist and misogynistic oppression and discrimination in the British church will prove very difficult and painful for Brown and Black women without self-love and self-confidence. Referring to Asian females, biblical theologian Mukti Barton demonstrates the impact of Westernized colonization on self-love and therefore a need for the decolonization and a realignment of self-imagine and self-love in society and the church.[35] How can anyone challenge systemic racism and sexism effectively when, as Black or Brown females, self-love of Black and/or Brown femaleness is lacking? So, for Brown and Black females, self-love must first take place, which can be obtained through the healing process from hurts of slavery and also from the past and present trauma of migration in the 1950s–1970s and/or currently as experienced by refugee and asylum seekers. Forgiveness of colonization and other forms of racialized sexism can then or simultaneously follow and more likely to truly take root. Similarly, when Iranian females self-love, their healing can begin since, for them, the reconciliation with their oppressors, the Iranian government, is unlikely to occur if they cannot return to Iran and do so. Besides, returning to Iran would be dangerous and possibly fatal for most if not all of them. For Iranian females, real forgiveness from historic slavery and persecution which was manifested through the torturous, military, and clerical regimes in Iran may take a lifetime but must start with self-love. Loving yourself and self-care is an act of resistance and protest[36] because oppressors cannot stop you from loving yourself. Furthermore, until Black and Brown women and girls accept ourselves, that is self-love ourselves, not only racially as Black and/or Brown, but as females too, we will struggle to counter institutional sexism and racism and this will prevent us from holding the British church to account for these isms. Self-love will lead females to challenge systems and structures, where Black and Brown females are underrepresented, that is, where no one in those systems or structure looks like them such as in

34. I develop the theme of forgiveness further in chapter 9.
35. Barton, "Skin of Miriam Became as White as Snow," 68–80.
36. bell hooks, *Sisters of the Yam*, 187.

some mainstream British churches. Together we will then be more mentally equipped to combat the combined effects of institutionalized racism and sexism, and individual racisms and sexisms too.

Self-love, self-appreciation, and self-acceptance are imperatives for navigating the British church as minority Black and Brown Loyal Sisters where racism and patriarchy are rampant. The impact of self-hate means that Black and Brown females can also be sexist and racist towards females of color, that is, sexism and racism may not only come from men. Only when Loyal Sisters' self-love is realized, their humanity and embodiment accepted and their racial insecurity overcome, will Loyal Sisters no longer seek the validation of white people or men to feel valued. When we truly appreciate and value ourselves as females of color, where we acknowledge ourselves as equally relevant as God's beautiful Loyal Sisters, like other humans (males or white women), will we do the same for other females like us too. Thriving Loyal Sisterhoods of love and support will then exist for every Sister.

Like Beckford in the *After the Flood* documentary[37] I also agree that reconciliation requires the role of the British church to relinquish power so that change can occur, since, for me, the requirement of Black and Brown women's forgiveness for racialized sexism and misogynoir alone will not bring institutional change to fruition in the British church nor reconciliation between, specially, women of color, and generally, people of color. Finding ways to self-love and self-care whilst healing and recovering from hurt by the church will combat the church's rejection of our self and help women of color to understand that there is a difference between the Love of God and the church—an institution which claims to love all humanity but may fail in its duty of love and care for all humans. Self-love can also aid our resistance against ecclesiastical, racist, and sexism oppression.

In his book, *Jesus is Dread*,[38] Beckford also proclaims that men should repent for their patriarchal sexism in the Black Church—something which he too is honest to admit is a personal requirement. I believe that male repentance can also aid self-love for women of color. Notwithstanding, for Christian Black and Brown females self-love should never be dependent or predicated on men's repentance since men may refuse to

---

37. Beckford, *After the Flood*.
38. Beckford, *Jesus is Dread*, 156.

repent and therefore refuse to reconcile with Christian women of color and therefore God's love for all humanity.

Kinouani and Hall also note that spirituality can be another form of therapy to combat racism for Black people.[39] In *Introducing Asian Feminist Theology*[40] Pui-lan surveys the cultural, social, and political context of Asian Chinese women's lives to discover the beginnings of Asian feminist consciousness in women's networks and organizations globally. From here she demonstrates Asian feminist theology and Asian religious traditions and critiques patriarchy in the church. She shows how God emerges and is reconstructed and immersed in the femininity and embodiment of Asian women's spirituality. I believe that this book is certainly informative and can be employed in the British context in terms of helping to explain some of what may also be happening to British diasporic Asian Christian women in British churches and can thus aid in their healing from racialized sexism in British Asian feminist spirituality and in the development of self-love and self-care.

Hall's interdisciplinary book[41] provides redemption and healing for Black people from racist trauma in the Eucharist. The bread is symbolic of Jesus's broken body and the wine, Jesus's shed blood in Jesus's crucifixion. Jesus's sharing of bread and wine with his disciples on the last Passover before his death and resurrection, now marked by Maundy Thursday in Britain, demonstrates Jesus's promise that s/he can similarly, share with Brown and Black females in our microaggressions and misogynoir. When the bread and wine are consumed in the Holy Communion it is a reminder of Jesus's deliverance from racist and sexist trauma. When Brown and Black women who struggle to self-identify and self-love their Brownness and Blackness and do not find answers in their everyday faith and in their churches, this is where more work needs to be done in the church context to engage Black and Brown women with themselves through recognizing the resurrected God in the *imago Dei* and the Communion/Eucharist.

The spirituality and pedagogy of self-love is not always practiced in our churches although the message of Christianity is one of God's love for humanity. We are told about God's love through Jesus but not encouraged to love-self in church. In our churches, we preach, sing, pray, and read Scriptures that God loves us such as demonstrated in John 3:16. However, some of our churches are void of self-love exaltations given our enslaved

39. Kinouani, *Living While Black*, 248. Hall, *Redemption Song*, 183.
40. Kwok, *Introducing Asian Feminist Theology*, 136.
41. Hall, *Redemption Song*, 183.

legacy of self-hate. The Scripture "love your neighbor as yourself" (Luke 10:27) is a rallying call to love others as we love ourselves. This Scripture assumes self-love. However, if our care for others is premised on a benchmark of self-hate of our womanhood and Blackness and Brownness and a failure to accept the mutual love relationship with God, this can be reflected in our hate for/unloved mistreatment of other human beings because we self-hate ourselves. However, spiritual redemption can also help us to self-love and self-care as discussed in chapter 9 in this book.

Conclusion

This chapter examined self-love and self-acceptance as a means to mental well-being, combating sexualized racism and misogynoir in the British church and communities at large, and for Black and Brown women to actively function in a Loyal Sisterhood. It shows that Black and Brown females also have some work to do on themselves in terms of self-love and the validation and acceptance of Black and Brown female identity. When Christian Brown and Black women have mental emancipation from sexualized and racialized inferiority complexes and fully accept our identities as women of color, we can then better understand the oppressive sins of racism and sexism and other intersectional factors which exist beyond us as humans; that is, within systems, structures, cultures, institutions, policies, and practices such as the British church.

The chapter notes that self-love and self-acceptance may not be easy for all Black and Brown females and Loyal Sisters due to racialized trauma associated with our inherited trauma from former generations, socialization, and sociality overtime. However, it recognizes that British diasporic Christian Black and Brown women can overcome traumatic self-hate for self-love and be productive Loyal Sisters in the British church and community. It is also only when Black and Brown women self-love and self-accept ourselves that Loyal Sisterhoods become meaningful, purposeful, and possible. It is when we self-love that we can appreciate others like ourselves, want to be among women who look like us, and question the absence of women and people who look like us in positive and affirmative roles in the church and in the public at large.

Finally, this chapter also recognizes that there is also a role for the church, that is, to change from its terror of intersectional racism and sexism and the oppression, discrimination, and repression of women of color in the church. With a willingness to change on the part of Black and Brown women in terms of self-love, self-care, and self-acceptance, and for the church to also change in terms of social injustice in the form of intersectional racism and sexism, this will hopefully and prayerfully bring about the full womanist spirituality and theology in praxis which is required in the British church.

Thoughts for Reflection and Appraisal

1. Love-self, for in doing so, Loyal Sisters can truly accept self as Black and Brown and female and beautiful and simultaneously value their self-worth. Discuss.

2. How can a Loyal Sisterhood support Brown and Black females as a relevant and affective network for therapeutic, spiritual, and pastoral self-care?

3. Is the British church, that is Black and multicultural churches and mainstream churches, doing enough so that effective womanist reconciliation can occur as discussed in this chapter?

9

Spiritual Redemption and Transcendence

Spirit of the Living God,
Fall afresh on me/[us];
Spirit of the Living God,
Fall afresh on me/[us].
Break me/us, Melt me/[us],
Mould me/us, Fill me/[us],
Spirit of the Living God,
Fall afresh on me/[us].[1]

How do we really engage the Anglican Church generally, and the CoE specifically, into purposeful womanist action in terms of change for women of color since it is the establishment church which still owns so much wealth and assets in the UK and globally? So far in this book, I stated that the British church, including the Anglican Church and Black and multicultural denominations, must acknowledge that there is racialized and sexualized patriarchy and other issues in the church, and the

---

1. Iverson, "Spirit of the Living God," 1926. I have added the word, Us for the purpose of this book. Later lyrics of this hymn have used the words "Melt me, Mold me, Fill me, Use Me."

adverse effects of such patriarchy on the spirituality, well-being, ministry, and productivity of Christian Black and Brown females; notably Loyal Sisters. Secondly, I pointed out that the British church needs to work towards eliminating the intersectionality of racism and sexism for the amelioration of the whole body of Christ and notably women of color. I showed that the impact and legacy of the Transatlantic Slave Trade, of racism and sexism, still remains today whilst also acknowledging that the British church's repentance is warranted to repair the damage and hurt done by it. Similarly, in chapter 8, I mentioned that womanist reconciliation requires women of color to forgive the systemic sins of racism, sexism, and misogynoir enacted by whiteness and/or maleness in the British church. The reconciliation requires both sides to change since for far too long Black and Brown people, including women of color, are required to forgive the British church's past and present sins of racism and racialized sexism and thus move on while the sinful pride and the failure to relinquish misogynist power continues in the British church. So given the present situation, my trust is in God for womanist action and change. In chapter 8 I also acknowledged that females of color are God's creation too, loved by God and can find healing from historic and current trauma for their holistic well-being.

This chapter starts with a section on womanist resistance and spiritual transcendence. The next section examines the theme of healing through the Holy Spirit. The third section addresses the spirituality of forgiveness. The following two sections explores womanist decolonization of Scripture and liturgical practices for application in the British church and communities. The next section discusses redemptive hope followed by a section on community solidarity. Section eight provides encouragement for Loyal Sisters, notably High Parish Sisters, to hope in God as spiritual redemption is possible when faced with the impacts of migration and suffering in the UK. Still building on the theme of hope, the next section attempts to provide spiritual answers to injustices in this current life, that is, through eschatological justice. The conclusion and final section provides and summation of this chapter.

Womanist Resistance and Spiritual Transcendence

Delores Williams argues that African American women's struggles and sufferings are redemptive through the cross.[2] A powerful gospel hymn demonstrates this. The chorus is below:

> Kneel at the cross.
> Leave every care.
> Kneel at the cross.
> Jesus will meet you there.[3]

Similarly, editing *Hope Abundant*, Kwok Pui-lan includes essays of emerging voices and new developments in the global South of indigenous women, Eastern Asians, and other women who face poverty, violence, and war and yet find abundant hope through their faith.[4] I would also concur that any analysis of social justice, recognition, appreciation, elevation, and emancipation of Brown and Black women must also consider redemption for British Loyal Sisters, Sisterhood faith, and Black and Brown women everywhere. Failure to do so leaves a significant vacuum in womanist spirituality and theology. For it is only through some type of redeeming grace that Brown and Black women can find hope, peace, solace, and a purposeful life as noted particularly by Emilie Townes when addressing concerns of African American women in her anthology and authored texts.[5]

I would argue that British Sisters do not "love struggle"[6] as Alice Walker states, but, as anything else life throws at us, British Loyal Sisters can deal and cope with struggles when they arise because of their strong faith in the Divine and established church Sisterhood bonds. An act of resistance and protest from oppression is to love God in spite of patriarchal oppression as Loyal Sisters demonstrate by their actions. Through metaphoric language, Laini Mataka, in her poem, *"Bein' a Strong Black Woman Can Get You Killed"*[7] also shows this. Black and Brown women are strong because they do feel stress and undergo struggle but they continue to serve the church and community tirelessly despite their unfortunate circumstances. Mataka allows the Black woman to be human,

---

2. Williams, *Sisters in the Wilderness*, 260.
3. "Kneel at the Cross." Composed by Charles E. Moody, 1924.
4. Pui-Lan, *Hope Abundant*, 288.
5. See Townes, *Embracing the Spirit*, 325. Townes, *Womanist Justice, Womanist Hope*, 228. See also Terrell, *Power in the Blood?*, 200.
6. Walker, *In Search of Our Mother's Gardens*, xi–xii.
7. Mataka, *Bein' a Strong Black Woman Can Get You Killed*, 112.

like Black and white men and white women. She is no superwoman. The Black woman can be excused for not being perfect and not having to live up to often unrealistic expectations of her from others:

> She died from myths that would not allow her to show weakness without being chastised by the lazy and hazy. She died from hiding her real feelings.

It would appear as you read Mataka that the lamentable life of the Black woman is doomed to destruction and hopelessness. But suddenly, and without warning, her momentary despair and supposed agony transforms into a mirage. A gospel spiritual, "I've Got One Thing You Can't Take Away,"[8] demonstrates this.

Simultaneously, the Black woman is made to seem invincible by Mataka because, despite her lamentable ordeal, she does not die. In reality, the Black woman lives. She *refuses* to die! Her mental and emotional strength is demonstrated in her commitment, figuratively, not to die. They are Loyal Sisters! As living visible beings, Black and Brown women bring hope which Loyal Sisters exude too in the British church and communities. They establish themselves overtime. They can thus be unique individuals and not necessarily be like another Black and Brown female, within and beyond the British church and Black and Brown communities. Instead, Black and Brown woman exchange death for life. They join with their Sisters in their incremental quest for emancipation, justice, elevation and hope. An African spiritual song, "If You Believe and I Believe,"[9] depicts this.

Obtaining freedom for Loyal Sisters is spiritually redemptive. However, complete freedom predicates redemptive healing which I shall discuss in the next section.

Healing by the Holy Spirit

In chapter 8 I mentioned that one of the possible reasons for self-hate, which some Loyal Sisters are still attempting to overcome in the British church, is due to the slave syndrome (physical, emotional, and psychological traumas) which dates back to the Transatlantic Slave Trade. I also discussed the necessity of Loyal Sisters' self-love and self-care in a church sorority of collective support which is free of selfishness, and for them to

---

8. Wallace and Might Clouds of Joy, "I've Got One Thing You Can't Take Away."
9. Bell, "If You Believe and I Believe," a Zimbabwean tradition hymn/folk-song.

also validate and accept their own Black and/or Brown female identity and selves. I pointed out that this is necessary since the absence of self-love and self-care can prevent Loyal Sisters from challenging combined racist and sexist practices in the British church and may prevent them from holding the British church to account for these practices if they have not fully accepted themselves and therefore are still questioning their worth. Loyal Sisters' self-hate can also enable the British church to continue its terror of systemic and intersectional racism and sexism and the oppression, discrimination, and repression of women of color in and out of the British church.

Black and Brown females can respond in various ways to healing their brokenness and to helping themselves to love and care for selves in the church; not only as individuals but as a community, a town/city, country, and world. One such way is by conducting annual healing services in which congregants are given space and time to seek and pray for healing of selves from the slave syndrome and other types of traumas which life has inflicted on them due to their combined race and womanhood. However, for Loyal Sisters to heal they must be willing to reconcile with the British church whether this is a Black, multicultural, and/or mainstream white church. This reconciliation means forgiving the sins of the present and past; not just the sin by the church but what others have done to them. In her biblical encouragement to women, Margaret Aymer recognizes the importance of confession as depicted in the beatitudes since God is for the oppressed.[10] In Matt 5:23–24 a spiritual instruction is given.

> Therefore, if you are offering your gift at the altar and there remember your brother or sister have something against you, leave your gifts there in front of the altar. First be reconciled to them; then come and offer your gift.

However, this reconciliation also means the British church has a responsibility to action change for its sins of misogynoir and racialized sexism towards Loyal Sisters and women of color everywhere. With a willingness to change on the part of both the church and Black and Brown women, together both agencies will hopefully and prayerfully bring about the womanist theological praxis which is required in the British church. Notwithstanding, womanist healing should never rely on the change from the British church. Womanist spiritual redemption requires Black and Brown

---

10. Aymer, *Confessing the Beatitudes*.

females to do whatever is necessary to obtain our healing, freedom, peace, and joy. Once we have done our part, godly justice and vengeance will be actioned by God for unrepentant churches; "vengeance is mine; I will repay, says God" (Rom 12:19), and as I shall discuss below. Spiritual transcendence often follows Loyal Sisters' commitment to God.

Healing services for the love of selves, especially among Black and Brown females, can possibly concur with Black History Month, International Women's Month, Christian seasons of Lent and/or Advent and/or other convenient times in the sacred calendar. These services may also recur for the whole church and not for Loyal Sisters alone. This time must also recognize Jesus's presence beside us every day when the burden gets too heavy to bear and when life's evils have impacted on our spiritual well-being too. Healing services from self-hate must also acknowledge that healing from trauma may require time; that is, it might necessitate a process and overtime rather than be instantaneous. Isa 61:3, "[S]He Gave Me Beauty for Ashes,"[11] is a process of healing in song.

For some Brown and Black females, seeking therapy and pastoral care from established faith institutions, such as the British church, is a big ask since, in some instances, much of the effects of self-hate have been generated from the same racialized and sexist faith systems of oppression. Healing services therefore must also be places which are free of guilt-tripping, shame and blame. Loyal Sisters should experience genuine love and pastoral care in these services. In other instances, I recognize that for some Loyal Sisters, Divine intervention is the only help necessary to heal and recover from self-loathing to self-love and self-acceptance and the effects of racialized sexism and misogynoir. It is therefore at these times that therapeutic self-care is most required and is effective, reliable, and spiritual in church Sisterhoods which are active supportive pastoral networks for Black and Brown females. Carol Wilson-Frith and Kevin Simpson reminds us of this in their song:

> Peace in my/[our] soul.
> Peace in my/[our] soul.
> What a wonderful peace in my/[our] soul;
> That comforts my[our] broken spirit,
> And makes me/[us] feel whole.
> What a wonderful peace in my/[our] soul.
> What a wonderful peace in my/[our] soul.[12]

11. Manzano, "He Gave Me Beauty for Ashes," composer; Robert Norton, arranger.
12. Wilson-Frith and Simpson, "Peace in My Soul." This song is composed by a

This now brings me to consider the spirituality of forgiveness more broadly.

Forgiveness

How does a Black mother, such as Gee Walker, find inner peace and emancipation without some form of redemption after the lost of her innocent 18-year-old son, Anthony Walker, on July 29, 2005? Anthony was brutally murdered by an ice axe in a racist attack in McGoldrick Park, Huyton, Merseyside, England. How does Mrs. Walker, and other mothers like her who have lost a child through tragic circumstances as in Anthony's case, get through each day without desiring to seek retaliation against the perpetrators and possibly even God? As devout Christians, how do they exist without resorting to redemptive salvation and hope? Despite the devastation experienced by Anthony Walker's family, friends, and mourners, the wake of Anthony's death—a type of undeserved suffering—can be redeemed. This is because the terrible killing of Anthony sets at fortissimo that good can be obtained from evil. It is substantiated in particular by the many virtuous responses. One remarkable response to the killing was the reaction of Gee and Anthony's sister, Dominique. My letter to Gee and Dominique in 2006 shows this.

> I have been particularly moved by your courage and devotion to God in the midst of adversity. Your willingness to forgive those who harmed not only Anthony with his life, but your family, emotionally and psychologically, has given fresh understanding to the meaning of the word "forgiveness." This is especially true as hate and revenge is commonplace in society. If this was all that you were able to teach humanity about God's love for the killing of your Anthony, then that would be redemptive enough. . . In my opinion, you are both women who are worthy of honour yourselves. Whilst you would certainly not wish to have become known through the death of Anthony, his death has nonetheless, revealed two female heroines as a model for all people; women, men and children, and especially for Black women, in the World.[13]

British Christian Black female and her Christian brother in the faith. This song was frequently sang in Church of God of Prophecy Conventions, nationally and locally in London. I have included the collective pronoun in brackets for sororities in the church or elsewhere.

13. McCalla, *Unsung Sheroes in the Church*, 4–5.

Whilst, understandably, many people who are unrelated to the killing would have chosen to hate the white males for killing a blameless Black youth, as members of Anthony's family, Gee and Dominique, nonetheless chose to forgive them. In 2017, 11 years on after Anthony's death, Gee Walker reveals in an interview with the then Archbishop of York, Rt. Rev. Dr. John Sentamu, that despite the loss of her son, she still forgives his killers and has found strength to carry on because of her Christian faith.[14]

It is the ability to find redemption in the midst of despair, in what is one of the most unnatural of human behaviors (through forgiveness), that I believe qualifies Gee and Dominique for Sisterhood status. Their forgiveness has thrust the Christian concept of forgiveness into the public domain and provoked others to question, whether for better or worse, their own dealings in this area. A more plausible and possibly a more acceptable reaction to such atrocity would be bitterness and resentment. Yet, Dominique and Gee decided against these; not solely for their own sake, but by doing so have also aroused the conscience of society. Of course, both women are humans and therefore it would be especially difficult for any loving mother and sister to forgive the perpetrators. They voluntarily chose to, as indeed, forgiveness should always be volunteered; not a forced action by anyone upon victims, and especially not by perpetrators and their associates. For forgiveness really comes from God and only God has the power to totally forgive, so it therefore follows that such acts of forgiveness requires godliness. Notwithstanding, further examination of the concept would reveal religious and philosophical complexities too. For example, does forgiveness mean forgetting? Is it a sign of weakness or strength to forgive? Does forgiving others mean that victims should not feel and manifest anger and pain? Does forgiveness constitute striving for justice for victims and others concerned? Even Gee and Dominique sought justice for their Anthony and expressed emotional pain, but they also decided to forgive the perpetrators. The white men who killed Anthony are now serving life-imprisonment "at Our Majesty's pleasure." They are being punished for their crime. Justice is seen in public action.

Womanist spiritual transcendence can occur in many other ways which is also spiritually redemptive. Another way is through womanist decolonization of Scripture where I focus my attention in the next section.

---

14. BBC, "Dr. John Sentamu Interviews Gee Walker."

Womanist Biblical Hermeneutics for the Decolonization of Scripture

In addition to the many inaccurate documentary evidences about Black and Brown women, the Bible itself is also found wanting. Its often imprecise portrayal of women has resulted in the legitimization of sexist and racist patriarchal discrimination and the misunderstanding of Scripture by readers, both men and women. Black and Brown female biblical scholars have thus responded by rewriting Scripture and other biblical texts to demonstrate the reality of Black and Brown women's experience in the Bible. In some cases, this has shown their glorification and at other times their unification, and similarly, their diversities. Renita Weems and Delores Williams, African American womanist theologians, discuss the significance of the social and political relationships of Black women in the Bible, such as revealed in the portraits of the queen of Sheba and Hagar.[15] Through close examination of the *Damascus Document*, one of the core documents of the Dead Sea Scrolls, Cecilia Wassen[16] discovers, in contrast to many scholars, that women were active participants in various biblical communities, despite patriarchal practices, especially with regards to the importance given to their womanhood. British Black and Brown females are also active in the contemporary British church. For the Bible and other theological sources to be applicable to real experiences of British Black and Brown females, womanist reinterpretation must begin and continue. Elaine Foster[17] and Valentina Alexander[18] argue that the way Black churches can begin to abolish sexism is to celebrate the achievement of Black women. Often homiletics and liturgical hermeneutics provide limited or no answers for specifically the emancipation of Black and Brown females. In fact, some rereading of Scripture only serves to suppress and oppress women and portray women negatively rather than liberate them and focus on their positive attributes. On the other hand, although some rereading may clearly demonstrate the struggles and survival of Black and Brown women, few seldom adequately go beyond the women's experiences. As enquiring readers we are thus left asking, how are Black and Brown women freed or elevated by their experiences? We do not know how this epistemology is emancipatory and

---

15. Weems, *Just a Sister Away*, 145. Williams, *Sisters in the Wilderness*, 260.
16. Wassen, *Women and the Damascus Document*, 272.
17. Foster, "Women and the Inverted Pyramid," 45–68.
18. Alexander, "Mouse in a Jungle," 85–106.

empowering for Black and Brown females of the African, Asian, and Caribbean diaspora in the British church, home, and community. Womanist biblical reinterpretations can answer these questions. They can represent and capture Black and Brown women's womanhood and sexuality, female derogation, and subjugation; their social and socioeconomic productivity and activism; their worldviews; and find solutions to their oppression and discrimination. Through womanist biblical and theological hermeneutics, the inaccurate documentary evidence about Brown and Black women in relation to the church and community can be rectified and provide spiritual redemption. With reference to the book of James and through biblical hermeneutics, Margaret Aymer asks how the Bible can be used as a liberationist tool by showing how community action in the diaspora can bring freedom from gendered[19] power relations for biblical migrants.[20] Wilda Gafney's Black feminist and womanist translations of biblical text is also revolutionizing our understanding of the racialized and gendered female stories for all the world and church to see.[21] We can do the same from stories of Black and Brown women in church and society and especially for migrant females in this book. The implication of rereading Scripture from and for Black and Brown female's perspectives would result in freedom and social justice for women of the Caribbean, African, and Asian diaspora in Britain and ultimately, Black and Brown females everywhere.

Trying to dismiss the gender inequalities in the Bible is plausible through context theology. The Bible generally favors males over females because of the biblical context of sexual/gender discrimination that existed in the lives of biblical characters. This is specifically in relations to leadership and in the roles they operated in their private and public lives; through their culture and ethnicities, nations and nationalities, and in specific timeframes. When applied to British diasporic women and in twenty-first-century Britain, biblical female discriminations are wholly unacceptable and cannot be justified. Black and Brown feminist and womanist theologies and Sisterhoods therefore play an integral role in levelling the gender playing field and liberating females of color.

---

19. Aymer uses gender here in its binary form as men and women.

20. Aymer, *James*, 102.

21. Gafney, *Women's Lectionary for the Whole Church: Year A*, 360; Gafney, *Women's Lectionary for the Whole Church: Year B*, 362; Gafney, *Women's Lectionary for the Whole Church: Year W*, 360.

Decolonizing Scriptures from a contextual stance thus enables the rereading of them from and for Brown and Black women's standpoints.[22] Take for instance the books of Esther and Ruth, Jesus's encounter with the Samaritan woman (John 4:1–42), Deborah (Judg 4 and 5 and Heb 11:32–34), Dorcas (Acts 9:36–43), Lydia (Acts 16:12–15, 40; Phil 1:1–10), Hannah (1 Sam 1; 2:1), and the parable of the persistent widow (Luke 16: 1–8). The biblical narrative can be adapted to demonstrate Brown and Black women's injustice and then the processes towards liberation, justice, and restoration in which Scripture is rewritten from Black and/or Asian feminist and/or womanist perspectives. These Scriptures can be used as theological underpinnings to illustrate a biographical version and interpretation of the personal, professional, and church lives of Brown and Black Christian females in Britain and the world in which the experience of the biblical women depicts their ontology.

These biblical texts can show how God can break down barriers of racism, sexism classism, ageism, colonialism, and other forms of biases, through her Divine encounter with Brown and Black women as demonstrated by Mukti Barton.[23] The Samaritan woman, for example, actively challenges sexism through countering conventional patriarchal stereotypes and the sexual tensions in biblical society in which women are regarded as inferior to men. She challenges racism, classism, and cultural and religious biases where the history of the Jewish and Samaritan conflict is addressed and racial, class, cultural, and religious antagonism is exposed and challenged. A womanist or Black and/or Asian feminist biblical hermeneutics of the Samaritan woman can be employed to deconstruct the relationship between patriarchy and colonialism and its effects on Brown and Black women in Britain. Thus this Scripture can be used to emancipate Brown and Black Christian women from oppressive patriarchy, racial discrimination, and class oppression[24] including the legitimization of severance of God's people which is purported within the infamous Indian caste system.[25] Notwithstanding, from my interaction

---

22. Dube, *Postcolonial Feminist Interpretation of the Bible*, 232. Hyun Kyung, *Struggle to Be Sun Again*, 200.

23. Barton, *Scripture as Empowerment for Liberation and Justice*, 195. Barton, *Liberation Spirituality as a Signal of Transcendence*, 26. Barton, *Creation and Fall and the Women of Bangladesh*, 56.

24. Barton, "Reinterpreting Hagar and the Woman of Samaria in the Context of Bangladeshi Women," 19. Barton, "Wrestling with Imperial Patriarchy," 7–25.

25. Kumari, "Untouchable "Dalits" of India and their Spiritual Destiny," 9–19. Barton, "Race, Gender, Class and the Theology of Empowerment," 225–37.

with British diasporic Christian Indian women it is clear that some of them belong to low Indian castes, such as Dalits, whilst they are more liberated in the UK than they would be in India. Others are also part of a higher strata but some also experience patriarchy in the British church regardless of their Indian caste position.

Biblical hermeneutics can aid in the analysis of identity articulations of Brown and Black church women in terms of their combined racial, gendered, religious, and leadership positions. It enables the expressed realities and the examination and re-examination of British Christian Brown and Black women in and beyond the church. From Jesus's discussion with the Samaritan woman and her immediate reaction to the conversation, we also get a sense of her as a leader. She returns to the city and starts an evangelistic campaign. Deborah was a leader of God's people and so was the woman at the well. Dorcas and Lydia were both professional businesswomen. Hannah was a spiritual, devout, and caring mother. Her value as a mother is equally recognized in Brown and Black women's biblical hermeneutics. Biblical hermeneutics dismisses the problematics of Brown and Black women in leadership and thus empowers women and aligns them in the will of God as they were created. These biblical church and secular leaders and others can be used to explore and/or develop appropriate leadership paradigms for Brown and Black women. Since the Bible is a manuscript which demonstrates the inclusive image of God (*imago dei*)[26] as well as the *lagos*, womanist biblical hermeneutics allows British Christian Brown and Black women to illuminate their unique identities and a Christian womanist or Black and Asian feminist ontology of being human. This section thus shows that it is possible to decolonize Scripture through womanist biblical hermeneutics. Womanist decolonization can also be applied to church liturgy and practice for spiritual redemption to which I now turn my attention.

Womanist Decolonization of Church Liturgy for Praxis

Womanist Liturgy and Messa Pentecostal and High Parish

In studying the liturgies, service sheets, and programs used at Messa Pentecostal and/or High Parish it is clear that they also lacked a womanist perspective in praxis although they attempted to include some racial and

---

26. Barton, *Liberation Spirituality as a Signal of Transcendence*, 26.

national diversity. In a discussion with one of the ministers at High Parish on January 6, 2021, it was apparent that racial and womanist liturgical reforms are required to the litany in the BCP, the traditional prayer book of the CoE since 1662. This is due to its overemphasis on the diction "miserable sinners" and therefore its apparent focus on metaphorical religious flagellation.

> Me: For people who suffer with guilt, low self-esteem, low self-acceptance, and self-condemnation, the constant reminder of them being "miserable sinners" when they are struggling with being themselves, can only affirm that guilt and prevent them from accepting God's love for themselves which is required in salvation and forgiveness from sins committed or omitted whilst acknowledging our sins and repenting of them every day.
>
> Priest replies: It's all been revised on later liturgies but this old version is still on the books and is still officially the prayer book of the church and is the root of Anglican Prayer. One of the abiding criticisms of 1662 is it's over concern with penitence as you also point out.
>
> Me: I agree with that.

The immigration process itself forces some Brown and Black women into an identity crisis in terms of race and womanhood. Some of the church's liturgies may not be helpful when faced with such trauma. The decolonization of some of the liturgy is therefore necessary for meaningful reconciliation between Black and Brown females and the church. By staying in mainstream churches despite their colonized liturgy, Loyal Sisters can assist attempts to decolonize the church, and High Parish specially, for all people of color and especially women of color.

In Anglo-Catholicism in the Anglican Church and Catholicism, worshipers entreat Mary to accompany them when they pray to God. According to Anglo-Catholics, Heb 12:1 refers to this accompaniment of saints and is especially noted for the "Hail Mary" prayers. By doing so worshipers show respect and reverence to Mary, the virgin mother of Jesus, and who was also a Jewish-Christian woman of Israel and therefore likely to also be a woman of color. The decolonization of church liturgy may also mean evoking female spirits of Black and Brown ancestors in prayers and preaching. This practice would not mean that intercessors and preachers are praying or preaching to these female ancestors or requesting of them any response to their prayers which can only be answered by God. Instead, this practice of invoking the spirits would be in keeping with biblical traditions. Religious patriarchs such as, Abraham, Isaac, and Jacob, are often mentioned by Jews during their prayers or religious actions and as they pray to YHWH. However, I am here suggesting the mentioning of ancestral spiritual matriarchs in our womanist decolonizing programs and worship and not the invoking of patriarchal presence into womanist prayers if such a practice is to be adhered to at all.

Some Christian traditions liken all Pentecostal worshipers to "happy clappy," because there is no defined liturgical expression as is common to Anglicanism. In Pentecostalism there is therefore more flexibility for womanist decolonization. Messa Pentecostal can also embrace womanist songs, prayers and language, to name some suggests, in its services, especially in women's ministries. Similarly, it is important that Messa Pentecostal seeks God so as to maintain and/or restore Pentecostal theology and spirituality in its worship generally. The outpouring of spiritual gifts such as divine healing, speaking in tongues (*xenolalia* and *glossolalia*), and prophesying, having a personal relationship with Jesus through salvation/repentance of sin (*soteriology*), sanctification and holiness, preaching and biblical authority, Christian missions and revivalism, genuine discernment of spirits and characters, immersion baptism and baptism of the Holy Ghost, and the eschatology and end-times, to name some manifestations of the Holy Ghost, and coupled with a strong Bible base[27] are common to Pentecostal theology and spirituality. Womanist spirituality can be incorporated into Pentecostal worship and services.[28]

Womanism: A Conversation on Liturgical Research

In a conversation with a CoE, Black female priest in 2022 we noted that the British church's liturgy requires womanist decolonization in order to serve the full body of Christ and the church. We discussed going beyond a general racial justice project since, in the CoE, Black and Brown people are often expected to engage in that area. We therefore determined that an intersectional and interdisciplinary research approach into women of

---

27. Land, *Pentecostal Spirituality*, 239 Hollenweger, *Pentecostals*, 588. Hollenweger, *Pentecost between Black and White*, 128. Hollenweger, *Pentecostalism*, 512. Cox, *Fire from Heaven*, 376. Cox, "Foreword," 13–15. Gerloff, *Plea for British Black Theologies*, 1086. Hill, *Black Churches*, 23. Hill, "From Church to Sect," 114–23.

28. Alexander, "Mouse in the Juggle," 85–106.

color was definitely required. It was also important to produce a practical liturgy that could help all races in our endeavors for greater equality/equity, diversity, and inclusion (EDI) as well as women of color and Black people in churches and congregants. We were not concerned with only a womanist liturgy for lifelong learning and/or professional and spiritual development of individuals. We therefore discussed the possibilities of producing church service womanist liturgy as well as prayers/devotionals. We stated that this could either be done by creating a new liturgical formation from either an already existing liturgy such as the BCP or by producing a completely new liturgy. The priest is of African descent and interested in hidden disabilities so we acknowledged some of the existing body of research which featured African women and HIV-AIDS.[29] We mentioned that a proposed liturgical study could not only draw and expand on these existing epistemologies into hidden disabilities and women of color but could also incorporate autobiographical and biographical ministerial experiences.

We imagined a liturgy in which the content would not comprise of or be influenced by the British and whiteness. Is it possible to produce such a project since all the Anglican liturgy appears to be influenced by white Britishness. For example, how could a completely African and/or Asian liturgy be produced since the Britishness of the Anglican Church is already very apparent in African and Asian churches globally through centuries of colonization? The Black female priest was very keen to point out that this was very apparent to her from her many travels to Africa and that BCP was a case in point where its layout and language is British and that this was disappointing to her when it was used in Africa. I pointed out that this is because these African churches belong to the Anglican Communion and therefore the Anglican Church. To decolonize the BCP is important as it presently focuses on Britain and therefore only Britishness. It fails to account for the national, racial, and cultural diversity of the global church too, that is the Anglican Communion. A womanist stance is also exempt from the current BCP. Currently, the BCP is therefore an exclusive and not inclusive prayer book which expects global assimilation as a given. It focusing on the universality of the Anglican Church and therefore the British diasporic community as a whole. I pointed out that as far as I am aware there are no current womanist liturgies of the type we were imagining in

---

29. See Dube, *The HIV and AIDS Bible*, 176. Dube and Musimbi Kanyoro, *Grant Me Justice*, 224. Gichaara, "Women, Religio-cultural Factors and HIV/AIDS in Africa," 188–99 Nadar and Phiri, "HIV Research, Gender and Religion Studies," 632–38.

Spiritual Redemption and Transcendence

the British Anglican Church. From a womanist interfaith stance, Jensen and Harris-Watkins produced a prayer book which allows women in the US (and elsewhere) to pray in their own gendered way in the Anglican tradition.[30] However, I pointed out that its focus on the US and Native Americans could mean that references and some of the language in it are not understood by and/or apply to diasporic British women of color or women of the African, Caribbean, Middle Eastern or Asian Continents. It was therefore apparent that a relevant liturgy is necessary for women of color from these continents and/or the British diaspora.

It was evident that what the British diasporic Black female priest and I were imagining was methodologically challenging but possible for specifically, in this case, diasporic British Black women and African and Caribbean women. I pointed out that in order to sufficiently decolonize the liturgy from Britishness, as far as this is possible, an ethnographic research project of an immersion into a traditional, African tribal community should be considered. This could involve carrying out research with the females of that tribe; that is an exploration into an African tribe which has not been colonized and still practices conventional African traditions and spirituality. In order to discover hidden disabilities, this immersive project could explore traditional prayers and rituals for healing the body, spirit, and mind and to whom these prayers are made and rituals given and the outcome of them. I pointed out that African American womanist theological anthropologist Linda Thomas, investigated healing in South Africa where African spirituality was also employed. However, her exploration was in a small Christian church[31] not a traditional African tribe. I pointed out that in this case, after the fieldwork is completed, the tribe's African spirituality and relevant traditions can then be translated into Christianity through hermeneutical tools. This translation of language, context, and spirituality can then be used to create a liturgy for the CoE and the wider Anglican Church. We named a few British universities and global academics and ministers who were likely to engage with this idea too and thus support the operationalization of it. We acknowledged that the required reason for research on the decolonization of liturgy with women and disabled people for the CoE is because the current Anglican liturgy is racist, sexist, and ableist. However, I noted that even with a study of this type it may not be completely void of European colonization

---

30. Richardson Jensen and Harris-Watkins, *She Who Prays*, 212.
31. Thomas, *Under the Canopy*, 174.

since the researcher's role plays a significant part in ethnographic research. I mentioned that a Christian Black female, like the priest who is African, is already affected by British colonization as would be any other researcher whose lived experience and ancestry is impacted by the empire and colonization. If possible, an insider researcher from the African tribe would therefore aid in the decolonization of the project and can be a gate-keeper in any prospective study since that person will come from an insider perspective. For example, although not ethnographers, being Christian Native Americans with knowledge and experience of a variety of religious experiences, including traditional Native American spirituality, certainly helped Jensen and Harris-Watkins produce their womanist interfaith prayer book.[32] The possibility of producing a womanist anthropological spiritual project of the discursive-type had between the priest and me, for Britain and the rest of the world, excited us.

It is with this excitement I now turn to address the topic of redemptive hope:

Redemptive Hope

In addition to forgiving the perpetrators of the horrific crime against their loved-one, Anthony Walker as mentioned above, Gee and Dominique

> sought other means of giving back to society, through establishing the Anthony Walker Foundation, whilst honouring Anthony's memory, amongst other things (My letter).[33]

Gee and Dominique, like Baroness Doreen Lawrence, Caribbean mother of 18-year-old teenager, Stephen Lawrence, who in 1993 was murdered in London through a similar racially motivated killing, have redeemed the deaths of their children by setting up memorials or charities, that is community projects which are chaired by Black females. Similarly, Caribbean mothers of teenagers Charlene Ellis and Latisha Shakespeare, in Birmingham, England, and Danielle Beccan in Nottingham, England, have done the same. These young women and girl were murdered through notorious Black-on-Black gang-style drive-by shootings in 2003 and October 2004 respectively. These memorials and charities are designed to promote worthy projects for youngsters in local communities

---

32. Richardson Jensen and Harris-Watkins, *She Who Prays*, 212.
33. McCalla, *Unsung Sheroes in the Church*, 57.

who are either related to an interest of the child victims or attempt to campaign against the evil that killed them. I also established Divine Ministries Education Enterprise (Nonprofit) Ltd in 2017 during my time of hardship. The PersonalCare Bank which I started in 2015, was one of the projects of spiritual redemption which emerged from this not-for-profit organization, and in which hope also emanated from establishing it. Although the organization and project is still developing and much work has yet to be done to improve it, the introduction of the PersonalCare Bank enabled girls (and persons of all genders) from low-income families to obtain personal care products, such as menstruation products and toiletries, in schools.[34] It is also due to redemptive hope and wider matters of spiritual redemption, which has enabled Black and Brown community womanists to establish their womanist, religious, social, political and/or economic projects in the public arena.[35] The resistance by some Loyal Sisters is not only for the increase in and return to matriarchal, theological structures, systems, worship, and doctrines in the Black church but also for the development of community womanist or womanist communities in the ecclesiology and the eradication of oppressive and discriminatory patriarchy. Hope for that realization is demonstrated in the song, "Everything Will Be Alright."[36]

Secondly, a willingness to seek God in prayer for change and to change is also necessary for such denominations to retain their young Sisters who are already beginning to establish community womanist projects outside the British church and/or are disloyal to it in other ways. Nonetheless, these young Sisters are becoming a significant beacon of spiritual light in the public secularization.

This section demonstrated that redemptive hope and womanist action can also accomplish community solidarity to which I shall now explore further.

Community Solidarity

From the various cultural communities represented in Birmingham and Nottingham, Charlene Ellis's, Latisha Shakespeare's, and Danielle Beccan's deaths demonstrated the community solidarity against gun- and

---

34. McCalla, "Bloody Cloth," forthcoming.
35. McCalla, *Community Womanism,* forthcoming.
36. Cleveland, "Everything Will Be Alright."

gang-rated crimes. The killings significantly united previously divided communities. About three decades earlier when Stephen Lawrence and Damilola Taylor were murdered in London, the British public showed its divisiveness concerning issues of race and police dealings. Many lessons were learnt from Stephen's and Damilola's murders about race relations and racism in Britain. Whilst countless further lessons have still to be learnt, undoubtedly, the lessons ascertained were instrumental in rallying public support for the Black female teenagers' families. Local, national, and international media coverage was laden with graphic detail about the murders, deaths, and aftermaths of these crimes. Readers were given sufficient context and up-to-date material on these cases as in Anthony Walker's situation. The speed with which the police reacted to arrest, sentence, prosecute, and imprison Anthony's and the female teenagers' killers was also significant since only in 2012 under the new partly changed double jeopardy laws were two of the murderers charged, brought to trial and now imprisoned for Stephen Lawrence's death. However, insufficient evidence prohibits justice with regards to the other three of Stephen Lawrence's murderers. Baroness Doreen Lawrence of Clarendon was honored in 2013 as a Life Peer and thus represents victims of crime in Parliament. She has manifested incredible resilience and stamina as a Black mother, as she continues to champion the cause of justice for her son and other Black youths in Britain.

Second, the deaths mentioned in the section above, of Danielle Beccan, Damilola Taylor, Stephen Lawrence, the three teenage girls, and Anthony Walker became catalysts of spiritual hope and redemption for others, mainly youngsters. Danielle's death, in particular, caused others to commit and recommit themselves to the Christian faith, British church, and faith communities. For some youngsters, this commitment was intrinsically related to the realization of the frailty and uncertainty of human life and the need to find a definite purpose to exist. For others, it was about spiritual conversion to faith itself. However, here lies the paradox. The physical death of Danielle, Stephen, the teenage girls, Damilola and Anthony, and the suffering of their families brought spiritual life to others, that is, the conversion to faith or a commitment to worthy/charitable causes. Their deaths have proven to be redemptive. They did not die in vain.

Although extremely sorrowful, the deaths of the youths aforementioned, nonetheless brought hope and reassurance for a considerable amount of humans in ways which would possibly not have been accomplished had they lived longer. In the words of Martin Luther King Jr., when referring to the unmerited suffering and deaths of four innocent African American girls (Denise McNair, Addie Mae Collins, Carole Robertson, and Cynthia Wesley) in the bombing of their Sunday School at the Sixteenth Street Baptist Church in Birmingham, Alabama on Sunday, September 15, 1963: "the innocent blood of these little girls may well serve as the redemptive force that will bring new light to this dark city."[37] Suffering can bring hope and redemption for Loyal Sisters too as I shall discuss in the next section.

> We are all in the army of God.
> We are all in the army of God.
> We gonna fight 'till the day we die.
> We are all in the army of God.[38]

Suffering, Hope, and Redemption for Loyal Sisters

When the first group of refugee and asylum-seeker congregants arrived at High Parish in 2017, mainly from Iran, they spoke of staying in the church building for several days and nights where they slept on the pews and took it in turns to wash themselves in the church toilets and vicarage bathrooms in the morning. The church pews are movable so the church nave generally served their multipurpose-use. Warm clothing and bedding were found through congregational donations and partner organizations. High Parish also has a kitchen; a large, community-center room, a Lady Chapel, and other side rooms, which were also available for use by the refugees. Until residential accommodation was sought for them through High Parish and partner organizations, Brown and Black female refugees would participate in some of the church social activities during the day to keep themselves occupied. Such was the hospitality shown by the vicar, associate priests, High Paris congregation, and partner organizations when the refugees first arrived. Although some of these women were alone and feared for their safety since they were squatting in the church with refugee and asylum-seeker men, there were many families amongst these squatters and some with young children and babies so

---

37. Dreier, "Martin Luther King's 'Eulogy for the Martyred Children." Martin Luther King Jr.'s "Eulogy of the Young Victims" is dated September 18, 1963.

38. Author and composer are unknown. I learnt this song in the Pentecostal Church where I was raised.

they said that this was a very supportive environment too. Together, they would find solace and safety among other women present as the women and men often, but not always, socialized separately during their homeless experience in the High Parish church building. They also occupied their time by sharing stories of life back home and ate whatever the wider congregation and support partner-groups provided for them. They were homeless but they found the church to be a safe place—a place of refuge.

When finally being housed, some of the asylum-seeking Black and Brown women of various nationalities, told of being housed in poor conditions and alone if they had not traveled to England with a family. They were often housed in HMOs or temporarily in hotels. They were frequently ordered by the Home Office to relocate to available housing at a whim and anywhere in England or Wales with very little notice thus having to leave whatever belongings they had at the accommodations they last stayed. For this reason they were forced to constantly rebuild their lives every time they moved. This whole experience was both frightening and traumatic for them. When they did find suitable accommodation, where they were often housed with other families or single people in shared accommodations for longer than the usual weeks or months, this brought some relief/respite from the frequent mobility but they always feared that until they got their ILTR statuses in England, they would be required to leave again.

Lockdown was especially difficult for everyone but a bad situation for these women in normal times became notably worse during lockdown as they could only communicate by phone (if they had one), could not meet in the church for worship or fellowship, and—because some did not have computers or internet access—could not meet online for church services. The church, however, became a place for keyworkers' activity to support as many of these refugees and asylum seekers as possible with basic necessaries such as food, clothing, phone supplies, and so forth, which were delivered to the homes in full Personal Protective Equipment (PPE) and left on the doorsteps of their accommodation entrances when social distancing was enforced. It was during lockdown that the community spirit of High Parish was clearly demonstrated for both men and women and the refugee and asylum-seeking community who especially required the church's support.

During my exploration of ministry at High Parish I also discovered that some women were in the country for almost 20 years, had children in England or Wales and at the time of writing were still waiting for ILTR in

Britain. In one instance, the Home Office threatened an African woman with deportation back to Africa. However, her nine-year-old daughter could stay in England because she was born in England although there were no other relatives in England to care for her daughter, thus intentional separation of mother and daughter if the Home Office acted on their threat. The church prayed, lockdown came, and the deportation was put on hold. Later the Home Office relented so the African women is still in England and now her immigration status to remain in England is upgraded to ILTR. Ecclesiastes 3:4 says it well in this incident:

> A time to weep and a time to laugh,
> A time to mourn and a time to dance.

Like some of the Iranian females at High Parish, Bishop Dr. Guli Francis-Dehqani and her family fled her country of origin to find refugee-citizenship status in Britain. During the Iranian Revolution in 1979 her family encountered an assassination attack which left her mother, Margaret, wounded. Her father, Hassan Dehqani-Tafti, was then serving as bishop of Iran. Guli's brother was murdered in 1980 by agents of the government so at age 14 she and her family settled in Hampshire, England. They rebuilt their lives in England with the knowledge that they would never be able to return to Iran. Her father remained the exiled bishop of Iran from their settlement in Hampshire until his retirement in 1990.

Dr. Guli's PhD thesis, which she obtained in 1999, is on religious feminism and Iranian missionaries in 1869–1934. She became Diocesan Advisor on women's ministry in the Diocese of Peterborough. She has also served in multi-faith ministries in various roles.[39] If anyone can relate to and empathize with the suffering and pain of Iranian refugees at High Parish and, perhaps, other asylum-seeker females, I think Bishop Guli is undoubtedly able to do so.

While the remit of this study did not fully allow the exploration of LGBTQ+ people as I was engaged in ministry endeavors rather than formal research when the data was collected, in 2019 I still remember having a conversation with a lesbian female African congregant at High Parish. This was during the church's community lunch one Sunday afternoon. We talked about her experience of being in Britain and the struggles to survive having not yet been granted LTR in the UK. She spoke with me in English which is not her first language. She was trying to improve her

39. Wikipedia, "Guli Francis-Dehqani."

English to sufficiently communicate with others although she has come a long way in her English fluency since arriving in England several years earlier where she could not speak any English. I asked her if she expected life in England to be so hard when she arrived. She immediately said no! She told me that she has struggled with acquiring suitable accommodation and with attempting to live in Britain in general while having total dependence on others to survive. However, she did say it was better here than in Africa because she was never loved by her family and community for being a lesbian and for being herself and that has existed since she was a child when she came out as herself. She said it was very hard when the people she expected to love her, like her family and friends in her African country,[40] do not love her because she is a lesbian and for her, that is a reality she is still trying to come to terms with and understand. She was then threatened with deportation back to the African country she fled. The Home Office felt it was safe for her to return to Africa. The threat was almost acted upon. However, a fierce campaign at High Parish for this woman to stay in Britain and not to return to danger in her country was led by the maverick white male vicar who is a known and fierce activist for social, economic, and political change, and also a contentious but lovable protagonist. A petition was signed by city residents and campaigners rallied support and traveled to London to stop the aeroplane departure from London through an act of social justice but where criminal and civil disobediences were avoided. After a last-minute plea to the Home Office on the morning of the deportation flight, the decision was suddenly reversed by them at the eleventh hour and the deportation was canceled.

That African woman is still in England since our conversation. She has improved her English tremendously and is living relatively comfortably. I had another conversation with her at an interfaith meeting in May 2022. She has now gotten LTR in Britain and is looking forward to finding suitable work in the UK. Another female experienced a similar plight because she is also a lesbian and the vicar intervened again. At the time of writing, she waits her next appointment with Home Office officials about her immigration status in Britain.

At High Parish where LGBTQ+ people are welcomed, at least Loyal Sister's LGBTQ+ genders are accepted. It is in this environment that self-love as a LGBTQ+ person can be encouraged and healing of self-hate can occur as discussed in chapter 8. Notwithstanding, this is despite the

40. I will not mention the African country by name since this could reveal her identity.

racial weakness of some of High Parish's congregants to love Black and Brown females holistically which includes heterosexual women too. To love a Loyal Sister because she is a lesbian must also mean her Blackness and womanhood too. Anything less than that is not God's love and this is something which the Anglican Church has to reconcile as a whole, let alone the Pentecostal Church. In a quotation with me, a Black Loyal Sister of the millennial generation, demonstrates the views held by many Pentecostals:

> Personally, I don't support LGBTQ+ and I think it's a shame that CofE and other churches have moved away from God's standards. I support their right to exist but I don't support their religion and fighting for standards to change. They're absolutely welcome in church but it went wrong when churches affirm their lifestyle when we should be teaching them to abstain.

What it means to justly and equitably love everyone in ecclesiastical and theological doctrine and praxis, where EDI also prevails, is a matter for all denominations to solve in prayer and humility—a contemplation which Kelly Brown Douglas also demonstrated in her reflection on homophobia in the American Black church from a womanist perspective.[41] I cannot standardize denominational doctrine for the whole British church from a social justice stance since, at the time of writing this book, any doctrinal decision making in any church is beyond my remit as an ecumenist and field researcher. My job is to carry out research, analyze what I believe can bring the emancipation of all God's Sisters and people as accurately and realistically based on the data-generation, and then to document the findings and disseminate the research accordingly.

Whilst many of the Loyal Sisters appreciate the warmth of the general congregation at High Parish they nevertheless acknowledge the sexualized racist superiority that sometimes expresses itself among some of the white congregants simply because the Loyal Sisters are women of color and/or immigrants. Being a heterosexual Black female myself, at times I also experienced racism from white congregants who regarded themselves as superior to me and thought that their British entitlement and rights were greater than mine although I am an automatic British citizen under the 1981 British Nationality Act. I am automatically a British citizen under the Act because I was born before 1983. Besides, on arriving in England in the 1960s my parents also are British citizens

---

41. Brown Douglas, *Sexuality and the Black Church*, 236.

under the 1948 British Nationality Act and, until their deaths in 2015 and 2016 respectively, were part of what is now known as the Windrush Generation. Furthermore, at High Parish I was often mistaken as an asylum seeker too by all congregants including refugees and asylum seekers. Many of the white congregants questioned my professional status as a professor and even my entitlement and British citizenship rights to paid work in the UK. Some of them felt I had limited or no rights. Some even thought I was mentally unwell when I claimed that I did have citizenship rights. This was perhaps partly because I had also fallen on economic and social, hard times when I was a congregant at this church, and since I was unknown to many of the congregation until I arrived there, I was seen as an asylum-seeking congregant too. My stories of better times, which I seldom told given the social deprivation of many of the people of color at the church, was disbelieved. On another occasion, during ministry work, one white male member was surprised that I owned a car when I required assistance to transport goods for storage until they were needed for ministry. However, he was unsurprised that the white female who also helped with the transportation of goods, owned a car. He did not question the white woman's ownership of her car. Similarly, being Black, the asylum seekers felt I should side with them and participate in many of the activities and benefits which were donated to refugee and asylum seekers. However, being a British citizen, I did not qualify for some of the support they received from charities and the church which supported asylum seekers and refugees. During my time of economic hardship, as a British citizen I qualified for other welfare benefits. Regrettably, this area still requires attention and change in practice in High Parish which claims to be an inclusive church since our identities are not just gendered but racial and sexual too as whole human beings. bell hooks puts it like this:

> I mostly want to remind her of the recipes of healing, and give her my own made-on-the spot remedy for the easing of her pain. I tell her, "Get a pen. Stop crying so you can write this down and start working on it tonight." My remedy is long. But the last item on the list says: "When you wake up and find yourself living someplace where there is nobody you love and trust, no community, it is time to leave town—to pack up and go (you can even go tonight). And where you need to go is any place where there are arms that can hold you, that will not let you go.[42]

---

42. hooks, *Sisters of the Yam*, 194.

From a womanist theological perspective, Loyal Sisters at High Parish are free to leave. However, unlike me who left after my ministry service there was complete, some do not do so as they have nowhere to go. So how far is choice to stay at High Parish real for Black and Brown females who attend it? Similarly, whilst not enslaved at High Parish itself, some of them are nevertheless enslaved by an immigration system which may disable them from becoming nationals and/or citizens and therefore this determines their choice to stay or leave High Parish. Furthermore, although my study has not revealed cases where women are enslaved by the Modern Slavery Act 2015, it does not mean they are not enduring extremely hard conditions in England. In some incidents their passports were confiscated while traveling to and after arriving in Britain, making it more difficult for them to obtain immigration rights in Britain such as LTR. It means that life as an asylum seeker and refugee in Britain is very difficult. It means that the choices for Black and Brown females as asylum seekers and refugees in Britain are limited. Anonymously, sharing their testimonies in this book in order to help other people who are also facing extreme difficulty for no fault of their own, is also redemptive and transcendent for them as it was for the apostle Paul in Phil 4:1–20 and in the lyrics of this gospel song, "Alabaster Box."[43]

Eschatological Justice

Finally, a common spirituality and theology, especially in Pentecostalism, is the eschatology, that is, the end times, the second coming of Jesus to judge the world and grant eternal life and reward for the righteous and eternal punishment and death for the wicked.[44] It is often referred to as the rapture. The Anglican season of Advent marks the eschatology also. The song, "Maranatha"[45] demonstrates Advent too.

Referring to the conversation between the priest at High Parish and me on January 6, 2021 about the litany in the BCP, it is clear that eschatology is a topic that some in the Anglican Church—and other churches too, no less the unchurched—would prefer to avoid discussing. Any discussion is also a reminder that "the wheat and the tares will grow together

---

43. Winans and Sjostrand, "Alabaster Box."

44. Hollenweger, *Pentecostals*, 588. Hollenweger, *Pentecostalism*, 512. Toulis, *Believing Identity*, 304.

45. Barstone and Maranatha Singers, "Maranatha."

until the day of harvest" (Matt 13:30) thus also acknowledging that it is not always clear who will be saved and who will be damned in the eschatology as the priest points out in the following conversation:

> Doreen: I did actually like the Epiphany section today. Very Trinitarian.
>
> Priest: The trinity bit is great but it's damning everyone to hell that I'm not so keen on. I'm not a Universalist these days but I'm not really into making emphatic statements about the state of other peoples' salvation. Neither my place to say God will save all or God will damn certain others. Kinda want to be more humble about it than that.
>
> Doreen: The later part needs refining as heaven is preferred over hell and this Epiphany [litany] does not recognize that preference. However, I do like the fact that hell is even acknowledged as many of our theologies, except for mainly evangelicals, tend not to look at hell at all as if only good exists and not evil so only heaven and not hell, however, contentious these issues are in our world of comfortable. Condemnation certainly needs to be secondary and minor to love at all cost in a social justice context. However, Jesus came not to condemn as in John 3:17 so neither should we. Hence, again, the wording requires refining so that there is a balance between good and evil whilst not condemning anyone to evil, preferring to leave everyone to "work out their own salvation with fear and trembling"[46] (respect, acknowledgement of God)
>
> Priest: Agree!

The incident of forgiveness on the part of Gee and Dominique, mentioned above, again plainly reveals divine characteristics of Christian Black and Brown women. Emile M. Townes demonstrates that African American women suffer and struggle.[47] It would appear that Black and Brown women do so the most of all racial and social groups in the US and around the world, and undeservedly at the hands of others. Yet, interestingly, when it comes to displaying spiritual or moral values, they practice them the most. It would thus follow that because British Brown and Black Sisters struggle the most, they are able to empathize the most. Surely, a just God is taking all of that into account! God is not only a redemptive

---

46. I refer to the Scripture Phil 2:12.

47. Townes, *Troubling in My Soul*, 257. Cannon, *Black Womanist Ethics*, 194. Townes, *Womanist Ethics and the Cultural Production of Evil*, 200.

God now on earth but is a God of justice in the resurrection and eschatology too. Like the parable of Dives and Lazarus (Luke 16:19–31), the encounter/vision of David in the sanctuary of God who envied the prosperity of the wicked until he discovered their plight (Psalm 73), and the apostle Paul who acknowledged we would experience human misery if our hope was only in this life (1 Cor 15:19), those who suffer the oppression and injustice at the hands of persons, systems, policies, structures, and the like, will find justice, peace, and emancipation in eternal rest in the presence of God as did Lazarus and repentant David, and in Paul's expectation for God's people. The God of justice will therefore act for oppressed and discriminated Black and Brown females, if not in this life, in the life to come/in the eschatology. This is clearly depicted in a familiar Jamaican spiritual:

> If you miss me shouting down here,
> If you miss me shouting down here,
> Take a walk up to heaven,
> And you'll find me shouting up there.[48]

The following Scripture says the same:

> Now if we are children, then we are heirs—heirs of God and co-heirs with Christ, if indeed we share in his sufferings in order that we may also share in his glory. I consider that our present sufferings are not worth comparing with the glory that will be revealed in us. (Rom 8:17–18 NIV)

Oppressed Black and Brown females will find eternal afterlife. The body will die but the spirit lives on into eternity because "the spirit is willing but the flesh is weak" (Matt 26:14). See also 1 Corinthians 15.

> We shall be changed, Hallelujah!
> We shall be changed, by and by.
> When the dead in Christ shall rise.
> To meet Jesus in the sky.
> We shall be changed in the twinkling of an eye.[49]

And:

---

48. The composer of this traditional Jamaican gospel spiritual is unknown. I sang this song in the Pentecostal Church in which I was raised. Sometimes the lyrics in the third line is "Oh come on up to bright glory." Shouting in this song refers to speaking in tongues (*glossolalia*) and/or charismatic worship in praise, song, prayers and/or the like.

49. A Caribbean spiritual. Composer unknown.

> My home is in heaven
> Waiting for me
> And when I reach there
> How happy I'll be.
> My home is in heaven
> No rent to pay
> My Jesus paid it
> On Calvary![50]

McClurkin's Caribbean medley[51] also demonstrates the eschatology too. On the other hand, oppressors will receive eternal punitive recompense in God's absence for their unrepentant and unapologetic sin of oppression as in the case of Dives and other evil persons. Black and Brown women's oppression and discrimination continues in the church and public because those to whom powers are given to change sinful racism and sexist systems still fail to do so despite the agency of resistance which Brown and Black women exercise to be emancipated and empowered. However, the institutional intersectionality of racist and sexist sin has led to oppression and discrimination for women of color. This sin can be eradicated too. However, this can only be done when people who operate systems of oppression and discrimination act to destroy them. The sin of misogynoir prevents oppressors' ability to change these adverse systems for the betterment of all humanity although God has given them the capacity to do so. A God of justice will act against those who are oppressing Black and Brown women, if not in this life, in the life to come. A social justice rereading of origin Sin is about failing to love all of God's humanity since we are called to love everyone as recorded in John 13:34–35 and 1 John 4:7–8.[52] A social justice and redemptive sermon for inflicting the suffering of racialized sexism and unrepentant sins of sexism and racism is one where oppressors will inherit eternal death:

> In the past God overlooked such ignorance, but now he commands all people to repent. For [s]/he has set a day when [s]/he will judge the world with justice.
> (Acts 17:30–31a NIV)

---

50. A Caribbean spiritual. Composer unknown. I sang this song in the Pentecostal Church where I was raised.

51. The original composer is unknown. However, McClurkin, "I've Got My Mind Made Up," popularized this Jamaican song.

52. See Further Reading on "Original Sin."

The same sentiment is expressed in the song, "There Is a Balm in Gilead."[53]

Conclusion

The significance of spiritual redemption and transcendence is realized in this chapter. It demonstrates that Loyal Sisters can heed Jesus's call to "occupy until I come" (Luke 19:13) by decolonizing Scripture and liturgy and to engage in community solidarity. However, they also suffer; must forgive the past, present, and themselves; heal; and therefore find peace. This is possible through pneumatology. Utopian hope and justice is forthcoming through Jesus's second coming which is fundamental to Pentecostalism, such as in Messa Pentecostal, and an important reassurance for liberal and progressive Anglicans, such as High Parish, because they are faithful to Jesus and the British church "come what may."

We pause for a moment to ready ourselves for the intercessory prayer which follows in chapter 10.

Questions

1. Is suffering redemptive and spiritual? How can we heal from suffering?
2. What suggestions would you give to church decision makers about doctrines on love in action for all humanity?
3. Forgiveness is easy. Discuss.
4. The British church should repent for misogynoir and racialized sexism. Discuss.

Further Reading

Original Sin

Given the Scriptures on the eschatology and social justice as mentioned in this book, it follows that original sin cannot only be about a personal commitment to the Christian faith as is fundamental to evangelical theology and an acceptance of Jesus's love for humanity made possible through

53. Mouskouri and Loubet, "There Is a Balm in Gilead."

God in the Christian faith. This is because not everyone practices the Christian faith and therefore it follows and appears that repentance from sins of injustice can be extended to persons beyond the Christian faith where eternal life seems possible too.

10

Altar Service[1]

Pneumatic Intercessions[2]

Holy Spirit, what a comfort You are;
Holy Spirit, what a comfort You are.
You lead us, You guide us, You dwell right inside us;
Holy Spirit, what a comfort You are.[3]

THE PRESIDING INTERCESSOR GIVES *instructions to the Congregation:*

When I say, Let the Church say, Amen, you respond with the gospel chant, in song by Jester Hairston.[4]

---

1. Clark Sheard et al., " God is Here," can be sang by a choir or soloist or a recording of it, can be played prior to the commencement of the intercession. The music and lyrics are by Meleasa Houghton, Israel Houghton, and Martha Munizzi.

2. See the Further Reading section at the end of the chapter for a brief analysis and narrative of the context and general background to this intercession.

3. Anonymous, "Heavenly Father, We Appreciate You."

4. The president sings the song a few times so that the congregation can hear the lyrics and the melody and can know how to respond during the intercession. "Amen" is a gospel spiritual by Jester Hairston. It was composed for the Sidney Pointier film, *Lilies of the Field* (1963), which popularized the song. It became a single by The Impressions on their album, *Keep on Pushing*, 1964.

1. We Pray for the Church of Christ

Today God, we come in humble submission and pray for your church everywhere—the body of Christ in England, the United Kingdom, and the world. We acknowledge you as Head of the church and we reverence you. We pray for our leaders in the Diocese of [name], headed by [bishop's name] and our area of [name of town/city], headed by [bishop's name]. We pray for [name of vicar], our incumbent vicar and all parishioners, leaders, congregants, regular attenders and visitors of [church name]. Despite our national, racial, ethnic, and cultural differences, remind us constantly that we are all created in God's image. Help us, Jesus, to see others as you see us. "Bind us together with cords that cannot be broken."[5] Help us to laugh together, pray together, share your word together, commune together, cry together, and be a loving and caring family together since we will all be together in heaven.

We pray for your church of other denominations who are the body of Christ too that "all of [us] may be one, as You, God the Father and Mother; Jesus, Son and Daughter, and Holy Spirit; are one."[6] For the sake of Jesus Christ, our Savior, I pray for unity, discipleship, and love as we share in the Communion, worship the almighty God, and fellowship as brothers and Sisters. Grant us your mercy to be patient and kind with each other in our differences and help us to find common ground and similarities in which to serve you and all humanity until we find harmony in you.

We pray for our interfaith families everywhere. Help us to stay true to our call to Christianity whilst reaching out to the faithful elsewhere. God, show us your way and how we can together be your people and be a beacon of your presence in a world lost and is desperately in need of you. Continue to strength us and bless us all through your grace.

Presiding Intercessor: Let the church sing, Amen!

Congregation: Chant in song, **Hairston's song,** *"**Amen**"*[7]

---

5. Gillman, "Bind Us Together," 1977. The lyrics of this hymn were composed by Bob Gillman for singing. However, in this prayer the lyrics were said and not sung. Hos 11:4, Matt 28:18–20, Eph 4:4–6, Col 3:14.

6. John 17:21.

7. See a performance of this song in Jester Hairston: Legacy of the Spirituals. "Sings 'Amen' at 90th Birthday."

2. We Pray for Sovereignty and Leaders

We pray for heads of state; for all who governor in this land and the world: For [name of current, British monarch], head of the Commonwealth of 54 nations with [name of incumbent], Secretary-General and [name of incumbent], Chair-in-Office. We pray for [name of incumbent], Secretary-General of the United Nations.[8] We pray for policy makers and in the British Parliament, Home Office, and Select Committee who in their roles have and are making policies that impact on the rest of society. We ask God for their wisdom, compassion, and mercy, especially in relations to immigration policies that impact directly on persons in this congregation and others throughout the world. We pray for local political councillors[9] who do not make the policies but administer them and support local constituents in local wards which are concerned with immigration policies that impact their lives. We pray for lawyers who implement the law by representing their clients in tribunals and courts and help others whom the law cannot readily and easily support. We plead to policy makers, local government officials, and lawyers of congregants of our church in our prayers for sympathy and understanding in every case especially those who were once themselves asylum seekers and refugees or economic migrants and have now obtained their British citizenship. Help them not to forget who they are in their treatment of people in similar positions as they once experienced. For those who have not forgotten the blessings of British citizenship afforded to them but operate in systems and structures which alienate them from supporting their own people and others, God support them in their work and give them strength. Heavenly God who is also earthly present, side with those who are still waiting to hear the outcome of their and their families' immigration statuses, bring relief and peace.

    Presiding Intercessor: Let the church sing, Amen!
    *Congregation: Chant in song, **Hairston's song**, "**Amen**"*

---

    8. At the time of leading intercessions and writing the book, the then monarch and Head of the Commonwealth was Queen Elizabeth II. Patricia Scotland is Commonwealth Secretary-General and Boris Johnson was Chair-in-Office of the Commonwealth. Antonio Guterres is the Secretary-General of the United Nations.

    9. Political councilors are elected representatives of wards in cities and towns in the UK. Local politics are administered through their office such as refuse collections and neighborhood services. They govern for local residents in their wards.

3. We Pray for Women and Children

Whilst we know that not all parents and guardians are women as men are also parents too, we acknowledge that childbirth is the domain of women and even in our modern world, women are still the predominate carers of children and thus we pray today for women and children. We pray for women of color who are impacted in communities by both race and gender, and others by low, economic statuses also. Partner with us, Jesus. We cast our burden on you, Jesus, in exchange for your peace.[10] For economic migrant, refugee, and asylum-seeking women in Britain, give them strength to overcome every obstacle, give them relief, and grant them justice. We pray especially for those migrant women in this congregation from Iran, Pakistan, Bangladesh, Iraq, India, the African Continent, and the Caribbean. For women who are at risk of FGM and breast binding, stay off these satanic threats to their health and general well-being and heal those who endure ongoing health problems and illnesses due to FGM and breast binding. We pray for all women with menstruation issues and menopausal symptoms. Help them to know they can just spiritually touch the hem of Jesus's garment and find wholeness[11] and hold your hand, God, as they seek appropriate remedies during their midlife.

We pray for lone mothers who have no relatives and limited friends to assist with childcare responsibilities. We remember those in the congregation too. Jesus, ease their burden and send them help! We invite your presence to be with children everywhere too.

(In song):

> Red, [Brown], yellow, Black and white, they are precious in his sight. Jesus loves the little children of the world.[12]

We pray for children of migrant parents who are treated differently to other children who were born and raised in England and thus have no recourse to public funds because of their parent's immigration status. May these children never lack![13]

---

10. See Matt 11:28.

11. See Matt 9:20–22, Mark 5:25–34, and Luke 8:43–48.

12. It was originally composed in 1864 to the words, Tramp, Tramp, Tramp for marching in the American Civil War then later changed to Jesus Loves the Little Children (see Hawn, "History of Hymns"). I have chosen to replace "and" with Brown to represent the diversity of the children in High Parish and the Parish community and children of the world.

13. Psalm 23.

Presiding Intercessor: Let the church sing, Amen!
Congregation: Chant in song, **Hairston's song,** *"Amen"*

4. The British Diaspora

We pray for the Windrush Generation and their descendants and especially those affected by the recent Windrush Scandal and are still awaiting compensation. We pray for persons affected by honor killings and forced marriages and those making progress in our country in these areas to bring justice. Our prayer is also for other Europeans, African, Asians and peoples in the rest of the world. For those who have made Britain their home and have found meaningful lives and social and economic security, we pray. For those who took and are still taking the treacherous journey by dinghies across the ocean fleeing persecutions and danger or for a better life and in doing so, lose theirs; for some who come for economic well-being and security only to experience a marginally better life than the one they escaped, we pray. For those caught up in human trafficking and modern slavery, we pray. How long must we cry for help? How long must we plead for justice? How long must we bear unbearable pain? We pray for all experiencing racism and xenophobia today.

We pray for our neighbors! Help us, God, to know and understand what it means, "To love our neighbors as ourselves."[14] Help us, Jesus Christ, to love, accept, and respect all people, of all nations, races, and ethnicities who live in our communities even when we do not understand their culture and way of living. Forgive us for neglecting "the other," refugees, asylum seekers, and economic and social migrants, for not welcoming everyone as fellow humans.

We pray for those who are suffering the loss of loved ones through enforced separation of families between foreign lands. God, we pray that you will "comfort those who mourn"[15] and are in grief.

For those suffering social and economic deprivation, please God, rescue them from this tyranny now and free them from servitude and total dependence on others. Come, Jesus, come!

For those who are poor, homeless, surviving daily with little to eat or limited clothing to wear, struggling to pay essential bills, and have virtually no toiletries, clothes detergents, and household cleaning products for

---

14. Mark 12:31.
15. Matt 5:4.

their personal and home hygiene and care, we pray. Forgive us for being judgemental and unduly unkind when we should have been sympathetic, benevolent, and generous where possible, like you, Jesus.

We pray that you will provide adequate resources for support and care services in our communities, for those who work and volunteer in these services and for policy- and decision-makers in these services whose actions effect practices and those who receive them.

We pray for people affected by the Coronavirus pandemic which has disproportionately impacting on people of color including women of color. We pray that God, you will contain the contagion.

Presiding Intercessor: Let the church sing, Amen!

Congregation: *Chant in song,* **Hairston's song,** *"Amen"*

5. We Pray for the Human Race and Light a Candle for

The presiding intercessor reads a list of individual, group, and family names. A candle is lit in the church by the vicar, deacon or a congregant after a name is read for everyone who requested our prayers.[16] *Alternatively, congregants in the service may also light candles and can stand or kneel at the altar or at the front of the nave as the presiding intercessor proceeds with prayers aloud and while other intercessors, the vicar and deacons or leaders lay their hands on them and pray in silence. The presiding intercessor then finishes with:*

We are yours, God. We are open to hearing your voice and obeying your will. Please stay with us and give us peace. Thank you for your mercy and grace. Thank you for being our God and loving us always.

God accept these prayers through Jesus Christ, who is alive and reigns with you, in the unity of the Holy Spirit, one God in three persons, now and for ever.

Presiding Intercessor: Let the church sing, Amen!

Congregation: *Chant in song,* **Hairston's song,** *"Amen"*

As the presiding intercessor leaves the lectern the congregation continues singing the hymn, stands and claps also. The singing continues as congregants "tarry at the altar."

---

16. During the week, prior to the service, congregants were asked if they require a special prayer in the service and if they would like to be added to the prayer list. These persons names who are called at this time and a candle lit for each person mentioned.

For Discussion:

1. Discuss Jesus's encounter with the Canaanite women in Matt 15:21–28 and Mark 7:24–30. See the Further Reading section of this chapter also.
2. With reference to the Canaanite women in Matt 15:21–28 and Mark 7:24–30, discuss the themes in this intercessory prayer.
3. In your preferred form/style or liturgy and homily of prayers, what is your intercessory prayers for Loyal Sisters and women of color based on what you have learnt from this chapter and about the Syrophoenician woman?

Further Reading

Context and Background to This Chapter

The intercession remains as I would write it for presentation in prayers to a congregation and is more or less a general written presentation in the CoE. Many Sunday worship congregational intercessions are normally much shorter than this one. However, this was a special service for prayers for the migrant women in the congregation, the local parish, and the world, so the length reflected this speciality.

The eleventh Sunday after Pentecost or Trinity 10 Sunday in the Anglican Church calendar marks the service of the Canaanite woman or Syrophoenician woman. This service centers on the controversial lectionary Scripture of Matt 15:21–28 and Mark 7:24–30. Whilst I shall not use this occasion to expand on these Scriptures, preferring to concentrate on the intercessory prayer itself, I shall say that it is controversial because of Jesus's encounter with the woman in it. Was Jesus racist, sexist, xenophobic, and anti-interfaith since the Canaanite women in these Scriptures is foreign, pagan, and gentile? What exactly are we to learn from this encounter about racial, gendered, social, and interfaith justices; EDI? I shall allow readers to explore, examine and discuss the Scriptures for themselves along with reference to online articles and the video titled, "Shouting at Jesus"[17] and "Did the Canaanite Women Teach

---

17. McDowell, "Shouting at Jesus."

Jesus Not to Be Racist?"[18] An exploration beyond these two references is also encouraged.

I accepted the invitation by the white British vicar of the diverse, inclusive, Anglican, parish church, High Parish, to lead intercessory prayers on Sunday, August 16, 2020—the service of the Canaanite woman. Being diverse, this means that the congregation is multi-ethnic and multicultural or intercultural which is a concept often used in sacred ecclesial contexts in Britain and other countries of the world such as the US. It positions cultural diversity in relations to a specific nation, in this case, Britain, with the rest of the world. I was one of the very limited Black British-born citizens in the church that day. It is a church which serves the community, pastoral, and spiritual requirements of predominately refugees and asylum seekers from mainly the Global South, Middle East, and the Africa Continent. This is evident in my intercessory prayers. Petitioning the Divine for people and ourselves is known as an intercessory prayer.

Spiritual prayers for others and oneself is an emancipatory tool of hope for emancipation, inclusion, justice, healing, comfort, and elevation as demonstrated in this intercessory prayer. It shows God's love and care for foreign Brown and Black women and their families who have either chosen to settle in Britain by choice as economic migrants or have fled their native lands abroad as refugees and asylum seekers. This womanist prayer is presented in a broader context of the Black and Brown women's relations to the human race and specifically for Loyal Sisters. I seized the opportunity to use my creative prayer to lead the congregation into intercessory prayer when invited to do so as an advocate for a womanist decolonization of church service liturgies and prayer homilies and litanies and in recognition of the limited presence of womanist theology in the British church. However, I recognize that womanist spirituality is present through Loyal Sisters and other Sisters of color.

In the CoE, an intercessory prayer is traditionally structured on the common worship. This structure of prayer usually features five parts: first, the church; second, creation, humans, sovereign and leaders; third, the local community; fourth, those who suffer; and fifth, individuals and families in the congregation and parish. It is not uncommon to deviate from the structure for special occasions. My intercession more or less followed the typical structure with the exception of replacing the third group—the local community—with prayers for women in general and

---

18. Paul, "Did the Canaanite Women Teach Jesus Not to Be Racist?"

specifically, local-community migrant women since it was the special service of the Canaanite woman. In addition to the structure, some intercessions include a response from the congregation which enables them to interact with the intercessor, be part of the prayer, and concentrate on the prayer itself. Some conventional call-and-responses are

> *Intercessor*: Lord, in your mercy
> *Respondents*: **hear our prayer.**

Or:

> *Intercessor:* Lord, hear us.
> *Respondents:* **Lord, graciously hear us.**

I preferred to engage with the congregation in a way that better represented their diversity and ways they are generally accustomed to worshiping, that is, drawing on spiritualities of their cultural traditions and experiences. I therefore chose to lead with:

> *Presiding Intercessor:* Let the church sing, Amen!
> And the congregation to follow with:
> *Congregation: Chant in song,* **Hairston's song,** *"****Amen****"*

Instructions for the congregation are usually in italics. The intercession is in normal type and responses are in bold type.

Bibliography

Adewunmi, Bim. "Women in Britain—from the Romans to the Windrush." *Guardian*, October 20, 2014. https://www.theguardian.com/lifeandstyle/2014/oct/06/black-women-in-britain-from-the-romans-to-the-windrush.
"Age Range by Generation." https://www.beresfordresearch.com/age-range-by-generation/.
Aldred, Joe, ed. *Sisters with Power*, London: Continuum, 2000.
Alexander, Valentina. "Africancentric and Black Christian Consciousness: Towards an Honest Intersection." *Black Theology in Britain* 1 (1998) 11–18.
———. '*Breaking Every Fetter'? To What Extent Has the Black Led Church in Britain Developed a Theology of Liberation?* PhD diss., University of Warwick, 1996.
———. "A Mouse in a Jungle: The Black Christian Woman's Experience in the Church and Society in Britain." In *Reconstructing Womanhood, Reconstructing Feminism—Writings on Black Women,* edited by Delia Jarrett-Macauley, 85–106. London: Routledge, 1996.
Alfred, Gloria. "If You Know the Lord Is Keeping You." https://youtube.com/watch?v=pqLoQpj9m3k&si=cjkod2eVyFfuuWXJ.
Anderson, Allen H., and Walter J. Hollenweger, eds. *Pentecostals after a Century: Global Perspectives on a Movement in Transition.* Sheffield: Sheffield Academic Press, 1999.
Anim-Addo, Joan, and Suzanne Scafe. *I Am Black/White/Yellow: The Black Body in Europe.* San Jose, CA: Mango Publications, 2007.
Anonymous. "Heavenly Father, We Appreciate You." https://hymnary.org/text/heavenly_father_we_appreciate_you.
Anonymous. "Sweep Over My Soul." https://www.songpraise.com/song/5d77f2b23f217b5ffc7c39d9
Arday, Jason, and Heidi Mirza, eds. *Dismantling Race in Higher Education: Racism, Whiteness and Decolonising the Academy.* London: Palgrave Macmillan, 2018.
Arthur, Linda B, ed. *Religion, Dress and The Body,* Oxford: Berg, 1999.
Association of Ambulance Chief Executives. "Reducing Misogyny and Improving Sexual Safety in the Ambulance Service." https://aace.org.uk/reducing-misogyny-and-improving-sexual-safety-in-the-ambulance-service/.
The Baptist Union of Great Britain. "Kate Coleman." https://www.baptist.org.uk/Articles/547636/Kate_Coleman.aspx.

Aymer, Margaret. *Confessing the Beatitudes*. Louisville, KY: Presbyterian Women Inc., 2011.

———. *James: Diaspora Rhetoric of a Friend of God*. Sheffield: Sheffield Phoenix, 2014.

Barstone, Bill, and Maranatha Singers. "Maranatha." https://youtube.com/watch?v=Q8Y_ko77fdQ&si=RK6FD561GdMgQu2P.

Barton, Mukti. *Creation and Fall and the Women of Bangladesh: A Contextual Study*. Dhaka: Netritto Proshikkhon Kendro, 1992.

———. "From Victim to Victor: A Black Feminist Re-Reading of Genesis 38." In *The Women's Christian Yearbook 2003*. Norwich: Canterbury, 2002.

———. "Gender-Bender God: Masculine or Feminine?" *Black Theology* 7 (2009) 142–66.

———. "I Am Black and Beautiful." *Black Theology* 2 (2004) 167–87.

———. *Liberation Spirituality as a Signal of Transcendence: Christian and Muslim Women in Bangladesh*. Oxford: Religious Experience Research Centre, 1998.

———. "Mukti's Story." In *Ethnicity: The Inclusive Church Resource*, edited by Michael Jagessar, 96. London: DLT, 2015.

———. "Race, Gender, Class and the Theology of Empowerment: An Indian Perspective." In *Gender, Religion and Diversity, Cross-Cultural Perspectives*, edited by Ursula King and Tina Beattie, 225–37. London: Continuum, 2004 and 2005.

———. "Reflecting on the Story of Ruth." In *Black Theology in Britain: A Reader*, edited by Michael N. Jagessar and Anthony G. Reddie, 236–38. London: Equinox, Oakville, 2007.

———. "Reinterpreting Hagar and the Woman of Samaria in the Context of Bangladeshi Women." *Rethinking Mission* (March 2012) 19.

———. *Scripture as Empowerment for Liberation and Justice: The Experience of Christian and Muslim Women in Bangladesh*. Bristol: Centre for Comparative Studies in Religion and Gender, University of Bristol, 1999.

———. "The Skin of Miriam Became as White as Snow: The Bible, Western Feminism and Colour Politics." *Feminist Theology* 9 (2001) 68–80.

———. "The Skin of Miriam Became as White as Snow: The Bible, Western Feminism and Colour Politics." In *Voices from the Margin*, edited by R. S. Sugirtharajah, 158–68. Maryknoll, NY: Orbis, 2006.

———. "Wrestling with Imperial Patriarchy." *Feminist Theology* 21 (2012) 7–25.

BBC. "Dr. John Sentamu Interviews Gee Walker." *Songs of Praise: The Yorkshire Dales*. April 9, 2017. https://www.bbc.co.uk/programmes/po4zd3k4.

———. "Misogyny and Sexism Rife in Dorset and Wiltshire Fire Service, Report Finds." https://www.bbc.co.uk/news/uk-england-dorset-67122900.amp.

———. "Narges Mohammadi: Iranian Woman Jailed for Rights Work Wins Nobel Peace Prize." https://www.bbc.com/news/world-middle-east-67026216.

———. "South Wales Fire Service: Bosses Tolerated Sexual Harassment, Report Says." https://www.bbc.co.uk/news/uk-wales-67872960.amp.

Beckford, Robert. *After the Flood: The Church, Slavery and Reconciliation*. London: Movement for Justice and Reconciliation (MJR), 2022. https://atfdocumentary.vhx.tv/.

———. *Decolonizing Contemporary Gospel Music Through Praxis: Handsworth Revolutions*. London: Bloombury, 2023

———. *Dread and Pentecostal: A Political Theology for the Black Church in Britain*. London: SPCK, 2000.

———. *My Theology: Duppy Conqueror*. London: DLT, 2021.
Bell, John L. "If You Believe and I Believe." 2005. https://hymnary.org/hymn/CH4/771.
Bible Training Institute (BTI). *Bible Training*, Volume 2. Cleveland, TN: White Wing House, 1969.
Brah, Atvar. *Cartographies of Diaspora: Contesting Identities*. London: Routledge, 1996.
Brown, Andrew, and Linda Woodhead. *That Was the Church That Was: How the Church of England Lost the English People*. London: Bloomsbury, 2016.
Brown Douglas, Kelly. *Sexuality and the Black Church: A Womanist Perspective*. New York: Orbis, 1999.
Bryan, Beverley, et al. *The Heart of Race: Black Women's Lives in Britain*. London: Verso, 1985.
———. *The Heart of Race: Black Women's Lives in Britain*. London: Verso, 2018.
Bush, Barbara. "Gender and Empire: The Twentieth Century." In *Gender and Empire*, edited by Philippa Levine, 77–111. Oxford: Oxford University Press, 2004.
———. "'Sable Venus,' 'She Devil' or 'Drudge'? British Slavery and the 'Fabulous Fiction' of Black Women's Identities, c.1650–850." *Women's History Review* 9 (2000) 761–89.
Caesar, Shirley. "Feel the Spirit (Live)." https://youtu.be/dp2qVlE3qu8?si=xd43u-ZbRF1zObDB.
Calley, Malcolm J. *God's People: West Indian Pentecostal Sects in England*. London: Oxford University Press, 1965.
Cannon, Katie G. *Black Womanist Ethics*. Atlanta: Scholars, 1988.
Casey, Louise. "An Independent Review into the Standards of Behaviour and Internal Culture of the Metropolitan Police Service." Metropolitan Police Service, 2023. https://www.met.police.uk/SysSiteAssets/media/downloads/met/about-us/baroness-casey-review/update-march-2023/baroness-casey-review-march-2023a.pdf.
Central Statistics Office. "Census of the Population 2022, Preliminary Results." https://www.cso.ie/en/csolatestnews/pressreleases/2022pressreleases/pressstatementcensusofpopulation2022-preliminaryresults/.
Cho, Sumi, et al. "Toward a Field of Intersectionality Studies: Theory, Applications, and Praxis." *Signs* 38 (2013) 785–810.
Church of England. "Criteria for Selection for the Ordained Ministry in the Church of England." London: Ministry Division of the Archbishop's Council, 2014.
———. *From Lament to Action: The Report of the Archbishop's Antiracist Taskforce*. Canterbury: CoE, 2021.
———. *Issues in Human Sexuality: A Statement by the House of Bishops of the General Synod of the Church of England, December 1991*. London: Church House, 2003.
———. "Prayers for God's Blessing for Same-Sex Couples Take Step Forward after Synod Debate." https://www.churchofengland.org/media/press-releases/prayers-gods-blessing-same-sex-couples-take-step-forward-after-synod-debate.
———. *Sending Candidates to BAP: A Guide to the Selection Process, A Reference Handbook for Diocesan Director of Ordinands*. London: Church of England, 2017.
Clark Sheard, Karen. "God Is Here." https://youtu.be/QS-Oj01NSVs?si=EdAGT6fGzrZBb_Vp.
Cleveland, James (and New Jerusalem Baptist Church). "Everything Will Be Alright," 1978. https://youtube.com/watch?v=uChlwyRRY6w&si=iPANftFvF_8HYteq.
Cole, Julie, and Graham Cole. *Faith and Fashion: How High Is a Holy Hemline*. Eugene, OR: Wipf & Stock, 2022.

Coleman, Kate. *7 Deadly Sins of Women in Leadership: Overcome Self-Defeating Behaviour in Work and Ministry*. Birmingham: Next Leadership, 2010.

———. "Being Human: A Black British Christian Woman's Perspective." In *The Whitley Lecture*, 1–63. Oxford: Whitley, 2006.

Coleman, Monica. "Introduction: Ain't I A Womanist Too?" In *Ain't I A Womanist Too?: Third-Wave Religious Thought*, edited by Monica Coleman, 1–31. Minneapolis: Fortress, 2013.

Cornelio, Jayeel, et al., eds. *Routledge International Handbook of Religion in Global Society*. London: Routledge, 2021

Cox, Harvey. *Fire from Heaven: The Rise of Pentecostal Spirituality and the Reshaping of Religion in the Twenty-first Century*. London: Cassell, 1996.

———. "Foreword." In *Pentecostals after a Century: Global Perspectives on a Movement in Transition*, edited by Allen Anderson and Walter Hollenweger, 13–15. Sheffield: Sheffield Academic Press, 1999.

Crenshaw, Kimberlé Williams. "Demarginalizing the Intersection of Race and Sex: A Black Feminist Critique of Antidiscrimination Doctrine, Feminist Theory, and Antiracist Politics." *University of Chicago Legal Forum* 139 (1989) 138–67.

———. "Mapping the Margins: Intersectionality, Identity Politics, and Violence Against Women of Color." *Stanford Law Review* 6 (1991) 1241–99.

Crosby, Fanny. "Blessed Assurance." 1873. https://en.m.wikipedia.org/wiki/Blessed_Assurance.

Crouch, Sandra. "Completely Yes." *We're Waiting*. Waco, TX: Light Records, 1985.

———. "Tell Him Yes v1.1." *We're Waiting*, Classic Gold. https://youtube.com/watch?v=nxogMOtwrpE&si=PeG-1F-Zuslb-ljX.

Davis, Angela Y. *Women, Race and Class*, USA: Penguin Books, 1981.

Day, Keri. *Azusa Reimagined: A Radical Vision of Religious Democratic Belonging*. Stanford: Stanford University Press, 2022.

———. *Religious Resistance to Neoliberalism: Womanist and Black Feminist Perspectives*. New York: Routledge, 2015.

Dixon, Lorraine. "At My Mother's Feet." In *Unsung Sheroes in the Church: Singing the Praises of Black Women Now!*, edited by Doreen W. McCalla, 69–83. New York: Author House, 2007.

———. "A Black Woman and Deacon: A Womanist Reflection on Pastoral Ministry." In *Sisters with Power*, edited by Joe Aldred, 50–64. London: Continuum, 2000.

———. "A Reflection on Black Identity and Belonging in the Context of the Anglican Church in England: A Way Forward." *Black Theology in Britain: A Journal of Contextual Practise* 4 (2000) 22–27.

Dreier, Peter. "Martin Luther King's 'Eulogy for the Martyred Children.'" *Huffington Post*, December 6, 2017, https://www.huffpost.com/entry/rev-martin-luther-kings-e_b_3930450.

Dube, Musa. *The HIV and AIDS Bible: Selected Essays*. Chicago: University of Chicago, 2008.

Dube, Musa, and Musimbi Kanyoro, eds. *Grant Me Justice: HIV/AIDS and Gender Readings of the Bible*. New York: Orbis/Cluster, 2004/2005.

Erel, Umut. *Migrant Women Transforming Citizenship: Life-stories From Britain and Germany*. London: Routledge, 2016.

Erel, Umut, et al. "PAR: Resistance to Racist Migration Policies in the UK." In *Transformative Research and Higher Education*, edited by Azril Bacal Roij, 93–106. London: Emerald Limited, 2022.

Bibliography

Fay, Brian. "Philosophy of Social Science." https://www.britannica.com/topic/philosophy-of-social-science.

Feminist Review. "Many Voices, One Chant: Black Feminist Perspectives." *Feminist Review* 17 (1984) 1–117.

Flynn, Don, et al. "The 'No Recourse to Public Funds' Policy in UK Immigration Law—A Source of Injustice, Inequality and Destitution." 2018. http://fass.open.ac.uk/sites/fass.open.ac.uk/files/files/PASAR/NRPF%20Report%20Jan20.pdf.

Foster, Elaine. "Women and the Inverted Pyramid of the Black Churches in Britain." In *Refusing Holy Orders: Women and Fundamentalism in Britain,* edited by Gita Sahgal and Nira Yuval-Davis, 45–68. London: Virago, 1992.

Gafney, Wilda C. *A Women's Lectionary for the Whole Church: Year A*. New York: Church Publishing, 2021.

———. *A Women's Lectionary for the Whole Church: Year B*. New York: Church Publishing, 2021.

———. *A Women's Lectionary for the Whole Church: Year W*. New York: Church Publishing, 2021.

Gentleman, Amelia. *The Windrush Betrayal: Exposing the Hostile Environment*. London: Guardian Faber, 2019.

Gerloff, Roswith, I. H. *A Plea for British Black Theologies: The Black Church Movement in Britain in its Transatlantic, Cultural and Theological Interaction with Special Reference to the Pentecostal Oneness (Apostolic) and Sabbatarian Movement*. London: Peter Lang, 1992.

Gichaara, Jonathan. "Women, Religio-cultural Factors and HIV/AIDS in Africa." *Black Theology* 6 (2008) 188–99.

Gillman, Bob. "Bind Us Together." Thank You Music, Maranatha! Music, 1977.

Glesne, Corrine, and Alan Peshkin. *Becoming Qualitative Researchers: An Introduction*. New York: Longman, 1992.

God TV News. "I Have Decided To Follow Jesus." https://godtv.com/true-story-behind-the-hymn-i-have-decided-to-follow-jesus/.

Gold, R. "Roles in Sociological Field Observation," *Social Forces* 36 (1958) 217–23.

Goodfellow, Maya. *Hostile Environment: How Immigrants Became Scapegoats*. London: Verso, 2020.

Gov.UK. "How Many People Do We Grant Asylum or Protection to?" Statistics, year ending June 2022. https://www.gov.uk/government/statistics/immigration-system-statistics-year-ending-december-2023/how-many-people-do-we-grant-protection-to.

———. *National Statistics: Immigration System Statistics, year ending December 2022*. https://www.gov.uk/government/collections/immigration-statistics-quarterly-release.

———. *Population of England and Wales: Ethnicity, Fact and Figures*, December 22, 2022. https://www.ethnicity-facts-figures.service.gov.uk/uk-population-by-ethnicity/national-and-regional-populations/population-of-england-and-wales/latest/.

The Grace Thrillers. "Holy Ghost Power Medley." South Africa: Sheer Publishing Ltd., n.d.

Graham, Elaine et al. *Theological Reflection: Methods (Second Edition)*. London: SCM, 2019.

Grant, Jacqueline. *White Women's Christ and Black Women's Jesus: Feminist Christology and Womanist Response*. Atlanta: Scholars, 1989.

The Guardian. "London Fire Brigade Put Into Special Measures Over Misogyny and Racism, Firefighters." *The Guardian*, December 14, 2022. https://www.theguardian.com/uk-news/2022/dec/14/london-fire-brigade-put-into-special-measures-over-misogyny-and-racism.

———. "Why Iran's Female-Led Revolt Fills Me With Hope." October 8, 2022. https://www.theguardian.com/world/2022/oct/08/iran-mahsa-amini-women-girls-revolt-hope

Gupta, Rahila, ed. *From Homebreakers to Jailbreakers: Southall Black Sisters*. London: Zed, 2003.

Hall, Delroy. *A Redemption Song: Illustration on Black British Pastoral Theology and Culture*. London: SCM, 2021.

Hall, Stuart. "The Local and the Global: Globalization And Ethnicity." In *Dangerous Liaisons: Gender, Nation, and Postcolonial Perspectives,* edited by Anne McClintock et al., 173–87. Minnesota: University of Minnesota Press, 1997.

Harvey, Nicolas Peter and Linda Woodhead. *Unknowing God: Toward a Post-Abusive Theology*. Eugene, OR: Cascade, 2022

Hatch, Edwin. "Breathe On Me Breath of God." 1878. https://hymnary.org/text/breathe_on_me_breath_of_god.

Hawn, C. Michael. "The History of Hymns: 'Jesus Loves the Little Children.'" Discipleship Ministries: The Methodist Church. https://www.umcdiscipleship.org/articles/history-of-hymns-jesus-loves-the-little-children.

Hays Daily News. "Give Me that Old Time Religion." *Salina Journal*. https://eu.salina.com/story/lifestyle/faith/2017/11/17/give-me-that-old-time-religion/17030122007/.

Herbert Woolston, Clare, and Federick Root, George. "Jesus Loves the Little Children." *Cedarmont Kids*. New York: Pleasantville Music Publishing, Inc., N.d.

High Parish. "An Order of Holy Communion for Pentecost Sunday." Service sheet, May 31, 2020.

Hill, Clifford. *Black Churches: West Indian and African Sects in Britain*. London: Community and Race Relations Unit of the British Council of Churches, 1971.

———. "From Church to Sect: West Indian Religious Sect Development in Britain." *Journal for the Scientific Study of Religion* 10 (1971) 114–23.

Hollenweger, Walter. J. *Pentecost between Black and White*. Belfast: Christian, 1974.

———. *The Pentecostals*. London: SCM, 1972.

———. *Pentecostalism: Origins and Developments Worldwide*. Peabody, MA: Henrickson, 1997.

hooks, bell. *Sisters of the Yam: Black Women and Self-Recovery*. New York: Routledge, 1993.

Hurd, Bob. "Envia tu Espiritu." https://youtube.com/watch?v=Y7EUVn7_TVk&si=_vIxge1ohQE8Pq8i.

The Impressions. "Amen." *Keep on Pushing*. New York: ABC-Paramount, 1964.

The Independent. "Ambulance Staff Afraid to Speak Out Amid a Culture of Sexism Racism and Bullying, Report Finds." https://www.independent.co.uk/news/health/ambulance-staff-sexism-bullying-b2288136.html.

———. "Report Reveals Shocking Examples Racist, Sexist and Bullying Behaviour in England's Fire and Rescue Services." https://www.independent.co.uk/news/uk/home-news/bullying-harassment-abuse-fire-and-rescue-services-b2311440.html

ITV News Wales. "Brave Whistleblower Speaks Out on 'Horrendous' Experience Exposing Sexual Harassment at Fire Service." https://www.itv.com/news/wales/2024-21-04/no-one-took-notice-says-cleaner-who-blew-whistle-on-sexism-at-fire-service.

Isin, Engin. "Performative Citizenship." In *The Oxford Handbook of Citizenship*, edited by Ayelet Shachar et al., 500–523. Oxford: Oxford University Press, 2017.

Iverson, Daniel. "Spirit of the Living God." N.d.: The United Methodist Hymnal, 1926.

Jagessar, Michael N., and Anthony G. Reddie, eds. *Black Theology in Britain: A Reader*. London: Equinox, 2007.

Jester Hairston: Legacy of the Spirituals. "Sings 'Amen' at 90th Birthday." https://youtube.com/watch?v=YT2w3_5nbZU&si=32-Qkt-_5xYdQz46.

Job, P. P. *Why God Why?* N.d.: Tortured for Christ, 2000.

Jordaan, Roxanne. "The Emergence of Black Feminist Theology in South Africa." *Journal of Black Theology in South Africa* 1 (1987) 42–46.

Kanyoro Musimbi, Rachel A. *Introducing Feminist Cultural Hermeneutics: An African Perspective*. New York: Pilgrim, 2002.

Kaptani, Ereni et al. "Methodological Innovation in Research: Participatory Theater with Migrant Families on Conflicts and Transformations over the Politics of Belonging." *Journal of Immigrant and Refugee Studies* 19 (2021) 68–81.

Kinouani, Guilaine. *Living While Black: The Essential Guide to Overcoming Racial Trauma*. London: Ebury, 2021

Kumari, Leela, B. M. "The untouchable 'Dalits' of India and their Spiritual Destiny." In *Another World is Possible: Spiritualities and Religions of Global Darker Peoples*, edited by Dwight Hopkins and Marjorie Lewis, 9–19. London: Routledge, 2009.

Land, Steven J. *Pentecostal Spirituality: A passion for the Kingdom*. Sheffield: Sheffield Academic Press, 1993.

Lareau, Annette. *Home Advantage: Social Class and Parental Intervention in Elementary Education, Second Edition*. London: Rowman & Littlefield, 2000.

Lartey, Emmanuel. *Black Theology: A Journal of Contextual Praxis*. Milton Park: Taylor and Francis, 1998.

Lawless, Elaine J. "Rescripting their Lives and Narratives: Spiritual Life Stories of Pentecostal Women Preachers." *Journal of Feminist Studies in Religion* 7 (1991) 53–71.

Lee, Lois *Recognizing the Nonreligious: Reimagining the Secular*. Oxford: Oxford University Press, 2015.

Liberty. *A Guide to the Hostile Environment*. https://www.libertyhumanrights.org.uk/wp-content/uploads/2020/02/Hostile-Environment-Guide---update-May-2019_0.pdf.

Linne, Shai. "Triune Praise." *Atonement*. N.d.: Shai Linne, 2008.

Lorde, Audre. *Sister Outsider*. New York: Penguin, 2019.

Louvin, Charlie, and Wynette, Tammy. "If I Could Here My Mother Pray Again." *And That's The Gospel*. Los Angeles: Playback Records, 1991.

Mahon, Michele. "Sisters with Voices: A Study of the Experiences and Challenges Faced by Black Women in London Baptist Association Church Ministry Settings." *Black Theology International Journal* 13 (2015) 273–96.

Mama, Amina, and Claudette Williams. "'We Are a Natural Part of Many Different Struggles': Black Women Organising." In *Inside Babylon: The Caribbean Diaspora in Britain*, edited by Winston James and Clive Harris, 148–66. London: Verso, 1993.

Manzano, Robert. "He Gave Me Beauty for Ashes." Kingsway Music, 1984.
Marley, Bob, and the Wailers. "Redemption Song," *Uprising*. Kingston, Jamaica: Tuff Gong Island, 1980.
Mataka, Laini. *Bein' a Strong Black Woman Can Get You Killed*. New York: Black Classic, 2000.
Matsikenyiri, Patrick. "Jesu Tawa Pano." General Board of Global Ministries, GBG Musik, 1996.
McCalla-Chen, Doreen W. "The Academic and Community Meet: Two Black Female Voices," *International Journal of Inclusive Education* 6, 2 (2002) 165–83.
McCalla, Doreen W. "Black Churches and Voluntary Action: Their Social Engagement With the Wider Society." *Black Theology: An International Journal* 3 (2005) 137–75.
———. "Bloody Cloth." In *Community Womanism: A Theological And Methodological Praxis of Black and Brown Sisterhoods in Britain*, Doreen McCalla. Eugene, OR: Cascade, forthcoming.
———. *Community Womanism: A Theological and Methodological Praxis of Black and Brown Sisterhoods In Britain*. Eugene, OR: Cascade, forthcoming.
———. "A Theoretical Framework of Benign Power in School Sector Decision Making: A Preface." *Discourse: Studies in the Cultural Politics of Education* 23 (2002) 39–57.
———. "Towards Greater Involvement of the British Black Church in the Secular Education of Black Youth: School Exclusion and British Black Males." In *The Black Church Studies Reader*, edited by Alton Pollard and Carol Duncan, 245–61. New York: Palgrave Macmillan, 2015.
———. *Unsung Sheroes in the Church: Singing the Praises of Black Women Now!* New York: Author House, 2007.
McClurkin, Donnie. *Caribbean Medley*. New York: Verity Records, 2000.
McDonald, Chine. *God Is Not a White Man and Other Revelations*. London: Hodder & Stoughton, 2021.
McDowell, Maria Gwyn. "Shouting at Jesus: The Canaanite Woman." *Women in Theology*, August 21, 2017. https://womenintheology.org/2017/08/21/shouting-at-jesus-the-canaanite-woman/.
Mirza, Heidi. "Decolonizing Higher Education: Black Feminism and the Intersectionality of Race and Gender." *Journal of Feminist Scholarship* 7/8 (2014/2015) 1–12.
Mirza Heidi, and Veena Meetoo. "Empowering Muslim Girls? Post-Feminism, Multiculturalism and the Production of the 'Model' Muslim Female Student in British Schools." *British Journal of Sociology of Education* 39 (2018) 227–41.
———. *Respecting Difference: Race, Faith and Culture for Teacher Educators*. London: Institute of Education, University of London: 2012.
Mouskouri, Nana, and Loubet, Roger. "Balm in Gilead." *Oh Happy Day*. Philips, 1990.
Moody, Charles, E. "Kneel at the Cross, 1924." https://hymnary.org/text/kneel_at_the_cross_christ_will_meet_you_?extended=true.
Murray, Charles, et al. *Charles Murray and the Underclass: The Developing Debate* Choice in Welfare 33. Civitas: Institute for the Study of Civil Society, 2000.
Nadar, Sarojini, and Isabel Phiri. "HIV Research, Gender and Religion Studies." In *Handbook of Theological Education in Africa*, edited by Isabel Phiri and Dietrich Werner, 632–38. Oxford: Regum International, 2013.
Nelson, Ralph, dir. *Lilies of the Field*. Beverly Hills: United Artists, 1963.

Bibliography

NISRA. *Northern Ireland Census 2021 Data.* https://www.nisra.gov.uk/statistics/census/2021-census. Northern Ireland: NISRA, 2021.

———. *Main Statistics for Northern Ireland Statistical Bulletin: Religion.* Northern Ireland: NISRA, 2022.

Oakley, Lisa, and Justin Humphreys. *Escaping the Maze of Spiritual Abuse: Creating Healthy Christian Cultures.* London: SPCK, 2019

Oakman, Johnson, Jr. "Hand in Hand with Jesus." https://hymnary.org/person/Oatman_Johnson.

Oduyoye, Mercy Amba. *Introducing African Women's Theology.* Sheffield: Sheffield Academic Press, 2001.

ONS. *Ethnicity and National Identity in England and Wales.* https://www.ons.gov.uk/peoplepopulationandcommunity/culturalidentity/ethnicity/articles/ethnicityandnationalidentityinenglandandwales/2012-12-11#ethnicity-in-england-and-wales.

———. *Harmonised Concepts and Questions for Social Data Sources, Primary Principles: Ethnic Group.* London: ONS, May 2015.

———. *Population and Household Estimates, England and Wales.* https://www.ons.gov.uk/peoplepopulationandcommunity/populationandmigration/populationestimates#:~:text=On%20Census%20Day%2C%202021%20March,census%20in%20England%20and%20Wales.

———. *Religion, England and Wales: Census 2021.* https://www.ons.gov.uk/peoplepopulationandcommunity/culturalidentity/religion/bulletins/religionenglandandwales/census2021.

O'Neill, Maggie, et al. "Borders, Risk and Belonging: Challenges for Arts-Based Research in Understanding the Lives of Women Asylum Seekers and Migrants at the Borders of Humanity." *Crossings: Journal of Migration and Culture* 10 (2019) 129–47.

Parker, Angela N. *If God Still Breathes, Why Can't I?: Black Lives Matter and Biblical Authority.* Grand Rapids: Eerdmans, 2021

Parker, Eve. *Trust in Theological Education: Deconstructing 'Trustworthiness' for a Pedagogy of liberation.* London: SCM, 2022

Paul, Ian. "Did the Canaanite Women Teach Jesus Not to Be Racist?" https://www.psephizo.com/biblical-studies/did-the-canaanite-woman-teach-jesus-not-to-be-racist/.

Pitts, Eve. "Black Womanist Ethics." In *A Time to Speak: Perspectives of Black Christians in Britain,* edited by Paul Grant and Raj Patel, 29–35. Nottingham: Russel, 1990

Pui-lan, Kwok. *Introducing Asian Feminist Theology.* Sheffield: Sheffield Academic Press, 2000.

———. *Postcolonial Imagination and Feminist Theology.* Louisville, KY: Westminster John Knox, 2005.

Reddie, Anthony G., ed. *Black Theology: An International Journal.* London: Taylor and Francis Group, 2002.

———. "Bring on the Sistas." *Black Theology in Transatlantic Dialogue.* London: Palgrave Macmillan, 2006.

Reynolds, Tracey. *Caribbean Mothers: Identity and experience in the UK.* London: Tufnell, 2005.

———. "The Success of Our Mothers: Caribbean Mothering, Childrearing and Strategies in Resisting Racism." In *Black Success in the UK: Essays in Racial and Ethnic Studies,* edited by Doreen McCalla, 85–100. Birmingham: DMee, 2003.

Reynolds, Tracey, and Elisabetta Zontini. "Bringing Transnational Families from the Margins to the Centre of Family Studies in Britain." *Families, Relationships and Societies* 3 (2014) 251–68.

Reynolds, Tracey, et al. "Migrant Mothers: Performing Kin Work and Belonging Across Private and Public Boundaries." *Families, Relationships and Societies* 7 (2018) 365–82.

———. "Practice Policy Briefing: Participatory Action Research-Engaging Marginalised Communities in Policy and Practice." 2017. https://www.runnymedetrust.org/projects-and-public.

Richardson Jensen, Jane, and Patricia Harris-Watkins. *She Who Prays: A Woman's Interfaith Prayer Book*. New York: Morehouse, 2005.

Robins, Roger Glen. *A.J. Tomlinson: Plainfolk Modernist*. Oxford: Oxford University Press. 2004.

Rudgard, Olivia. "Anglican Church Congregation Numbers Have 'Stabilised.'" *The Telegraph*, May 14, 2017. http://www.telegraph.co.uk/news/2017/05/13/anglican-church-congregation-numbers-have-stabilised/.

Sareen, Ashish. "Spiritual Calling Is Not A Job, Employment Tribunal Says." https://www.law360.co.uk/articles/1566585/spiritual-calling-is-not-a-job-employment-tribunal-says.

Scafe, Suzanne. *Feminist Review: Black British Feminism* 108 (2014) 1–141.

Scotland's Census. "Religion, 2022." https://www.scotlandscensus.gov.uk/census-results/at-a-glance/religion/.

Sky News. "Gracie Spinks: Derbyshire Police Made Multiple Errors After Stalking Allegations Ahead of Woman's Death, Inquest Concludes." https://news.sky.com/story/gracie-spinks-limited-investigation-into-stalking-allegation-ahead-of-womans-death-inquest-concludes-13007295.

———. "West Midlands Police Put Into Special Measures Over Poor Investigations, Inspector Say." https://news.sky.com/story/west-midlands-police-put-into-special-measures-over-series-of-failings-13014865.

Small, Stephen. *Racialised Barrier: The Black Experience in the United States and England in the 1980s*. London: Routledge, 1994.

Smith, Io, and Wendy Green. *An Ebony Cross: Being a Black Christian in Britain Today*. London: Marshall Pickering, 1989.

Spielberg, Steven, dir. *The Color Purple*. Burbank, CA: Warner Bros., 1985.

Spradley, James P. *Participant Observation*. London: Routledge and Kegan Page, 1980.

Stewart, Dianne M. *Black Women, Black Love: America's War on African American Marriage*. New York: Hachette, 2020.

Stone, Samuel J. and Samuel S. Wesley. "The Church's One Foundation." https://www.hymnsite.com/lyrics/umh545.sht.

Stone, Selina. "Holy Spirit, Holy Bodies? Pentecostalism, Pneumatology and the Politics of Embodiment." PhD diss., University of Birmingham, 2021.

———. *The Spirit and the Body: Towards a Womanist Pentecostal Social Justice Ethic*. Leiden: Brill, 2023.

———. *Tarry Awhile: Wisdom from Black Spirituality for People of Faith*. London: SPCK, 2023.

———. "Toward a Holistic Pentecost: Pentecostalism, Embodiment and Social Justice." *Pneuma* 45 (2023) 21–39.

Strauss, Anselm L. *Qualitative Research for Social Sciences*. London: Cambridge University Press, 1987.
Strauss, Anselm L., and Juliet Corbin. *Basics of Qualitative Research: Grounded Theory Procedures and Techniques*. Newbury Park, CA: Sage, 1990.
———. "Grounded Theory Methodology." In *Handbook of Qualitative Research*, edited by N. K. Denzin and Y. S. Lincoln, 273–85. Thousands Oaks, CA: Sage, 1994.
Swaby, Nydia A. "'Disparate in Voice, Sympathetic in Direction': Gendered Political Blackness and the Politics of Solidarity." *Feminist Review* 108 (2014) 11–25.
Swinton, John, and Harriet Mowat. *Practical Theology and Qualitative Research (Second Edition)*. London: SCM, 2016.
Terrell, JoAnne Marie. *Power in the Blood?: The Cross in the African American Experience*. Maryknoll, NY: Orbis, 2003.
Thomas, Linda Elaine. *Under the Canopy: Ritual Process and Spiritual Resilience in South Africa*. Columbia, SC: University of South Carolina Press, 1999.
Thompson, Phyllis, et al., eds. *Here to Stay: A Collection of Stories by Women*. Oxford: Lion, 1990.
Thurman, Howard. "Thou Shalt Love." In *Meditations of the Heart*, by Howard Thurman, 46. Boston: Beacon, 1953.
Toppin, Shirlyn. "'Soul Food' Theology: Pastoral Care and Practice Through the Sharing of Meals: A Womanist Reflection." *Black Theology: An International Journal* 4 (2006) 44–69.
Toulis, Nicole. *Believing Identity: Pentecostalism and the Mediation of Jamaican Ethnicity and Gender in England*. Oxford: Berg, 1997.
Townes, Emilie M., ed. *Embracing the Spirit: Womanist Perspectives on Hope, Salvation, and Transformation*. Maryknoll, NY: Orbis, 1997.
———. *A Troubling in My Soul: Womanist Perspectives on Evil and Suffering*. Maryknoll, NY: Orbis, 1993.
———. *Womanist Ethics and the Cultural Production of Evil*. New York: Palgrave Macmillan, 2006.
———. *Womanist Justice, Womanist Hope*. Oxford: Oxford University Press, 1993.
Townsend Gilkes, Cheryl. *If It Wasn't for the Women: Black Women's Experience and Womanist Culture in Church and Community*. Maryknoll, NY: Orbis, 2001.
Trinity College London. "Leave to Remain." https://www.trinitycollege.com/qualifications/SELT/UKVI/leave-to-remain.
Troup, Carol. "Engagement with Mission Magazine Archives: A Black Laywoman's Perspective." *Black Theology International Journal* 19 (2021) 101–21.
Truth, Sojourner. *Narrative of Sojourner Truth: A Bondwoman of Olden Times, with a History of Her Labors and Correspondence Drown from Her "Book of Life."* Schomburg Library of Black Women Writers, edited by Henry Louis Gates Jr. and Jeffrey C. Stewart. New York: Oxford University Press, 1991.
Turner, Carlton. *Caribbean Contextual Theology: An Introduction*. London: SCM.
"Understanding Generation Alpha." https://mccrindle.com.au/article/topic/generation-alpha/generation-alpha-defined/.
University and College Union. "Precarious Work In Higher Education: Insecure Contacts and How They Have Changed Overtime." October 2021. https://www.ucu.org.uk/media/10899/Precarious-work-in-higher-education-May-20/pdf/ucu_he-precarity-report_may20.pdf.

Waite, Hannah. *The Nones: Who Are They and What Do They Believe?* London: Theos, 2022.

Walker, Alice. *The Color Purple*. New York: Harcourt Brace Jonvanovich, 1982.

———. *In Search of Our Mother's Gardens: Womanist Prose*. London: The Women's, 1984.

———. "Womanist." In *The Womanist Reader*, edited by Layli Philips, 3–20. New York: Routledge, 2006.

Wallace, Richard, and Might Clouds of Joy. "I've Got One Thing You Can't Take Away." *God Bless America*. Santa Monica, CA: Universal Inc., 1970. https://youtube.com/watch?v=a2WW4HXXdTc&si=ZzH9PhOMfYdCadhd.

Wassen, Cecilia. *Women and the Damascus Document*. Atlanta: Society of Biblical Literature, 2005.

Watt, Diane. "Praying, Playing and Praising." In *Unsung Sheroes in the Church: Singing the Praises of Black women now!*, edited by Doreen W. McCalla, 84–104. New York: Author House, 2007.

Webster, Wendy. *Imagining Home: Race, Class and National Identity, 1945–64*. London: Routledge, 1998.

Weekes, Debbie. "Shades of Blackness: Young Black Female Construction of Beauty." In *Black British Feminism: A Reader*, edited by Heidi Mirza, 113–26. London: Routledge, 1997.

Weems, Renita. *Just a Sister Away: A Womanist Vision of Women's Relationships in the Bible*. San Diego, CA: Laura Media, 1988.

Wesley, Charles. "Love Divine, All Loves Excelling." 1747. https://hymnary.org/text/love_divine_all_love_excelling_joy_of_he.

White, Nadine. *Barrel Children: The Families Windrush Left Behind* trailer by Nadine White. https://youtu.be/A_EJF14WddQ?si=6yaG_2Z8nsTBZTgl.

Whitfield Vaughan, John. "If I Could Hear My Mother Prayer Again." 1922. https://en.m.wikipedia.org/wiki/If_I_Could_Hear_My_Mother_Pray_Again.

Wikipedia. "Ambrose Jessup Tomlinson." https://en.wikipedia.org/wiki/Ambrose_Jessup_Tomlinson.

———. "Amen (gospel Song)." https://en.m.wikipedia.org/wiki/Amen_(gospel_song).

———. "Barrel Children." https://en.m.wikipedia.org/wiki/Barrel_children.

———. "Chris Goldsmith." https://en.m.wikipedia.org/wiki/Chris_Goldsmith.

———. "Demography of Scotland." https://en.m.wikipedia.org/wiki/Demography_of_Scotland.

———. "Guli Francis-Dehqani." https://en.wikipedia.org/wiki/Guli_Francis-Dehqani.

———. "Nazanin Zaghari-Ratcliffe." https://en.wikipedia.org/wiki/Nazanin_Zaghari-Ratcliffe.

———. "Old Time Religion." https://en.wikipedia.org/wiki/Old-Time_Religion.

———. "Rose Hudson-Wilkin." https://en.wikipedia.org/wiki/Rose_Hudson-Wilkin.

———. "Rosemarie Mallett." https://en.wikipedia.org/wiki/Rosemarie_Mallett.

———. "Smitha Prasadam." https://en.wikipedia.org/wiki/Smitha_Prasadam.

———. "Siyahamba." https://en.m.wikipedia.org/wiki/Siyahamba.

Williams, Delores S. *Sisters in the Wilderness: The Challenge of Womanist God-talk*. New York: Orbis, 1999.

William Walsh, Peter. "Briefing: Asylum and Refugee Resettlement in the UK." 2022. https://migrationobservatory.ox.ac.uk/resources/briefings/migration-to-the-uk-asylum/.

Winans, CeCe, and Sjostrand, Janice. "Alabaster Box." N.d.: Wellsprings Gospel, 1999. https://youtube.com/watch?v=EQgro1QKlFY&si=cHlKo7oqIKbNMFaP.

Wolf, Naomi. *The Beauty Myth: How Images of Beauty Are Used Against Women*. New York: Vintage, 1990.

Woodhead, Linda, and Paul Heelas. *The Spiritual Revolution: Why Religion Is Giving Way to Spirituality*. London: Blackwell, 2005.

Worldometers. "UK Population." http://www.worldometers.info/world-population/uk-population/.

World Population Review. "United Kingdom Population." https://worldpopulationreview.com/countries/united-kingdom-population.

Wyatt, Tim. "British Social Attitudes Finds 'CoE' Respondents Halved in 15 Years." *Church Times,* September 7, 2018. www.churchtimes.co.uk/articles/2018/14-september/news/uk/brtish-social-attitudes-finds-c-of-e-respondents-halved-in-15-years.

"Yalsa Night: Longest Night of the Year." https://www.tappersia.com/yalda-night/#:~:text=One%20of%20the%20oldest%20Persian,on%20the%20year's%20longest%20night.

www.ingramcontent.com/pod-product-compliance
Lightning Source LLC
Chambersburg PA
CBHW050847230426
43667CB00012B/2189